'This timely publication offers real practical solutions to the challenges of teaching Chinese in schools. Its rich examples will be invaluable to teachers and teacher trainers.'

Li Wei, Chair of Applied Linguistics, UCL Institute of Education

'This is a much-needed work, as it puts the spotlight firmly on the teaching of Chinese in the school context. All colleagues involved in this area will find it a fascinating, informative read with the potential to promote the subject more widely and to enhance practice in meaningful ways.'

**Colin Christie, PGCE Languages subject leader,
UCL Institute of Education**

'Second language education and second language acquisition are two separate subjects, but this book combines them together, providing insight into Chinese and practical teaching methods.'

**Zhao Yang, Professor, School of Chinese as a Second Language,
Peking University**

Mandarin Chinese Teacher Education

Mandarin Chinese Teacher Education

Issues and solutions

Edited by Fotini Diamantidaki,
Lin Pan and Katharine Carruthers

IOE Press

First published in 2018 by the UCL Institute of Education Press, University College London, 20 Bedford Way, London WC1H 0AL

www.ucl-ioe-press.com

British Library Cataloguing in Publication Data:
A catalogue record for this publication is available from the British Library

ISBNs
978-1-78277-223-1 (paperback)
978-1-78277-230-9 (PDF eBook)
978-1-78277-231-6 (ePub eBook)
978-1-78277-232-3 (Kindle eBook)

Typeset by Quadrant Infotech (India) Pvt Ltd
Printed by CPI Group (UK) Ltd, Croydon, CR0 4YY
Cover image © Jonny Abbas / Alamy Stock Photo

Contents

Acknowledgements

We would like to thank all the contributors of the book who have made the current collection possible. This collection is the result of hard work and determination in an effort to ensure we start addressing the lack of research surrounding Mandarin Chinese pedagogy. The aim is to support teachers in their classroom and find some solutions to the issues arising in teaching and learning Chinese. It is the first in a series of UCL Institute of Education Confucius Institute *Teaching Chinese* publications (to be edited by Katharine Carruthers and Lin Pan).

The UCL Institute of Education Confucius Institute would also like to extend its sincere appreciation to the PGCE Languages team at the Institute of Education for making the PGCE Mandarin pathway possible and to Hanban for its support for our teacher education, resource and research programmes.

This book project is a bilateral endeavour with Peking University and Peking University High School and its Chinese version will be published with Peking University Press.

In addition, the authors of Chapter 5 gratefully acknowledge the assistance they have received from Yang Renwang in finding the raters from a Beijing senior high school and with initial data analysis. They are also thankful for the support and continued professional guidance throughout the process of conducting this research that they have received from Ruth Heilbronn and also the support from Ding Jia and Yu Bin with the research design and data collection.

Rob Neal (Chapter 6) gratefully acknowledges the assistance he has received from his colleague Yang Renwang in finding the raters from a Beijing senior high school and with initial data analysis.

About the contributors

Victoria Allen studied Chinese and Japanese at the University of Leeds and then went on to complete a PGCE in Japanese with Chinese at the University of Nottingham. She then taught in a junior high school and its four feeder primary schools in Suibara, Niigata, Japan as part of the Japan Exchange and Teaching (JET) Programme. As a result of her experience in Japan, she wrote a bilingual handbook for JET teachers and their Japanese primary school teachers entitled *All Things English*. It detailed lessons, games and teaching activities for the learning of English in Japanese primary schools. Since returning to the UK in 1997, she has worked in various state secondary schools teaching Chinese and Japanese to non-native speakers of all abilities. Victoria also works as a consultant for a UK exam board to contribute to the development of Chinese language GCSE examinations aimed at non-native speakers. She is currently Head of Oriental Languages at a school in the southwest of England and teaches Chinese and Japanese to secondary school students. Her research foci include accuracy of written work for exam purposes, and development of non-European script languages in the mainstream curriculum.

Katharine Carruthers is the Director of the UCL Institute of Education (IOE) Confucius Institute for Schools and Pro-Vice-Provost (East Asia) for University College London. She was awarded an OBE for services to education in the 2018 New Year Honours list. Katharine has played a leading role in promoting and developing the study of Mandarin Chinese and China across the curriculum in schools in England. This work has been facilitated by the establishment of the IOE Confucius Institute and 45 Confucius Classrooms in partnership with Peking University and Peking University High School. Katharine is an experienced teacher and examiner of Chinese. She is the series editor of the textbooks for teaching Chinese for 11–16 year olds, and is Chief Examiner for Cambridge Pre-U Mandarin Chinese for Cambridge International Examinations. She leads on the delivery of the PGCE Mandarin pathway at the IOE. Her research interests centre around the teaching and learning of Chinese as a foreign language in schools, the notion of intercultural competence in Chinese and UK schools, and globalization and language policy.

Fotini Diamantidaki is a lecturer in Languages in Education for the Postgraduate Certificate in Education (PGCE) in Languages and other teacher education routes at the UCL Institute of Education. Her research interests involve the integration of literature in the language classroom in combination with the use of the internet and digital technologies, as well as the integration of world languages into the curriculum, including the growth of Mandarin teacher education in England. Teacher education pedagogy and cultural and intercultural understanding in classroom contexts are fundamental strands to her research interests.

Rob Neal has an MA in Teaching English to Speakers of Other Languages from Lancaster University and an MEd in Educational Research from the University of Cambridge. He is currently a PhD candidate at the University of Cambridge. For his doctoral dissertation, he is investigating the intelligibility of young beginner learners of Chinese.

Haishan Pan was working as a Mandarin teacher in a community Chinese school for over 6 years, before she attended the PGCE in MFL and EAL course at the IOE in 2012. She established a particular interest in the usage of target language in classrooms, and was fortunate to receive good support from the teachers and students in her placement schools, where she had access to resources and an academic environment that she needed to complete her assignment. As a current Mandarin teacher in a prep school in London, she continues to practise the ideologies she has learnt from these studies.

Lin Pan is Mandarin Excellence Programme Coordinator and Masters of Teaching Tutor at the UCL Institute of Education. Her research interests are language ideologies, globalization and multilingualism. Lin has had publications in *Language Policy, Journal of Sociolinguistics, Visual Communication, Applied Linguistic Review, Language Learning Journal*, and *English Today*. Her book, *English as a Global Language in China: Deconstructing the ideological discourses of English in language education*, is published by Springer.

Emily Preston is a teacher of Chinese as a foreign language in Singapore. Emily spent half of her life growing up in Asia. She completed her BA and MA degrees in Chinese at the University of Leeds before embarking on her teacher training in Mandarin Chinese at the IOE. Emily taught Mandarin in UK schools before relocating to Singapore to teach Mandarin as a foreign language at the United World College of Southeast Asia.

Xu Qian is working as an EAL teacher in an international school in China. She completed her BA in her hometown Tianjin and then obtained her MA from the UCL Institute of Education in 2014. As a bilingual learner herself, she has a keen interest in second language acquisition and bilingualism. She always aims to cultivate a learner-friendly atmosphere in multilingual classrooms in order to facilitate the language learning.

Paul Tyskerud graduated with a degree in Psychology from Cardiff University. He then worked as a British Council language assistant in China from 2006 to 2008, studying Mandarin part-time during that period at Suzhou University. After training for a PGCE in Mandarin and French at Sheffield University, in 2009 he began teaching Mandarin at Dartford Grammar School and later training new Mandarin teachers entering the profession. His Mandarin department was awarded UK Confucius Classroom of the Year 2013 by the Chinese Department for Education. Paul has presented at the annual National Conference for Mandarin Teachers on three separate occasions, worked on sabbatical as Curriculum Development Coordinator for the UCL IOE's Confucius Institute, and worked with the UK Department for Education on video projects to demonstrate how pupils studying in the UK can learn Mandarin. In September 2013, Paul moved to Spain to teach Mandarin at The British Council School in Madrid and is currently Head of MFL in the school.

Yi Xiang is a PhD candidate in Education at the UCL Institute of Education. She gained her BA in Teaching Chinese as a Second Language at East China Normal University, and her MA in Linguistics and Applied Linguistics at Shanghai Jiao Tong University. Her PhD research focuses on the experiences of native Mandarin-speaking teachers from China, exploring how this group of teachers construct their professional identities during their first years in UK schools, and the structural, educational, social and personal influences on the process.

List of abbreviations

AQA	Assessment and Qualifications Alliance
BC	British Council
CALL	computer-assisted language learning
CC	Confucius Classroom
CFL	Chinese as a foreign language
CI	Confucius Institute
CiLT	Centre for Information on Language Teaching and Research
CLA	Chinese language assistant
CLT	Communicative language teaching
CMC	computer mediated communication
CPD	continuing professional development
EAL	English as an additional language
EFL	English as a foreign language
ESOL	English for speakers of other languages
GTP	graduate teacher programme
HSK 6	Hànyǔ Shuǐpíng Kǎoshì/ Chinese Proficiency Test
IB	International Baccalaureate
ICT	information and communications technology
IDTs	internet and digital technologies
IOE	Institute of Education
KS	Key stage
LO	learning objective
MFL	modern foreign languages
NQT	newly qualified teacher
OTT	overseas trained teacher
PKU	Peking University
PPP	present–practise–produce
QTS	qualified teacher status
TCFL	teaching and learning Chinese as a foreign language
TL	target language
UCL	University College London

Introduction

Fotini Diamantidaki, Lin Pan and Katharine Carruthers

> What may have been overlooked is the sheer exhilaration of the
> journey into a foreign language and a foreign culture *for its own sake.*
> (Hawkins, 1999: 84)

The introduction of Mandarin Chinese as a curriculum subject in UK
schools is enabling that sense of the exhilaration of language learning
to flourish: students are learning about a character-based language and
exploring a different culture and a different way of thinking. How better
to start this short book than with a quote from the late Eric Hawkins,
linguist and educationist, who was head of Calday Grange Grammar
School on the Wirral from 1953–65. Calday Grange Grammar School was
one of the first five UCL Institute of Education Confucius Institute (IOE
CI) Confucius Classrooms formed in 2007, where Chinese was encouraged
to flourish in the mainstream curriculum alongside European languages
and where the school created links with China and was amongst the first
maintained schools to develop and mentor outstanding teachers of Chinese.
The school's head teacher at that time, Andrew Hall, saw Chinese as the
means by which he could continue Hawkins's legacy at the school.

The UCL Institute of Education Confucius Institute (IOE CI)

England has approximately 3,750 secondary schools and 21,500 primary
schools. The school system is highly autonomous and secondary schools
have considerable control over their own curriculum. How can they
be encouraged to consider the introduction of Chinese? What is the
infrastructure that is needed for success?

The IOE CI works to support the development of Mandarin Chinese
as a language on offer in schools, taught in the mainstream curriculum
alongside French, German, Spanish, and other languages that may be
available at the school. In a rapidly globalizing environment, there is a
demand and interest shown by students, their schools, their parents, and
their future employers. In a recent British Council report (Tinsley and
Board, 2014), Chinese is cited as the fourth most important language for
UK trade.

The work of the IOE CI, which began in 2007, has been to focus on removing the barriers to teaching Mandarin Chinese by working to ensure there are good teaching materials, accessible and appropriate examinations, flourishing support networks, and, most fundamentally, trained teachers.

The IOE CI is a bilateral project with Peking University (PKU) and Peking University High School, and supported by Hanban, which runs the Confucius Institute programme. As well as a small team of specialists in London, the IOE CI has a network of more than 40 UCL IOE Confucius Classrooms (IOE CCs) across England, schools which have Chinese firmly embedded in their own curriculum, with their own local teachers of Chinese. These schools also give advice, support, and taster classes to other schools in their region looking to start offering Chinese. This outreach development work is made possible through the support of Peking University High School and a team of over 60 (Hanban) teachers from China who come to work with the IOE CCs each year and to support the local teachers of Chinese.

In partnership with Pearson and with the support of Peking University and Hanban, the IOE CI has worked on the development of teaching materials for Chinese: three student books (进步一、二 for 11–14-year-olds and GCSE Chinese for 14–16-year-olds), two work books, and three teachers' books. This was the first time that textbooks for teaching Chinese have been published by a mainstream publisher in England; they have brought Chinese more closely into line with provision for other languages. The books were written by teachers from the first five IOE CCs alongside authors and editors from the PKU and the IOE CI team of Chinese specialists.

The IOE CI offers a wide range of continuing professional development (CPD) courses for teachers of Chinese each year and also courses in China for existing teachers of other languages to learn Chinese. The IOE CI supports an e-forum of over 800 members. The forum is a national resource for advice and information and holds an annual two-day Chinese conference. The conference grows significantly in size each year and is the CPD event that teachers of Chinese in schools do not want to miss.

Mandarin Chinese teaching in the UK

Native-speaker Chinese teachers who work on secondment from their teaching positions in China are one of the sources of Chinese teachers in UK schools. They come through the British Council's Chinese Language Assistant (CLA) programme and also under the auspices of Confucius Institutes across the country – Hanban teachers. Both groups (CLAs and Hanban teachers) complement the work of local Chinese teachers, both native and non-native speakers.

Most Hanban teachers are trained for up to three months in China before they come to the UK. The training is delivered by a Chinese university, with large groups of about 200–300 training together. This group of teachers will then typically be deployed in various countries other than the UK (see Xiang, current volume). However, in the case of the cohort of around 60 Hanban teachers destined for the IOE CI, this Chinese university training is supplemented by the IOE CI's own one-week pre-departure training programme. This short training programme is delivered by the IOE CI with the support of its partner university or school in China and is specifically for teachers who will be based in IOE Confucius Classrooms. Teacher trainers come from the UK to deliver the training.

Pre-departure training facilitates Hanban teachers' transition from the educational landscape in China to that of the UK. It provides important knowledge on how to teach in a Mandarin classroom in the UK, which is a crucial first step in providing teachers with adequate preparation, especially to those without the experience of teaching Chinese as a second or foreign language (Yi, current volume).

Xiang Yi, a PhD student, made a very detailed investigation of the professional identity of Hanban teachers in British schools and found that pre-departure training is insufficient in terms of the knowledge and understanding it provides on the nature of the teachers' learning in a new sociocultural environment. In particular, the pedagogical knowledge provided by the Chinese university training programmes is mainly theorized and developed based on the experience of teaching Chinese as a second language for adult learners within China. This context can be very different from the UK school context, in terms of the language learning environment and the academic and linguistic needs of learners. What works in the Chinese adult context may or may not work in the UK school context. The consequential impact of this is a sense of confusion about a teacher's teaching practices and a subsequent impact on confidence. Xiang Yi argues for the need to develop a training programme curriculum that is better targeted and includes a greater appreciation of the UK school environment (see Xiang, current volume).

UCL IOE Postgraduate Certificate of Education (PGCE): The mainstreaming of the Mandarin Chinese pathway

When working to mainstream Mandarin Chinese in any secondary school system, addressing teacher education is of fundamental importance. The mainstreaming of the subject requires a cohort of locally trained teachers with qualified teacher status. The UCL IOE, in collaboration with the IOE

CI, has developed a unique programme to train its student teachers of Mandarin Chinese.

The PGCE Mandarin Chinese pathway was introduced at the UCL Institute of Education by its director Katharine Carruthers, following discussions with the PGCE Languages team and the director of the Institute of Education at the time, Professor Chris Husbands. The introduction of the PGCE Mandarin pathway comes as an organized response to equip Chinese teachers with the necessary principles and training to teach in secondary British schools. The first cohort of student teachers began in September 2011.

Teachers wanting to train to teach Chinese follow a pathway of either Mandarin with another European language or Mandarin Chinese with English as an additional language (EAL). They spend about a third of their time at the UCL IOE and two thirds of their time in schools teaching Chinese in two separate school placements.

Whilst at the IOE, the students join with other Languages PGCE students for lectures in Subject Studies and Professional Studies, but also attend tutor group sessions, which focus specifically on the nature of teaching and learning Mandarin Chinese. This is a unique feature of the course. Numbers of applicants for the course far exceed availability, and numbers on the programme have increased from 10 in 2011 to 15 in 2016. The link between the UCL IOE and the UCL IOE CI means that it has been possible to find excellent placements for student teachers in schools teaching Chinese and that our student teachers receive the vital support they need.

Student teachers on the course come from a variety of native and non-native speaker backgrounds. The native speakers are from China, Taiwan, and Singapore as well as British-born Chinese and Chinese people who have settled in the UK. There are also student teachers who have learnt Chinese at university (some of whom started their learning at school) as well as others who have learnt Chinese seriously whilst living in China and who have reached level 6 of the Chinese proficiency test (HSK6) whilst living in the country. It is a mutually enriching experience for student teachers of European languages and of Mandarin Chinese to work with and learn from each other.

The unique approach of the PGCE Mandarin teacher education route at the UCL IOE is that all languages are mainstreamed. PGCE Mandarin has become one of the main pathways offered alongside European language pathways. This means that, regardless of the pathway they are following, all student teachers benefit from the same enriching opportunities of lectures, specialist tutor groups, workshops, enhancement opportunities, and cross-cultural course tasks. The course was developed in response to growing interest in China across the world, from both an economic and a historical perspective. This has led to a corresponding demand for Chinese speakers in England. The course develops teachers who can reliably and sustainably increase the number of Chinese speakers, using appropriate teaching methodologies to nurture language competence amongst school-aged learners.

The Mandarin Chinese pathway students: The survey

In anticipation of the present publication, Fotini Diamantidaki has organized a survey among the students who have attended the course since its infancy in 2011. The purpose was to find out how the students feel about the way Mandarin Chinese has been integrated into the PGCE Languages course, what challenges the students may have faced as Mandarin specialists during their PGCE year in relation to other specialist language groups, what enrichment opportunities were offered, and how they generally feel they were prepared for teaching in British schools. The results have helped us shape this publication.

The survey was conducted anonymously on Survey Monkey, and the students who chose to reply only filled in the year they attended the course. The majority of the students who participated in the survey (42.86 per cent) were from the first year the course was established (2011), followed by students from the most recent academic year (2015) with a response rate of 28.57 per cent. It is interesting to note the evolution of the PGCE Mandarin course as revealed by the perspectives of students who attended in different years.

The Mandarin Chinese pathway students: Summary of responses

Integration of Mandarin Chinese into the PGCE Languages course

The general consensus from the answers in the first cohort (2011/12) was that Mandarin Chinese student teachers did not feel that the integration into the PGCE Language course had been very smooth. In answer to the question: 'To what extent did you feel that Mandarin Chinese was completely integrated into the PGCE Languages course?', one respondent said: 'I was in the first cohort so maybe not so much. I am sure this has improved over the years.' Another respondent felt that a lot of the examples and case studies were more relevant to Western languages: 'At that early stage, we felt a little apart from the Western languages. A lot of the cases discussed in class were more relevant to those.' However, students from subsequent years 2013, 2014, and 2015 said that the structure of the course, with lectures and tutor group sessions, was useful to them. '[...] I think that it was reasonably well integrated into the PGCE Languages course. For example, we had main lectures with other MFL PGCE students while having Mandarin-specific group activities, which I think is very helpful.' The balance between theoretical (lectures) and practical input (tutor group sessions) was valued by all students.

Rewards and enrichment opportunities

The most valuable reward as highlighted by students 'was the opportunity to forge relationships with esteemed language experts' and finding 'both main lectures on MFL teaching in theory and case studies in general and certain language-specific group teaching ... very useful'.

Responses also highlighted the variety of enrichment opportunities shared across the entire PGCE intake, and where Mandarin PGCE students had the opportunity to 'compare/discuss approaches and methods with teachers from other cultures and with different languages'.

Tutor group sessions were a very rewarding opportunity for all to share ideas, and certain students highlighted specific sessions of particular importance to them: 'I think that PPP teaching exercises by tutor groups at the beginning and the film-based group presentations are excellent sessions.'

School visits for Mandarin specialists (one visit per placement) were also mentioned as a particularly rewarding opportunity, along with the practical reward of 'getting paid to learn and teach at the same time!'

PGCE students also commented upon the ability 'to pass on knowledge and become an educator', but they also acknowledged other gateway opportunities for further networking channels and 'being able to present at the Chinese conference'.

Preparation during the PGCE year to face the challenges in a UK secondary school context

According to students' answers, preparation has improved since the first year the course was introduced, varying from 'fairly well prepared' (2012) to ending in 'very well prepared' (2015).

Students felt 'fairly well prepared in terms of planning and delivering lessons' (2012) and 'well prepared in tailoring a lesson that fits the pupils' needs', but the general consensus from 2012 was that 'the course was well-structured, with balanced theory and practice learning as well as essay writing sandwiched with two placements, which have well prepared student teachers for their teaching careers at schools, whether in a well-established Mandarin teaching department or working on one's own'.

The 2013 cohort highlighted the added variable of the support one receives while in school placement: 'It really depends on what support and experience we have got from the placement schools. Generally, I would say the course provided a good opportunity.'

The following year's cohort (2014) highlighted the significance of the specific assigned subject tutor: 'I feel confident in teaching and I have learnt a lot from my subject tutor.' One respondent noted a wish for longer school placements, highlighting that MFL lessons were allocated little time as part of the curriculum, which had an impact on motivation levels and teaching with only the exam in mind: 'I believe the placements could have been longer. A challenge I think I would face is the amount of time given to MFL lessons and the pressure of exams. This means lessons have less potential to encourage and motivate students. This drops attitude to learning levels and enthusiasm for MFL.'

The 2015 cohort felt 'very well prepared' and expressed the idea that they 'would have definitely enjoyed more collaborative teaching and planning at the university'. One person reiterated the idea mentioned in 2013 that the placement school is important: '[...] the level in which somebody feels prepared very much depends on the placement school the student teacher is based concerning numerous factors e.g. whether school policy fits with that person's personal views towards education, their relationship with their mentor, individual personality and so on.'

Challenges faced by Mandarin specialists

One of the main challenges PGCE students were faced with, regardless of the year they attended the course, was the lack of research in Mandarin Chinese to inform their practice and nurture critical thinking: 'There are not many research publications, i.e. books or journals available, whether theoretical or classroom-based comparative studies compared with say French.' As a result, students felt that the 'amount of Mandarin-specific input was hindered' due to 'limited available resources'.

Another challenge that was expressed by non-native English speakers was that 'the use of language in academic use was the biggest challenge', meaning that they found it difficult to adopt the academic style required for their M-level assignments.

Finally, students found the approach to teaching Mandarin characters in schools variable and felt that a standardized way of teaching characters was needed: '[...] as there was no unified applicable method that teachers were using. I feel stroke order and radicals are something that needs to be formally assessed at GCSE to standardize the way that characters are taught.'

Since Mandarin Chinese is indeed a new element added to the curriculum, the challenge is always to find appropriate materials to prepare the students for the lectures and inform their critical thinking. Initiatives such as the present book aim to fill some of these gaps in research and the case studies that follow seek to advance the discussion in the field of teacher education and pedagogy in Mandarin Chinese, in the specific context of Mandarin Chinese as a foreign language in UK secondary schools.

The survey shows how a new language has been woven into the fabric of the IOE's PGCE Languages offering and how placements have been identified. Thoughts and feedback from graduates of the course – a combination of native speakers of Chinese from China and the Chinese diaspora and non-native speakers of the language – give insight into the programme, so that it can be continuously developed and improved. This multicultural approach to teacher education provides a forum for a rich debate on the pedagogy of teaching Mandarin Chinese.

How this book is structured

This book is being published in two versions: in English by UCL IOE Press, and in Chinese by Peking University Press. It is divided into two parts.

The first part of the book looks at four case studies and strategies with respect to teaching Chinese in secondary school settings in England, in order to provide readers with context. The first part also reflects on issues in teaching Chinese, considers various approaches, and presents some practical ideas. It draws on work written by the IOE's own PGCE students, our PhD students, and the PGCE tutors themselves, with two chapters on teaching Chinese characters, one on target language use, and one on literature in the Mandarin Chinese classroom. Each chapter ends with some practical ideas for teachers of Chinese to use in their own classrooms.

Chapter 1, written by Haishan Pan, investigates the use of target language (TL) in Mandarin classrooms and how it impacts the students' learning and progress. Numerous research studies and findings show that use of the TL is important in the language classroom, and teachers should become role models by integrating this key element into their planning and teaching. However, Neil (1997) acknowledges that no matter how much the TL is used by teachers, some students' use of it is still limited. Pachler *et al.* (2009) acknowledge that use of the TL should be enabling learners' progress rather than becoming a hindrance with its maximal use. Data collection and analysis resulted in several key findings, based on which Haishan Pan develops recommendations for using the TL in the mainstream classroom. It should be mentioned that, while the data has been collected in one school only, the recommendations can be widely applied.

In Chapter 2, Emily Preston discusses strategies for teaching Chinese characters. The reason characters have historically been considered a significant challenge for foreign language learners is the huge difference between the Chinese writing system and that of alphabetic languages. The author suggests that many of the challenges learners face whilst learning Chinese characters have less to do with the difficulty of the Chinese language itself and more to do with the methods of instruction, inadequate resources, and a lack of awareness of the skills that students need to become autonomous learners. The chapter looks at how Chinese characters are taught in a sample of schools in England, what methods teachers use, how much lesson time they allocate for it, and the problems teachers perceive that they face. Findings are corroborated with the literature and suggestions are given for improved teaching strategies.

Chapter 3, written by Xu Qian, investigates strategies for teaching Chinese characters to pupils from non-Chinese-speaking backgrounds, aiming to provide recommendations for teaching Mandarin characters at both theoretical and pedagogical levels. Qualitative research was conducted in two secondary schools in the UK. In order to investigate a wide range of data from different school types, classroom observations were carried out in both a private school and a state school in Britain. Vignettes of two Chinese lessons observed in these schools are presented. They demonstrate that Mandarin character recognition is one of the major challenges for pupils who are only familiar with alphabetic language systems and is of huge importance to language learners. Teaching and learning strategies for Chinese characters are further discussed and analysed. Finally, further research on Mandarin character teaching beyond the limitations of this study is proposed.

In Chapter 4, Fotini Diamantidaki explores the differences between using literature in the European language classroom and in the Mandarin Chinese classroom. Challenges and perceptions of using literature in the language classroom are discussed and new technologies for approaching literature are suggested.

The second part of the book looks at action research, which is an important area for development with respect to teaching Chinese in schools. Practitioners should be at the forefront of research into their classrooms: it helps them to reflect on, review, and improve their own practice, and also provides information that will be of use to others in the field. There has been a promising start to this work, with a researcher at the IOE providing guidance and support where necessary to a group of teachers involved in action research in their own schools, and this section documents their findings. There are chapters on the nature of action research, the intelligibility of young Anglophone beginners, teaching Anglophone beginners to read and write Chinese, and developing proofreading skills.

Chapter 5 is written by Lin Pan, Rob Neal, Paul Tyskerud, and Katharine Carruthers and contends that modern foreign language teachers should consider being involved in research to explore their classrooms in order to have a better understanding of their students' learning and their own teaching, and as a means of professional development. Language teachers play a central role in their classrooms: they monitor learning and evaluate their students' day-by-day performance and progress. To this end, it is crucial that teachers develop a range of skills in planning, monitoring, and evaluating their own professional activities and the results of the teacher–student interaction. Research has increasingly become a useful skill that teachers can include in their professional repertoire and an interesting and meaningful journey on which to embark. The authors propose that it is important and necessary for language teachers to have a range of specific research skills for exploring and solving immediate problems in their own classrooms and institutions (Walker, 1985; Nunan, 1993; Mertler, 2014).

Chapter 6, written by Rob Neal, is set within the context of teaching and learning Mandarin Chinese at a comprehensive secondary school in the north of England. The author investigates the intelligibility of five Anglophone young beginner learners of Mandarin Chinese. Audio files taken from the learners' role plays were sent via email to five Chinese students at a senior high school in Beijing, who were invited to transcribe what they thought they had heard in Chinese characters. Particular attention was paid to areas where the rater had transcribed a different character from what the speaker had intended to say. Working at the syllable level, the source of the breakdown in intelligibility was categorized as being a result of: the tone, the initial consonant of the syllable, the final part of the syllable deviating from the standard form, or a combination of two or all three of these factors. While it was difficult to be certain about the exact cause of the intelligibility breakdown, it was argued that participants' pronunciation problems ran far deeper than non-standard tones, which have been the focus of the majority of research into Chinese as a Foreign Language (CFL) pronunciation studies. An increased focus on initials and finals alongside tone was proposed as an appropriate pedagogical intervention.

In Chapter 7, Paul Tyskerud addresses a key question about his own practice, which is what strategies pupils believe to be most effective for supporting them to learn to read and write Chinese characters. In addition, the action research was aimed at filling a current void in research into how Anglophone learners learn Mandarin. A sample group of beginner learners of Mandarin from two UK secondary schools completed two questionnaires prior to and after the intervention period. The intervention period involved teachers introducing and familiarizing pupils with the three seemingly most effective strategies for supporting non-native learners to read and write Chinese characters. The questionnaire gauged learners' opinions of the most effective strategies. A second sample group of teachers completed the same questionnaire based on their perception. Results show rote learning for writing to be the most favoured strategy by both pupils and teachers. Rote learning was also considered by pupils to be most effective for reading, whereas teachers preferred the use of radicals. Implications for practice are discussed as well as what further research into Mandarin learning strategies would be useful.

In Chapter 8, Victoria Allen investigates strategies for proofreading written work using Chinese characters with students from non-Chinese-speaking backgrounds. This is to enable students to proofread and spot errors in their own work in a non-Romanized script text. Four strategies are trialled with a GCSE group preparing for their written controlled assessment. Feedback is provided from the students as to their preferred method. The advantages and disadvantages of each method are discussed, with conclusions drawn as to the most useful of the strategies, particularly under exam conditions. The limited action research project reminds staff and students to consider how a first draft is exactly that and not a finished product. This research was originally conducted for the UK GCSE Mandarin controlled assessments, but is also relevant for the new specification GCSE examinations that were due for first teaching in 2017 and first examination series in 2019.

It is hoped that our book will provide a useful reference for PGCE Mandarin students, teacher trainers, and those involved in the development of Mandarin Chinese in schools across the UK and further afield. The Chinese version of the book provides insightful reading material, particularly for those studying for a master's in Teaching Chinese as a Foreign Language in universities across China and for those going abroad to work as teachers of Chinese.

There is a relatively small amount of material available to read on Chinese teaching and learning in schools and on second language acquisition with respect to Chinese at secondary level. Our book starts to look at ways to address this, through the collaboration of researchers, teachers involved in action research, and our student teacher cohort.

References

Hawkins, E. (1999) *Listening to Lorca: A journey into language*. London: Centre for Information on Language Teaching and Research.

Mertler, C.A. (2014) *Action Research: Improving schools and empowering educators*. London, New York: Sage.

Neil, P. (1997) *Reflections on the Target Language*. London: Centre for Information on Language Teaching and Research.

Nunan, D. (1993) 'Action research in language education'. In Edge, J. and Richards, K. (eds) *Teachers Develop, Teachers Research: Papers on classroom research and teacher development*. Papers from a conference held at Aston University, 3–5 September 1992. Oxford: Heinemann, 39–50.

Pachler, N., Barnes, A. and Field, K. (2009) *Learning to Teach Modern Foreign Languages in the Secondary School: A companion to school experience*. 3rd ed. Abingdon: Routledge.

Walker, R. (1985) *Doing Research: A handbook for teachers*. London: Methuen.

Tinsley, T. and Board, K. (2014) *Languages for the Future: Which languages the UK needs most and why*. London: British Council.

Part One

Teaching Chinese in
secondary schools
in England

1

How to encourage students to use more target language in the Mandarin classroom

A study of mixed ability groups

Haishan Pan

Introduction

Mandarin Chinese has been viewed as one of the most difficult languages in the modern foreign languages (MFL) family. A 2007 report by the Centre for Information on Language Teaching and Research (CiLT) confirms that the decline in MFL is due to their difficulty; this makes the introduction of Mandarin into the mainstream curriculum even more challenging.

Indeed, the intrinsic linguistic features of the Chinese language, for example its unique tonal phonetic system and the logographic script, make it difficult for learners to master (Walton, 1989); consequently, 'to reach such a high standard the students have to have a lot more exposure to the language than European languages' (CiLT National Centre for Languages, 2007: 13). However, the recent growth in online resources, mobile apps, and software has made learning Chinese easier. Liu (2006) points out that Mandarin teachers should strictly follow the 'immersion approach' and exclusively use Chinese in class to enhance the learners' experience, while Xu (2008) identifies different ways for teachers to use English sensibly and judiciously in the Mandarin classroom.

The focus of research has been on how teachers can use the TL more effectively to enable learners' linguistic progress. The recent debate has shifted from teachers using a 'virtual position' (exclusive TL use) to an 'optimal position' (mixed use of TL and L1) in answer to the question of how best to improve students' foreign language skills (Pachler *et al.*, 2009: 115). However, Neil (1997) acknowledges that, no matter how much the TL is used by teachers, some students' use of it is still limited. He believes that the focus should be on these students. The issues learners face in using the TL more were outlined in different studies. Dickson (1996) highlights that the maximal position (extensive TL use) alienates low achievers, making mixed ability teaching impractical. Strategies for teachers to enable learners to use more TL in European language classrooms can be found in quantitative and qualitative studies (see list in Macaro, 2000: 178), but there are fewer studies about students, let alone Mandarin Chinese students.

To explore the question of how to encourage students to increase their TL use in classrooms further, and thereby facilitate their linguistic progress, the author has observed mixed ability groups in the author's second placement school. Observation notes are attached in Appendix 3. It became evident that TL use among these groups varied, but TL use by lower ability students was especially limited. The two Mandarin teachers had their own strategies, although they admitted that they avoided using the TL exclusively in their lessons. After gaining permission from both Mandarin teachers and the sample students, drawn from Year 9 to 13, interviews were conducted with them individually to investigate what thoughts they had on increasing Mandarin use during lessons. The questionnaires used are attached in Appendix 2.

This paper first reviews the latest developments regarding TL use in the MFL classroom, particularly its links to Mandarin teaching and learning, followed by a discussion of associated issues and difficulties. It also discusses the question of whether teachers' maximum use of the TL is sufficient to enable students to use it more as well. Then the data collated from the qualitative study, including lesson observations, follow-up interviews with students, and subsequent discussions with teachers, are presented and analysed to identify the latest Mandarin TL practice in a real classroom setting. Limitations, such as the size of the target sample, the number of research areas, the limited timescale, and the interpretation of the data, are considered. The final part of the paper summarizes the findings, restates the author's position, and considers the best way forward with regard to meeting the needs of both teachers and students while achieving the goal of encouraging students to use the TL more in the classroom.

Research on TL use in MFL and Mandarin classrooms

The MFL national curriculum, updated in 2012, emphasized the importance of TL use as the 'normal means of communication' in the classroom (DES and Welsh Office, 1990: 6). This concurs with empirical research (Dickson, 1996; Neil, 1997) and a large body of pedagogical literature (Macdonald, 1993; Jones, 2002) about how teachers can maximize TL use and implement it effectively. Three key positions – virtual, maximal and optimal – are often cited in literature, with support from different authors (Macaro, 2000; Barnes, 2007; Meiring and Norman, 2002).

The virtual position is generally regarded as a sign of a successful lesson (Ofsted, 2004). However, various issues associated with it have been well documented (Mitchell, 1986; Dickson, 1996), while Jones *et al.* (2002) insist that L1 should only be used to fulfil certain well-defined purposes. The most common issues are that exclusive TL use can be time-consuming, it can be hampered by lack of confidence from teachers, and it is difficult to implement it for certain tasks, including grammar teaching and explaining meaning. At the same time, different projects studying TL use in MFL classrooms (Macaro, 1997; Crichton, 2009) prove that teachers' non-exclusive use of TL also enables students to make effective linguistic progress and enhance their learning experience.

Most of the literature and studies mentioned above are based on European language teaching, whilst research on TL use in Mandarin lessons, as the newly introduced language, remains limited (Wang and Kirkpatrick, 2012). A number of language scholars, including Ma (2003), Wang (2007), and Liu (2006), confirm that the pedagogical tradition for Mandarin teaching has long been dominated by the Chinese-only principle, although Wang's research has not just focused on schools. Xie *et al.* (2007) and Wang (2010; 2013), however, argue against exclusive use of the TL, by providing empirical evidence that Mandarin teachers have, in practice, successfully applied the non-exclusive pedagogy. Mandarin, similar to the rest of the MFL family, has gone through the same debate about TL use in the classroom, with TL use by teachers being preferred.

TL use difficulties faced by students

Neil (1997) argues that focus should shift to students whose TL use is limited despite the amount of TL use by teachers. This is reiterated by the findings of a survey (James *et al.*, 1999) that analysed students' language skills across four different languages and identified speaking skills as the weakest even when teachers pursued a practice of maximum TL use. Dickson (1996) states that it is dangerous to be too reliant on the quantity of teachers' TL input and to overlook the students' opinions and needs.

Pachler *et al.* (2009) list many factors associated with the amount of TL use by learners in the classroom, including the ability and size of the group, motivation and confidence, group dynamics, and the receptiveness of students. Dickson (1996) reports that students in KS4 used proportionately less TL than KS3; they lost interest as it became more complex, and those who were not 'high-fliers' found it even more frustrating if TL was overused. Franklin's research (1990: 21) reiterates that 79 per cent of teachers did not use the TL because of 'the presence of many low ability pupils in the class'. Dickson (1996) states that maximum TL use in mixed ability groups, especially in large groups, often undermines the learners' interest and good working relationships in the classroom. Meiring and Norman (2002) suggest that certain areas, including grammar teaching and explanation of meanings, should be taught with a modest proportion of TL use for lower ability students.

The ability and achievement of students seems to dictate the use of the TL in the classroom. Brown and Fletcher (2002) highlight other factors that can impact on learners' language learning, including social skills, self-esteem, and commitment to learning. Their study on a group of lower set Year 10 students' behaviour in MFL lessons indicates that the reality of classroom experience is in conflict with expectations created by policy on MFLs and official statements.

Recommended strategies for TL use in the Mandarin classroom

For Mandarin teaching and learning, the above factors may be compounded by the fact that Mandarin is a very different language for UK students, who may find themselves taking longer to grasp the language. This is acknowledged by MFL KS3 (DfES and QCA, 2004), which notes that the attainment level for Chinese needs to be modified, e.g. it needs to be spoken at a slower speed and using a limited range of topics. Hu's preliminary study on UK learners' perception of learning Chinese reports that pronunciation presents challenges, as the changes in tones dictate the meanings of words (2010).

However, Utah's successful Chinese immersion programme, which requires beginners to use TL exclusively in lessons, may change the perception of the difficulty learning Mandarin poses for Westerners (Weise, 2012). One may argue that the programme is still in a relatively early stage, and Wang and Kirkpatrick (2012) insist that codeswitching between L1 and TL – optimal position, favoured by many MFL practitioners, is beneficial for beginner classes; they describe the scope of L1 in Mandarin lessons as covering three distinct areas – the explanatory, managerial, and interactive functions. Hu (2010) believes students' learning styles and proficiency levels play an important role in the choice of teaching strategies. Xing (2006) argues that students' motivation and learning abilities need to be taken into consideration before the teaching strategy can be determined. Tse and Tan (2011) suggest that a differentiated approach, instructional materials, and appropriate pedagogy should be included in planning to cater for the diverse needs and backgrounds in the primary setting. The existing literature shows that there is clearly room for further research to continue exploring how Mandarin learners perceive TL use in their classroom and how they can be supported to use more TL.

Qualitative study on TL use in mixed ability groups

A small-scale qualitative study was carried out in the author's second placement school to explore Mandarin learners' perceptions of TL use in classrooms. Observations were held in most Mandarin lessons throughout the placement, and notes were taken on TL use by both teachers and learners. The intention of observing TL use in lessons was not disclosed to the teachers and students until the interview stage. The author was treated as an additional teacher supporting the group, so that the influence of her presence on what happened in the classrooms was minimized (Wragg, 1999).

It became evident from the initial observation stage that these classes consisted of mixed ability groups, and their use of the TL varied, particularly for lower ability students. Teachers adopted the optimal position in most lessons, with L1 for instructions/commands, classroom management, pedagogical grammar, and culture. The assistant director of learning, who was the former head of Chinese, stated that 'it is our strategy to form smaller classes after our students enter into Year 9, in fact, most of them were selected based on language abilities and performances in Year 7, as we need to guarantee our exam results'. When she was asked if it was challenging to teach mixed ability groups, she answered quickly: 'Indeed, and we just need to find the most suitable teaching strategies. They all have their own personalities and learning styles. It is about how they learn and make progress.'

When the author first disclosed the purpose of this study, both Mandarin teachers welcomed the idea, although both admitted they were not confident in their TL use and it would be impractical to use TL exclusively due to the differing abilities of students and the nature of certain tasks. The head of Chinese commented: 'I don't know much about TL use, but it would be impossible to use it for certain exercises such as grammar, culture, or explaining characters' meanings. My students will be too tired if I use Chinese throughout the lesson, and me too.' She gave permission to the Year 9–13 students to attend the scheduled interviews.

School and department background: Mixed ability Mandarin learners

The study school, SB, is a fairly new school which opened in 2007. It is a comprehensive inner London school with half of the students' ethnicity being described as White British and the rest with multi-ethnic heritage. Based on its last Ofsted report in 2010, the proportion of students entitled to free school meals is high, and a few are at the early stages of learning English as an additional language.

This ratio corresponds to the proportion of ethnic students in Mandarin classes. The head of Chinese introduced herself as the new teacher; she only started teaching three years ago, and she confirmed that Mandarin was introduced to the school five years ago. 'The department is still in an early stage, and we are dedicated to enabling students to achieve excellent GCSE results, that's why you will find some years only have 3, 4, or 7 learners; most of them are our hopefuls and they are all willing to learn.'

Two pupils with differing abilities from each year were identified for the interviews. It can be inferred from their background summary (Table 1.1 in Appendix 1) that gender, ethnic background, and size of class are not major factors influencing Mandarin learners' achievements, although it should be taken into account that student C comes from a Chinese background with basic knowledge of the language. In terms of the support they received, it seems that those in the lower ability range received more support outside lessons, except for student G who had studied Mandarin to GCSE level. When I shared this information with the teachers, they both responded that students from the lower range needed extra tuition: 'they usually feel more comfortable and motivated in the classroom if they are more prepared before the lessons'.

Analysing Table 1.1, the major factor influencing the linguistic achievement of students seems to be their 'motivation to study Mandarin'. Those with clearer and higher motivation are more likely to be in the high achievers' range. This agrees with Meiring and Norman's (2002) recommendation that teachers should be encouraged to create the sort of 'cultural island' that will significantly influence the motivation of learners and consequently their use of the TL. Although the sample students may have motivations other than just 'being part of the cultural island', it is clear that they need to be motivated to use the TL in the classroom, but there are other factors influencing achievement, which are explored below.

Qualitative study

During the initial observation stage, a few factors which influenced the learner's TL use in the classroom were identified, i.e. teachers' use of TL, resources, peer support and classroom interactions. Other factors, such as grammar and cultural knowledge, were also considered, although it was recognized they had less impact on TL use by these learners. At the interview stage, a structured interview questionnaire was developed, integrating the identified factors. Then an individually recorded interview with each student was held, with an allocated time of 20 minutes. The recorded data were analysed at a later stage.

These structured interviews garnered some interesting facts, which means that the author was able to use more targeted questions when conducting the subsequent interviews with the two Mandarin teachers. Although the interview questions for the teachers were structured around similar topics to the students' ones, the teacher interviews did not necessarily follow the questions strictly to allow more spontaneous discussions with the teachers.

There were a few constraints with this methodology, as the structured interview questions may not be applicable to each individual learner. The author tried to extend the interview time, so that certain questions could be discussed in more depth by the learners. However, the scheduled slots were either at lunch time or after school, when most learners had further commitments, so the data collected may not give the full picture of their perceptions of the topic. Another concern is the small sample size that may impact the research findings, although it may be argued that the number of learner interviewees, at 10 out of 34, was reasonable, and that the only two teachers in the department were both interviewed.

Interviews with students from Y9 to Y13
Before starting each interview, the author clarified its purpose and explained what TL means, so that the interviewees had clear expectations. However, during the interviews, some interviewees seemed to digress from TL use to language learning and talked more about the language skills they had acquired during Mandarin lessons and the tasks they had been set. Macaro (2000) outlines different interpretations of TL use. He believes that TL use covers all aspects of a lesson, including giving information, interactions, instructions and class management. This terminology was frequently used by the teachers and hence was familiar to them. But the concept was probably unfamiliar to students, who were confused when asked questions about the topic. Nevertheless, during the interviews, their enthusiasm and excitement about participating in the discussion enabled the process to run smoothly, with the resulting data being divided into different categories as detailed below.

Eight of the interviewees were taught by one teacher and two by the other. As different teachers may have different teaching strategies and styles, it could be argued that it would have been more appropriate to compare data among the same teacher's groups. However, data analysis has confirmed that students from each year had a similar perception of the amount of TL use in lessons, although the more capable ones rated the TL use slightly higher than the rest. Please refer to Figure 1.1 in Appendix 1.

When the lower ability students were asked why they thought their TL use was limited, the answers were unanimous: 'I don't think I can cope with more than 40 per cent of TL use in lesson, as I am nervous to use it and I'll have a breakdown if the teacher uses it too much'; 'I am embarrassed to speak it in the classroom as I don't want to make mistakes, and everyone seems better than me'; 'I think I'm not good at speaking and using the language. It is very hard.'

The higher ability students concurred with the above comments, stating: 'it is about learning for everyone, and the teacher has to look after the less able ones, so I can't imagine that we will use more TL when someone can't understand it'; 'I know the teacher feels guilty not being able to use more TL as we all need to concentrate on the exams and we need to use English to understand rules and grammar.'

Exam preparation seemed to play a major role in the limited use of the TL regardless of the ability of learners, while those who were not involved with exams rated their TL use higher than the others. A number of higher ability learners expressed their desire to speak more TL in classrooms: 'I want to use longer sentences to interact with Miss, I am not good at speaking, and I want to do well in the oral assessment'; 'it will be good if I can talk to Miss in a few sentences about anything so that I can be corrected, I'm worried about my speaking exam'.

Those in the medium and higher ability groups had a more positive view on the impact of the teachers' TL use than students from the lower ability groups. 'I want the teacher to use more TL in lessons to explain meanings, give instructions and even classroom conversations; it will help me to use more', G said. 'But what if you don't understand them?', 'I'll ask, and Miss can translate them afterwards, and if she keeps doing it in every lesson, I'll learn and use more TL'. 'I like challenges, and if you ask me to come to the lesson with English only, I'd rather spend these two hours at home learning more vocabulary. More TL is better for me', claimed I. 'It's not about more

TL use by the teacher. It's about building up my confidence in learning. It's good to know the basic rules for the time being, as it'll ease my way in', H stated. 'I think I am more confident than last year, but if Miss speaks too much in Mandarin, I'm confused', F commented.

Student J gave a similar statement as H and F, although he spent some time talking about 'Chinglish' – a system he thinks helps him to use more TL in lesson. 'It's like a set of rules taught by Miss if you want to memorize how to say things in Chinese. It can be used for a simple sentence. By imagining it in English but in a Chinese way, then I translate it into Chinese, it's usually correct'; 'for example, I go to lessons at 7 this morning', it can be put into English as 'I this morning at 7 go to lessons – 我今天早上7点上课'.

When the rest of the interviewees were asked about this Chinglish system, there was mixed feedback: 'It worked really well for me at the beginning to get the gist of the language, but once it gets harder, I'll switch back to English.' 'I have speaking difficulties: sometimes it works, sometimes not. I'll still struggle despite knowing what I want to say.' The author explored this point further with the teacher in subsequent interviews and it was acknowledged that the system was useful for certain sentence structures and basic word order, but it would not be applicable for more complex sentences. The teacher believed that Chinglish might be a good starting point for lower ability students to develop their confidence in responding and interacting in the TL in classrooms.

Resources were welcomed by learners as a means to support their TL use: 'I like to use the commands list given by Miss. If I can't remember how to say it, I can always refer to it'; 'I use my mini dictionary sometimes, not often, but it helps me to understand what teacher says sometimes'; 'the vocabulary on the walls helps a lot, and I can pick it up straight away without asking others'. However, most interviewees hesitated when they were asked if their peers could be a resource in lessons.

PEER SUPPORT AND INTERACTIONS IN THE CLASSROOM

When the question about peer support as a resource was raised, higher ability learners reported that they did not think supporting or interacting with lower ability peers would be useful in improving their TL use. They preferred talking to the teacher or with someone who was at the same level: 'If I help someone, I will usually use English in our conversations, although the vocabulary or sentence will be in the TL. It may be better if I'm paired with X, as we are at the same level and we can use more TL in lessons', G stated. 'I think there is some sort of competition going on and the interactions usually take place in English instead of Chinese', claimed I.

The lower ability group, however, stated that it was beneficial to have their peers support them by using the TL. However, most said that it did not occur often unless the teachers arranged them into pairs or groups or when the capable ones were asked to do peer-tutoring. 'I may ask them if I don't know how to say a word, but it does not happen often as I'll usually ask Miss.' When this was raised in the teacher's interview, the teacher stated: 'It is difficult because everyone is competitive, and they don't want to be embarrassed in front of their peers, especially if they don't know'; 'it's about creating a classroom culture, and it takes time to build up this environment where they can get used to it.'

In terms of interactions in the classroom, nearly everyone confirmed interactions with peers were held in English. 'They usually communicate in English as not everyone knows it in Chinese, and I'll respond in English. If I'm next to someone speaking in the TL, I'll speak in the TL.' The more able ones welcomed more interactions with teachers in the TL: 'I am here to learn Mandarin, and I think my interactions with Miss will develop my language skills'; 'I have learnt Mandarin for some time now, and I just don't want to know only basic vocabulary. I like to use Mandarin for everything, even jokes'.

For the less able ones, 'confidence' and 'encouragement' were the words occurring most in their response. 'I don't mind Miss using the TL a bit more, but I need more confidence, as I don't want to make mistakes'; 'It's all about confidence, and I think Miss encourages me all the time as I have problems in speaking, and I need words repeating'.

In the subsequent interviews with the teachers, both stated that interactions with students was of the foremost importance in their lessons: 'I think everything else comes after having good relationships with your students, and I'll use a mixture of the TL and English in our interactions flexibly: I like to make jokes in English'; 'I know my classes. I sometimes use TL to make simple jokes in certain classes, but I use English to explain grammar, teach culture, or make comments on their work.'

According to most learners, grammar and culture were not necessarily linked to TL use, and most of them agreed that grammar and culture should be taught in English, except for two higher level users who would have liked grammar to be taught in the TL and then translated into English. For the final question of what would increase their use of the TL, most of the lower ability learners stated that they were happy with their current lessons. Only two of them wanted the teacher to use more TL in lessons, which corresponded with the responses from the rest of the higher ability learners.

Teachers' strategies of TL use and reflections on the findings

Both teachers admitted in subsequent interviews that their use of the TL was limited to 'giving instructions', 'asking/answering questions', and basic classroom interactions like greetings and giving compliments/comments. They both highlighted the importance of differentiation in TL use based on individual learners and classes.

'I used more TL for the Year 11 group before. Now they have exams to prepare for, so you will notice I use English to cover things to save time, and I use more TL for Year 9', one teacher commented. 'It is a mixed ability group, and I need to push everyone to achieve well in their mock exam, so they don't have much time for TL in my lessons, but there'll be a lot more soon', the other teacher stated. Although they had their own teaching strategies, both agreed that it took time to develop students' habits of TL use. The head of Chinese stated: 'Teachers' influence is massive because most of them are still at an early stage of learning. How frequently they use TL is based on how much we interact with each other, so I'll add things gradually based on their progress, especially for the mixed ability groups. I have a set of basic classroom commands that everyone should know, but I will only introduce more complex ones to the able students. It all depends on the class.' The other teacher then commented: 'For my class, I tend to stretch the more capable ones by providing detailed instructions and having spontaneous interactions with them in the TL because they like challenges, but the rest will just follow my normal routine, they pick up from me and peers.'

In terms of departmental strategies towards TL use, the assistant director of learning commented that there was no such overall strategy of using TL in Mandarin lessons: 'I don't see the need to create rules and boundaries. If the teacher is capable enough to enable the students to make progress and achieve results, I am not bothered about how things are implemented.' She then talked about some new mobile phone apps for learning Mandarin phrases in the classroom: 'Resources are a useful tool to build up their confidence. Considering we are in a digital era, I'll encourage my students to download them.'

By comparing the students' and teachers' interview data, it can be inferred that both target audiences have similar perceptions of how much TL was used in their classrooms. The reason why certain year groups or certain students rated higher use of TL are also revealed. Teachers' strategies for TL use, resources, and interactions between students and teachers have a much bigger influence on learners' use of TL than peer support and interactions, although each individual learner may have their own strategy. Mixed ability groups have presented challenges for both teachers and learners when it comes to using the TL more. Moreover, academic results seem to occupy their teaching agenda and codeswitching becomes the norm for classroom interaction, commands, and certain language functions. Nevertheless, teachers are aware that if appropriate strategies are implemented gradually, based on the learners' differing abilities and their progress, and if this is complemented by certain techniques and resources, a cultural learning environment can still be created to motivate learners to become more confident users of the TL.

Summary

Considering the recent debate on which of the three key positions in TL use enables effective linguistic progress, this qualitative study has confirmed that Mandarin teaching and learning faces the same dilemmas as other European languages, despite its perceived difficulty. The idea that the exclusive use of the TL is a sign of a successful lesson and has invariably a positive impact on learners has been contradicted not only by the experience of numerous practitioners (Xie *et al.*, 2007; Wang, 2010; 2013) but also by the data collated in this paper. The maximal position has also become a long-term goal for Mandarin teachers at the school in this study, who endeavour to increase learners' TL use, but need to take account of their different needs and abilities.

Pachler *et al.* (2009: 117) state that 'the objectives of any series of lessons are for pupils' learning to progress rather than to maintain maximal (teacher) TL use'. This statement is a true reflection of the school's Mandarin classrooms. The optimal position is preferred in this real setting and the focus of TL use has changed from teacher-centred to student-oriented. Macaro (2000) points out that L1 may deprive learners of exposure to TL models, meaning that teaching in the TL needs to be systematic in order to be effective. For mixed ability classes, codeswitching has not only helped the lower ability groups, but most importantly allowed 'real' interactions to take place to enable learning progress.

For the teachers, students' motivation and confidence in learning the language is the top priority. This correlated with the students' interview data, as encouragement and interactions with teachers stood out from the other factors impacting their TL use. However, according to the data, teachers' TL use, resources and peer support/interactions were also useful in encouraging more TL use, depending on individual circumstances. For example, Chinglish is somehow favoured by lower ability users, and it can become a stepping stone for their future language acquisition. On the other hand, higher ability users favoured more TL use by their teachers and therefore wanted more complex instructions and conversations to stretch their abilities.

There is no doubt from the analysis above that teachers play the most important role in driving TL use. However, for mixed ability teaching, the key is not the amount of TL use by teachers, but, more importantly, their professional judgement as to how much TL is appropriate. They need to take into account the ability of the class, the level of difficulty and nature of tasks, and how they build up their 'cultural island' to motivate the learners to use more TL (Meiring and Norman, 2002).

Despite the limitations of this study, the existing practice in these Mandarin classrooms confirms that Mandarin, in common with other MFL subjects, faces the challenge of balancing results-driven teaching strategies with linguistically oriented ones. As Dickson (1996) states, there is a perceived gap between the principle of maximizing TL use and the reality of classroom practice, and the 'expressions of belief in the exclusive use of TL tend to be more idealistic than realistic' (1996: 26).

PRACTICAL IDEAS

- Tailor the lessons to the language level of learners. For example, for beginner and intermediate learners it could be more efficient to use target language that is familiar to them as well as body posture and real objects/items to show what you mean.
- Gradually build up a bank of target language phrases you would like to use in the classroom, making sure that learners understand them.
- Don't be afraid to use English in the classroom, but try to limit it to detailed explanation of tasks or to supporting learners as needed.
- Show learners positive examples of using target language in the classroom. For example, the Chinglish phrases used by the director of learning at the school in the study helped learners more confidently translate the target language into English and vice versa; lower ability learners also appear to be able to use it.
- Target language should be used for each lesson activity. Plan each activity carefully before the lesson and consider what target language you should use. Choose language that is simple and effective, then use it in the classroom. You will be surprised at how much this will help you and the learners in completing each activity with ease.

- Do not forget that using some very simple but effective phrases will help you excel in lessons. Encouragement phrases: 很棒！太好了！你好厉害！对！真不错！Assessment phrases: 对不对？ 是不是？有没有？好不好？ Instruction phrases：听我说! 看黑板！请坐！请回座位！The list goes on, and you can develop a list for yourself.
- Once your learners are confident with simple phrases, you may consider asking simple questions in the target language. You can start by asking questions of higher ability learners, but be flexible and allow them to answer in English if need be, since they may not yet have enough TL to express themselves. If this does not work in one lesson, it does not mean it cannot work in another. Always have a 'can do' attitude.
- Last but not least, never forget you are the person in charge in the classroom, and using the target language naturally will not only enable you to gain better attention from the learners, but also help you to develop more confidence in your lessons as a language teacher.

Appendix 1

Table 1.1: Summary of the characteristics of interviewed students

Student letter	Year	Gender	No of St.	Ethnic background	Linguistic achievement and other supports	Motivation to study Mandarin
A	9	M	3	White British	medium level; no other support	inspired by Chinese Gong Fu and culture
B	9	M	3	Black African	medium level; no other support	loves Chinese food and dislikes Spanish
C	10	F	7	Chinese – HK	higher level; learnt Cantonese in HK and community schools in the UK	family expectations and her own origin, as part of her family came from China
D	10	F	7	Mixed – African and White	lower level; extra tuition at home	not sure why, but likes to join her Mandarin peers
E	11	F	15	White British	higher level; no other support	wants to do well in GCSE exam
F	11	F	15	Mixed – Chinese and White	lower level; occasional family support	family expectations and Chinese origin
G	12	F	4	White European	higher level; studied Mandarin to GCSE level	knows a few MFLs and wants challenges
H	12	M	4	Black African	lower level; no other support	Mandarin is most difficult MFL – family is proud of him
I	13	M	5	Black African	higher level; no other support	wants to go to China to find a job
J	13	M	5	Black African	lower level; extra tuition at school	wants to go to China but finds Mandarin too hard

Notes: 1. Letters were used to represent each student; the students' year, gender, number of students in class, ethnicity, linguistic achievement and motivation to study Mandarin are also included.

2. Sixth form students (Y12–13) study International Baccalaureate (IB) Mandarin *ab initio*. Neither I nor J had ever studied Mandarin before the course. H was new to Mandarin and had speaking difficulties. Linguistic achievement refers to their four language skills levels/abilities in Mandarin.

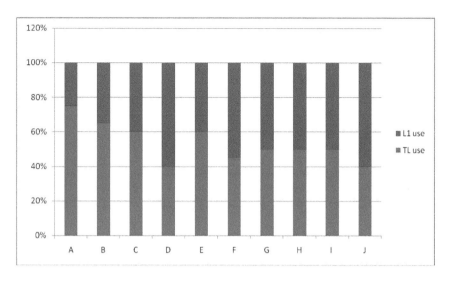

Figure 1.1: Summary of the perceived amount of TL use by individual students in the Mandarin classrooms

Appendix 2

Interview questions for Mandarin students at the study school

1. How much TL do you think you have used in your Chinese lessons?
2. If not a lot, why do you think this is the case? Will the teacher's TL use impact on yours?
3. What activity will enable you to feel confident to use the TL in the classroom? How often do you think this activity occurs in each lesson?
4. What about grammar? Can the teacher use the TL to explain grammar, or do you prefer English?
5. Do you think Chinese is the most difficult MFL subject? Why? How much do you know about Chinese culture, and do you think the teacher should use the TL to teach culture?
6. Who do you think is the best user of the TL in your class? Why? Can he/she help you in improving yours? If you pair with him/her, will you use more TL? What language do you prefer when you interact with the teacher and students?
7. If you were allowed to use different resources in lessons, do you think you could be more creative and spontaneous in your use of TL?
8. Finally, what else can enable you to use more TL during your Mandarin lessons? Just one or two ideas are sufficient.

Interview questions for Mandarin teachers at the study school

1. Do you agree that your learners' TL use in the classroom will be influenced by the amount of TL you use yourself? If you use more, do they also use more? Does use increase more for senior groups or for those who are not in the exam period?

2. If the answer for question 1 is 'no', what strategies increase the learners' use of the TL in the classroom?

3. How much pedagogical value does grammar contribute to the above process? Do you think grammar should be taught in English or in the TL?

4. How much scaffolding do you provide for each task/activity to develop students' TL use? Name a few tasks or activities, e.g. questioning, pair work, or interactive activities. What about reference sources, using vocabulary lists, and dictionaries?

5. Do you think culture should be taught in English or in the TL? If in the TL, what can help students learn it easily? Will the increased use of TL in the classroom affect the relationship between teachers and learners?

6. In the mixed ability group, what are the best strategies to encourage everyone's access to the TL? How would you motivate lower ability learners to use it while challenging higher ability learners?

7. What is the department's policy towards TL use? How much do you think this will affect the teaching and learning?

Appendix 3

Table 1.2: Notes taken from each of the five Mandarin classes; observations in identified Mandarin classes were taken throughout the placement period

Pupil Target Language Use		
Class: Y9 Language: Mandarin	No. of pupils: 3	
Time	**Activity**	**Pupil Target Language Use and Reflections**
0–10 mins	'Copy the text and fill in the gaps in Chinese.' Teacher circulates.	
10–20 mins	Teacher goes through the exercise with the class.	Pupils read Chinese and translate sentences: one sentence each.
5 mins	'Follow me: how to pronounce 牛肉.'	爸爸喜欢喝。。。和吃。。。
	'Ask questions based on the text: 他爸爸喜欢吃什么？他们是谁？他妈妈几岁？几月几号？'	Pupils ask and answer questions in the TL based on the text.
20–30 mins	'Can you describe some features of the Chinese text? Something different from English writing.'	Pupil tries to think how to answer. (Need to leave gaps in the beginning, and the date at the bottom.) Exchange in L1.
	'You may learn how to write letters in Chinese for the GCSE.'	Pupil struggles to come up with one or two words. 'What is 中国菜？' List different dishes in the TL, and they get it in the end. Exchange in L1.
	'Can you remember what you learnt during the last lesson?'	How do you remember the characters for bowl and veggie? Exchange in L1.
	饭馆儿 – usually comes with 儿 in Mandarin.	
	多吃菜，少吃饭: cultural aspect	Pupils try to translate the phrases to L1, and understand better after the cultural part. 菜和茶的区别。

30–40 mins 8 mins	Translation from L1 to TL: how to say 1 glass of water; 2 cups of coffee; 4 cups of juice TL: 谁喜欢吃冰淇淋？谁喜欢吃…？谁喜欢喝可乐？谁喜欢吃中国菜？谁喜欢去饭馆？ Grammar: 想 I want to … translate sentences in the TL. Explanation is in L1.	TL use: each student has a go and they all do well. Less able student struggles a bit, but the others do well. People put up hands to answer instead of speaking in the TL. Pupils translate sentences one by one; they all do well by using the new grammar point. Pupils go through all the new vocab. One does not pronounce the words well, but repeats them one more time. Each student is given time to practise repeatedly.
40–50 mins	Point to the right characters: reading and listening, each student has a go at the pointing exercise. The teacher says, and pupils point. Listening exercise based on *Jìn bù*: answer questions in L1.	Pupils are eager to play the game. Pupils concentrate on reading questions and answering. All listen and answer well. 'How do you say 巧? Is it the same as 炒?'
50–60 mins	The teacher goes through the answers with the pupils. Mixture of L1 and TL. Questions and answers in TL but explanation in L1. 'Let's have a look at another one': speaking and writing. 想要；要；teacher explains use in L1; asks pupils to write them down in the TL and some vocab in the vocab book (green). Homework: get ready for a play in a restaurant, and also do the *Jìn bù* workbook. L1.	TL use is corrected. Phrase use explained in L1. 'How many did you get correct out of 5? Mark each other's work.' L1. Read and translate: TL and L1 conversion. Two pupils respond and exchange in L1: 'I want to be a waiter, customer etc.' How do you write the characters? 淋，冰，力，菜。

Pupil Target Language Use		
Class: Y10 Language: Mandarin		No. of pupils: 6
Time	**Activity**	**Pupil Target Language Use and Reflections**
0–10 mins	Starter: use phrase 离我家 to make sentences; pupils are given time to think what they need to say before being asked. 3 able pupils to demonstrate and then the others to follow. Instructions and explanations in L1. Demonstrations in TL.	Exchange in L1/TL: pupils to make sentences using what they have learnt. Expand sentences: use more phrases, guided by the teacher. One example: 离我家不远有一个超市，我常常去买菜；我觉得超市里的鸡很新鲜；我妈妈用鸡来做清蒸鸡。
10–20 mins	Conversations: teacher with pupils to stretch their ability; pupils to expand sentences as much as they can, based on the above example. Codeswitching between L1 and TL.	Spontaneous and challenging. In TL; key words explained in L1. Encouragement given in a mixture of L1 and TL. Pupils listen and try to understand (TL); opinions given in L1.
20–30 mins	Hobbies: 我喜欢。。。；因为。。。所以。。。；但是；除了。。。以外；一边。。。一边。。。； Listening and speaking; using connectives and key grammar words to make sentences (opinions to be given). Pupils need to include time frame; with whom?; connectives. Again, instructions and explanations in L1 with content in TL.	Oral practice: able pupils demonstrate first and are followed by less able ones; pupils are stretching their ability to a higher level. Conversations on sports: 我（的）爱好是。。。；我也要去看。。。；你踢足球时，你喜欢做什么？
30–40 mins	Homework: 'Describe your hobbies and surroundings in the neighbourhood!' (due on Friday); Lin to write songs and whatever genre you like. (differentiation)	Communicating and dialogue in mixture of L1 and TL.

40–50 mins	Revision of words and learning new words about local places: check pronunciation.	More able pupil to deliver the lesson; asks the groups to repeat.
	Teacher gives clues in L1 on how to memorize some words (less able pupils respond well) – reading and listening.	Mixture of TL and L1.
50–60 mins	极了: extremely	Speaking and writing skills.
	how to use the phrase:	Pupils copy down the phrase then put the phrase together with 好吃/好看/好 to do oral practice.
	好极了: extremely good; it can be used to replace below:	
	太好了; 非常好; 很好; 特别好	Interactions in L1.
	好吃极了: 'extremely delicious';	
	Can phrases be replaced by this?	
	In L1 and TL.	

Pupil Target Language Use		
Class: Y11 Language: Mandarin	No. of pupils: 16	
Time	**Activity**	**Pupil Target Language Use and Reflections**
0–15 mins	LO: to learn festival and food words.	Write the LO down in exercise book.
	Starter: vocabulary translation Chinese to English	Reading and writing skills.
	Instructions given in L1.	The more capable pupils finish first and help the weaker ones. Interactions in L1.
	Teacher circulates to check progress. Weaker pupils are reminded to attend individual sessions to catch up. L1.	
15–25 mins	Go through the vocab with all; weaker pupils are selected to answer, errors are corrected and explanations are given in a mixture of TL and L1.	Notebooks exchanged for peer assessment.
		Answers were given in L1.

25–40 mins	New vocab: displayed on board with characters and pics only. Differentiation strategy was adopted.	Two able pupils were picked to teach how to pronounce and memorize the words – pronunciation was corrected by the teacher. Mixture of L1 and TL.
40–50 mins	Vocab revision: teacher goes through the new vocab in TL; explains vocab meaning and usage in L1 and gives a quick talk about the festivals and their culture in L1.	Speaking and reading skills. Mixture of L1 and TL, but mainly L1; TL for vocab only.
50–60 mins	Game: touching the right words on the board Teacher says one word, two or three pupils compete to see who touches the right word first.	Boys like the game and do really well. All interactions in L1 except for the content.

Pupil Target Language Use

Class: Y12 (IB) Language: Mandarin Total no. of pupils: 4

Time	Activity	Pupil Target Language Use and Reflections
0–10 mins	Starter: translation Q&A: read questions in Chinese and answer based on the translation above. Instructions in L1	Read and write Both pupils do well, as they have learnt it for GCSE. Support from each other on how to say the words 周末，衣服，套装，
10–20 mins	Reading: read 3 passages and answer 3 questions. Circulate to check how they do and assist in their learning. Instruction and explanation is carried out in L1. Time is used for encouraging the pupils to come up with correct words for challenging questions. Mixture of L1 and TL	The two pupils discuss how to answer the questions in L1. Both do well reading and translating all passages. 几 use: in questions it means how many; in statements it means a few/some.

20–30 mins	要和应该：differences in their use (L1) 应该带: what it means, how to use it in 3 different samples. L1 她应该带什么衣服去？ 她应该带。。。。	The pupils handled that very well. Exchange in L1 on the use of the phrase. Both copy the TL down and answer in the TL.
30–40 mins	The pupils continue completing the task given by the teacher. The teacher circulates to check their answers and make corrections. All tasks were completed well, although explanation was given more to the third person. L1	A third pupil arrives and starts to copy things down. Encouragement given in TL and L1
40–50 mins	Colour word board: words are displayed in different colours. Pupils are to make sentences by using as many colour words as possible. Instructions in L1 Teacher writes the pupils' sentences on the board, then explains where 应该should be placed. L1	Reading and speaking, also integrating the grammar point 应该 Pupils are not used to this type of game and would like to have a go. Interactions in L1 and Q&A in TL Pupils write down its use.
50–60 mins	More examples are displayed to check understanding, and all seemed to get it right. Further explanation of the word is given. Guessing game: based on PowerPoint	All give correct answers. Oral practice

Pupil Target Language Use		
Class: Y13 (IB) Language: Mandarin No. of pupils: 4		
Time	Activity	Pupil Target Language Use and Reflections
0–20 mins	Word translation: exchange among pupils about the unknown words in English. L1 instructions. Sentence sample: 口味很地道 风味小吃 他们做的中国菜很地道 蜂蜜和蜜蜂的区别 我家有三个房间。 我家有两层。二层有... 你和他一样都上13年级。 红火 / 热门；温暖 / 温馨 他做的事情让我觉得很温暖。	English is used to explain the Chinese words. Teacher-led exchange, can't separate their use of English and Chinese. Exam-focused, no pronunciation. Teacher offers: 'If you have interest, I can show you after the lesson.' Explanation in L1 and TL depending on words usage; pupils listen attentively. What is the pinyin? How do you translate this? How do you translate this phrase? L1. Not much pupil TL due to the exam focus.
20–40 mins	Exam questions in reading: teacher goes through them one by one with the pupils who are preparing for exams. 什么是别的？什么是一样？ 'Make sure you know all the key words.' The teacher gives thinking time for one student to explain the reason. 快点 – 'Quicker. You don't need to copy the second sentence.' 'Separate the words into characters to explain the meaning and usage'. L1.	Translation of reading exercises: each pupil to give a reason for the answer they have chosen. What is the meaning of this sentence? In L1 for most interactions. Good, but what can make it better? Oh, it can ... (L1) 'Don't tell her, ok? I am trying to get her there.' In L1, using strategies to support each individual. Less able pupils don't know the difference between the two.

	Translation of paragraph in the exam paper: certain pupils are selected to translate in order to check their understanding. 放学／上学：differences between the two. 'Refer to the paragraph in the reading exercises.'	More able pupils read out two/three sentences in Chinese, and translate very well. Less able students struggle to read whole sentences, but can translate a few correctly.
40–50 mins	图书馆查资料：how to translate it? L1 instructions and explanation. Reading questions: What are the key words to translate here? How do you say 'a long time ago'? Long time? How long? 多久／多长时间。 Explanation in L1 with contents in TL	Even the able pupil didn't know the phrase. 'It's a bit tricky for this question, yes, you need to know what 一个半月 means before you know how to respond.' More able pupil says what they think should go into the writing exercise, and mentions 天气／每天我的课都是很无聊。
50–60 mins	Writing an essay based on instructions.	Interactions in L1.

References

Barnes, A. (2007) 'Communicative approaches to modern foreign language teaching and using the target language'. In Pachler, N. and Redondo, A. (eds) *A Practical Guide to Teaching Modern Foreign Languages in the Secondary School*. London: Routledge, 4–11.

Brown, K. and Fletcher, A. (2002) 'Disaffection or disruptive engagement? A collaborative inquiry into pupils' behaviour and their perceptions of their learning in modern language lessons'. *Pedagogy, Culture and Society*, 10 (2), 169–92.

CiLT National Centre for Languages (2007) *Mandarin Language Learning: Research study* (Research Report DCSF-RW019). London: Department for Children, Schools and Families.

Crichton, H. (2009) '"Value added" modern languages teaching in the classroom: An investigation into how teachers' use of classroom target language can aid pupils' communication skills'. *Language Learning Journal*, 37 (1), 19–34.

DES (Department of Education and Science) and Welsh Office (1990) *Modern Foreign Languages for Ages 11–16*. London: Department of Education and Science.

DfES (Department for Education and Skills) and QCA (Qualifications and Curriculum Authority) (2004) The National Curriculum for England Modern Foreign Languages. London: DfES. Online. https://tinyurl.com/ycdbnqvj (accessed 28 November 2017).

Dickson, P. (1996) *Using the Target Language: A view from the classroom*. Slough: National Foundation for Educational Research.

Franklin, C.E.M. (1990) 'Teaching in the target language: Problems and prospects'. *Language Learning Journal*, 2 (1), 20–4.

Hu, B. (2010) 'The challenges of Chinese: A preliminary study of UK learners' perceptions of difficulty'. *Language Learning Journal*, 38 (1), 99–118.

James, C., Clarke, M. and Woods, A. (1999) *Developing Speaking Skills*. London: Centre for Information on Language Teaching and Research.

Jones, B. (2002) 'Encouraging more talk in the modern languages classroom'. In Swarbrick, A. (ed.) *Aspects of Teaching Secondary Modern Foreign Languages: Perspectives on practice*. London: RoutledgeFalmer, 82–98.

Jones, B., Halliwell, S. and Holmes, B. (2002) *You Speak, They Speak: Focus on target language use*. London: Centre for Information on Language Teaching and Research.

Liu, X. (2006) *Hanyu zuowei di'er yuyan jiaoxue jianlun*. Beijing: Beijing Language University Press.

Ma, Q. (2003) 'Guanyu duiwaihanyu jiaoxue de ruogan jianyi'. *Shijie Hanyu Jiaoxue*, 3, 13–16.

Macaro, E. (1997) *Target Language, Collaborative Learning and Autonomy*. Clevedon: Multilingual Matters.

Macaro, E. (2000) 'Issues in target language teaching'. In Field, K. (ed.) *Issues in Modern Foreign Languages Teaching*. London: RoutledgeFalmer, 171–89

Macdonald, C. (1993) *Using the Target Language* (Concepts Handbooks for Language Teachers 1). Cheltenham: Mary Glasgow Publications.

Meiring, L. and Norman, N. (2002) 'Back on target: Repositioning the status of target language in MFL teaching and learning'. *Language Learning Journal*, 26 (1), 27–35.

Mitchell, R.F. (1986) *An Investigation into the Communicative Potential of Teacher's Target Language Use in the Foreign Language Classroom*. PhD thesis, University of Stirling.

Neil, P.S. (1997) *Reflections on the Target Language*. London: Centre for Information on Language Teaching and Research.

Ofsted (2004) *OFSTED Subject Reports 2002/03: Modern foreign languages in secondary schools*. London.

Pachler, N., Barnes, A. and Field, K. (2009) *Learning to Teach Modern Foreign Languages in the Secondary School: A companion to school experience*. 3rd ed. London: Routledge.

Tse, S.K. and Tan, W.X. (2011) 'Catering for primary school pupils with different Chinese language proficiencies in Singapore through differentiated curricula and instructional materials'. In Tsung, L. and Cruickshank, K. (eds) *Teaching and Learning Chinese in Global Contexts: Multimodality and literacy in the new media age*. London: Continuum, 29–43.

Walton, A.R. (1989) 'Chinese language instruction in the United States: Some reflections on the state of the art'. *Journal of the Chinese Language Teachers Association*, 24 (2), 1–42.

Wang, D. (2010) 'A study of English as a lingua franca in teaching Chinese to speakers of other languages'. *International Journal of Learning*, 17 (6), 257–72.

Wang, D. (2013) 'The use of English as a lingua franca in teaching Chinese as a foreign language: A case study of native Chinese teachers in Beijing'. In Haberland, H., Lønsmann, D. and Preisler, B. (eds) *Language Alternation, Language Choice and Language Encounter in International Tertiary Education* (Multilingual Education 5). Dordrecht: Springer, 161–77.

Wang, D. and Kirkpatrick, A. (2012) 'Code choice in the Chinese as a foreign language classroom'. *Multilingual Education*, 2, Article 3, 1–18.

Wang, H. (2007) 'Duiwai hanyu jiaocai zhong de meijieyu wenti shishuo'. *Shijie Hanyu Jiaoxue*, 2, 111–17.

Weise, E. (2012) 'Chinese immersion school consortium launched'. Mandarin Immersion Parents Council blog, 1 August. Online. http://miparentscouncil. org/2012/08/01/chinese-immersion-school-consortium-launched/ (accessed 4 October 2017).

Wragg, E.C. (1999) *An Introduction to Classroom Observation*. London: Routledge.

Xie, M., Huang, N. and Li, C. (2007) 'Jiangxi gaoxiao duiwaihanyu zhuanye shuangyu jiaoxue xianzhuang fenxi'. *Yichun Xueyuan Xuebao (Shehui Kexue)*, 29 (3), 117–19.

Xing, J.Z. (2006) *Teaching and Learning Chinese as a Foreign Language: A pedagogical grammar*. Hong Kong: Hong Kong University Press.

Xu, P. (2008) 'Chuji jieduan duiwaihanyu ketang jiaoxue zhong meijieyu shiyong wenti tantao'. *Xiandai Yuwe*, 9, 119–21.

Chapter 2

How Chinese characters are taught in UK schools

A survey of twelve teachers

Emily Preston

Introduction

Teaching and learning Chinese characters is one of the most difficult aspects of Chinese instruction (Huang, 2000; Ke, 1996; Samimy and Lee, 1997; Shen, 2005). The reason characters have historically been considered a significant challenge for non-Asian background learners is the huge difference between the Chinese writing system and that of alphabetic languages. It is generally recognized that learning to read and write Chinese takes learners longer than a European language. Nonetheless, whilst Chinese orthography is challenging, it is also the aspect of Chinese that appeals to many learners because it is different and aesthetically pleasing. In fact, many of the challenges learners face whilst learning Chinese characters have less to do with the difficulty of the Chinese language itself and more to do with the methods of instruction, inadequate resources, misunderstanding, and lack of awareness of the skills learners need in order to become autonomous learners. With this in mind, this paper seeks to address how Chinese characters are being taught in a sample of UK schools. Findings will be referenced to the literature and suggestions will be given on how to improve the teaching and learning of Chinese as a foreign language (TCFL) in the UK further.

To date, the vast majority of research into TCFL has been conducted among learners and practitioners at higher institution level, predominantly in the United States. This study will provide valuable insight into the methods for character instruction at secondary level as well as the particular challenges that need to be addressed. It also aims to synthesize the most compelling research about TCFL and discuss ways in which findings can be adapted to school contexts in order to build TCFL pedagogy around character literacy in schools.

Literature review

Zhang and Li (2010: 95) outline five problems with Chinese language teaching in the UK. These include a lack of an adequate syllabus and examination system for Chinese teaching; a lack of adequate teaching materials in Chinese; a scarcity of qualified and experienced teachers of Chinese; limited research and debate concerning the learning and teaching of Chinese; as well as insufficient coordination and cooperation between various organizations and institutions. The first three problems have begun to be addressed. The Mandarin GCSE was reformed in 2009, new textbooks were published for KS3 (*Jìn bù 1 and 2*) and KS4 (*Edexcel GCSE Chinese*) and a new Mandarin PGCE course was established at the Institute of Education, University of London. There is now a need for more school-based research and debate about learning and teaching Chinese, as well as cooperation and resource-sharing between institutions within the UK and abroad. Zhang and Li (2010) mention the lack of consideration about how L1 English speakers learn Chinese and the specific linguistic aspects of Chinese that have not adequately been accounted for, yet they do not elaborate on what these aspects include.

According to Shen (2005), the particular linguistic challenges in learning Chinese characters include the complexity of the character structure (e.g. ranging from a simple two stroke character, like 十, to the seventeen strokes of 赢) and the lack of an obvious correspondence between character and sound. Zhao (2013) highlights two further challenges to character learning: recognition and differentiation. He provides the following examples:

读四个句子: 卖四个包子
(Read four sentences: sell four steamed buns)

中国银行: 中国很行
(Bank of China: China is amazing)

In the first example, 读 (to read) can easily be misread as 卖 (to sell), just as 句子 (sentence) can be mistaken for 包子 (steamed bun). The same is true in the second example of 银 *yín* (silver/money) and 很 *hěn* (very). To complicate things further, certain characters can have multiple pronunciations and meanings, depending on the context. For example, 行 can be pronounced as háng meaning company or profession (so 'money company' = bank) or it can be pronounced as 行 xíng, which in this context means to be competent or OK (so 'very OK' = amazing).

Research demonstrates that the components of Chinese characters, the functional radicals (both semantic and phonetic), are essential to character and word recognition (e.g. Carr, 1981; Chu, 2004; DeFrancis, 1984; Everson, 2009; Hayes, 1987; Ke, 1998; Lǔ, 1999; Xiao, 2009; Xing, 2006; Zhang, 2009). For instance, in the first example above, if students knew that the semantic radical 讠 means 'language', they would be able to differentiate between 读 and 卖 more easily, because reading involves language. They would also be less likely to make writing mistakes if they are told that a certain set of strokes actually constitutes a form with a meaning. The difficulty that remains, however, is accessing the sound, because although 读 is composed of 讠 + 卖, it is not pronounced mài, but dú. This is where the phonetic radicals can aid recognition (Xing, 2006: 111–5; Zhang, 2009). In the same example, 句子 jùzi and 包子 bāozi can easily be confused. Yet if learners are told that that the character 包 can be used as a phonetic component in other characters, they may be more sensitive to the subtle differences in form (see examples in Table 2.1).

Table 2.1: The functional components of eight characters pronounced 'bao'

Character	Phonetic radical	Semantic radical	Meaning
抱	包	Hand 手 （扌）	Hold; embrace
鲍	包	Fish 鱼	Abalone (dried fish)
饱	包	Food 食 （饣）	Full up (after eating)
胞	包	Moon, month 月	Womb; placenta
苞	包	Grass 艹	Bud of a flower
雹	包	Rain 雨	Hail
龅	包	Tooth 齿	Projecting teeth
刨	包	Knife 刀 （刂）	To level; make smooth (e.g. in carpentry)

Researchers generally agree that learning the structure of a character and its relationship to sound and meaning should be the starting point of all character study (Chu, 2004; DeFrancis, 1984; Everson, 1998, 2009; Huang, 2003; Ke, 1996, 1998; Lǔ, 1999; Yang, 2000; Xing, 2006; Zhang, 2002). Yet this is not how learners are taught in most higher education institutions or schools. In 2008, Scrimgeour (located in Australia) writes in a now defunct online forum that curriculum designers have long overlooked the extent to which the rules, principles, and representations of sound and meaning in the Chinese character system contrast to learners' own language. He urges educators to rethink the current Chinese curriculum in schools and build in systematic metalinguistic training at the early stages of learning to enhance learners' reading and vocabulary acquisition (Scrimgeour, 2011). Concerns over current approaches to character instruction have also been echoed in the US (Zhang, 2009) and the UK (Zhang and Li, 2010).

Despite increased research findings about how best to teach characters to CFL learners, characters are represented in textbooks as individual, unrelated units comprised of a set number of strokes (see Figure 2.1).

Figure 2.1: The stroke order for the character 明 míng

Further information about the character's etymology, structure, or functional units is largely omitted (Scrimgeour, 2011). Analysing a character's functional components increases the depth of concept-driven processing, which is a more effective approach than rote memorization of stroke formation (Everson, 2009: 103, Shen, 2005). A simple example includes characters that always appear in textbook topics about time and daily routine (see characters below). The first four all have the same semantic radical (日 rì sun) and the last character 期 shares the functional component 月 with the first character 明.

Tomorrow   evening   morning   star   +   period of time = week

(bright 明 +day 天)

Figure 2.2: How functional radicals can be recycled in topical language

However, textbooks currently do not take into account learners' prior knowledge of functional components, instead providing the full stroke order for every new character (Zhang, 2009: 76). This perpetuates a practice whereby learners recognize how to construct the characters (mostly independently at home) rather than understand them. Furthermore, only the semantic radicals are featured as an interesting add-on. Zhang (2009) questions the pedagogical advantages of those semantic radicals that are featured. The phonetic radicals, which research demonstrates are key to character learning, do not feature in textbooks. Zhang (2009) cites plenty of pedagogical advantages to what he terms the 'phonetic approach' to character instruction. In this vein, Scrimgeour calls for a move away from reliance on textbooks, which mainly focus on developing oral proficiency, and for the increased introduction of interactive resources that allow for more in-depth study of the Chinese character system (Scrimgeour, 2011).

Conversely, Liu and Lo Bianco (2007) contend that despite devices that seek to make character learning more intuitive by displaying inter-character connections and roots, the huge endeavour of character learning still proves too much of a psychological barrier that discourages most learners (Liu and Lo Bianco, 2007: 102). They highlight the debate surrounding the possibility of dispensing with characters altogether at some levels of schooling and just using Pinyin Romanization during transitional periods or focusing on verbal Chinese communication. According to them, once characters are taken out of the equation, the learning task is easier and the rate of acquisition faster (Liu and Lo Bianco, 2007). However, it is unrealistic to teach Chinese without teaching characters, due to their functional importance in Chinese society.

Survey background

An online survey was sent to ten teachers in the UK. The survey was also posted on the Mandarin Chinese forum moderated by the UCL IOE Confucius Institute, which is used by teachers of Chinese in HE and FE institutions. The survey was posted on this forum, as its aim is to facilitate discussion and research into teaching methods for Mandarin Chinese and to develop best practice. The twelve schools who responded and participated in the survey are outlined in Table 2.2.

Table 2.2: Schools represented in the survey

No.	School	Type	Learners' age range	Teachers' background	Experience teaching Chinese
1	A	State selective BOYS	11–18	British, PGCE Nottingham	19 years
				British, PGCE Exeter	3 years
2	B	Academy selective BOYS	11–18	Mainland Chinese, QTS UK;	15 years
				Mainland NQT	Not stated
3	C	Independent GIRLS	11–18	Mainland Chinese, QTS, 15 years in UK	8 years
4	D	Independent	5–18	2 British teachers 4 Chinese teachers	Not stated
5	E	Academy	13–18	British, GTP	
6	F	Comprehensive faith school	11–18	British, PGCE	6 years
7	G	Complementary school	6 months–19	PGCE No QTS	Not stated
8	H	Selective academy BOYS	14–6	Taiwanese, OTT, 24 years in the UK	9 years
9	I	Girls-only faith school GIRLS	11–18	Mainland Chinese	7–9 years
10	J	State comprehensive	11–16	Mainland Chinese	Not stated
11	K	Independent co-ed	6–7, 13–18	Taiwanese, PhD, 12 years in the UK	7 years
12	L	Independent day school for girls	11–18	3 part-time teachers from mainland China	6–10 years

Six of the schools are 'Confucius Classrooms'. Schools that are awarded IOE Confucius Classroom status have Chinese fully embedded in their curriculum, and they give advice, support, taster and outreach classes to other schools in the region interested in starting a Chinese language programme. Of the Confucius Classrooms in this survey, two were selective academies for boys, a further two were non-selective schools from the state sector, one was a faith school for girls and the final school was a co-educational independent school, which has made Mandarin compulsory throughout secondary school and offers Mandarin in the curriculum for students in its pre-prep and prep-schools (5–18). Besides the Confucius Classrooms, the other schools include an independent girls' school in London, a co-ed independent school, another selective academy for boys, a comprehensive faith school, as well as a complementary Chinese school that caters for pupils from the age of 6 months to 19 years. Even though the sample size is relatively small, the schools in the sample are varied and thus are a valid representation of schools teaching Chinese more generally. These schools are also most active in the Chinese teaching community, by offering outreach programmes and participating in national Chinese-speaking competitions; teachers from these schools contribute regularly at conferences and in online forum discussions. Nonetheless, the majority of the schools in the survey are situated in the south of England, which is a limitation of this study.

The teachers

Four British, four mainland Chinese and two Taiwanese teachers of Mandarin completed the survey. The nationality of the teacher from the complementary school was uncertain. Most of the teachers underwent teacher training in the UK (PGCE, GTP, OTT), and with the exception of teachers at the complementary school, almost all had obtained qualified teacher status (QTS). The teachers in this survey are all experienced teachers, ranging from 6–19 years' experience teaching Chinese in UK schools. One of the teachers has written a PhD thesis on aspects of Chinese language education among native-speaker Chinese children. Another teacher has recently self-published a monograph which aims to provide a new approach to teaching English students to read and write Chinese (Robinson, 2012).

The learners

The background of the learners is quite wide. In five of the schools, the teachers reported that learners were all British who were learning Chinese as a foreign language. In the other six schools, there were learners who spoke another Chinese dialect at home, British-born Chinese (heritage learners),

learners who had English as an additional language, and other learners, such as students from the United States.

Mandarin in the curriculum

In half of the schools, Mandarin is offered throughout secondary school to pupils aged 11–18. In one school, Mandarin is only offered from Year 9 upwards (13–18). In another school, learners only study to GCSE, as the school does not have a sixth form, whilst in yet another school learners only study two years of Mandarin for GCSE (aged 14–16) and, despite their excellent results (almost 100 per cent A*), the school will not allow pupils to continue their study of Mandarin to A-level.

In all but one secondary school, Mandarin lessons take place on curriculum, with lesson time ranging from 35 minutes to 80 minutes. In the complementary school, lessons are two hours in length. This is encouraging, however, it may not be reflective of the situation in many schools, as the schools in this survey generally all have established Mandarin programmes. The hours of Mandarin tuition received at school each week range from one hour to five hours, depending on the year groups.

Four of the schools also have access to a Mandarin teaching assistant who provided in-class support as well as extra-curricular support. The majority of schools, whether they have an assistant or not, offer extra-curricular support to their students during break, lunch, and after school, as well as online support through a teaching blog. These sessions cover reading and writing Chinese characters in addition to other skills.

Course books and schemes of work

The most popular textbooks for KS3 chosen by teachers in this survey are the *Jìn bù* books 1 (Carruthers, 2010) and 2 (Carruthers, 2011). However, most of the schools do not use *Jìn bù* in isolation, preferring to mix and match textbooks such as *Chinese Made Easy* and *Easy Steps to Chinese*. The latter textbook series was also used for KS4 study in addition to the popular textbook *Edexcel GCSE Chinese* (Carruthers, 2009). At key stage 5, *Chinese for AS* (Zhang and Heppell, 2008), *Edexcel Chinese for A2* (Tate *et al.*, 2009) and *Chinese for A level* (Zhang, 2006) were listed as the chosen course texts. Only one school listed *Nǐ Hǎo* (Fredlein, 2001) as a core textbook, whilst another school used *Jìn bù* as a supplementary text. The complementary Chinese school followed the *IQ Chinese* textbooks and online resources, whilst another used the *IQ Chinese* online resources at the start of every lesson for reading practice. All schools bar one used the accompanying workbooks in varying capacities.

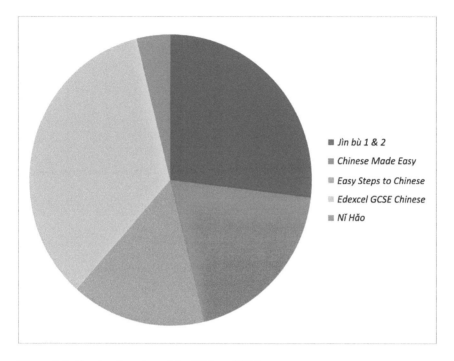

Figure 2.3: Textbooks selected for KS3 and KS4

Asked whether they recommend other supplementary materials, most teachers responded no. The teachers who did recommend supplementary materials used those materials to give students further support with reading and writing characters, for instance, *The Chinese Classroom* for character-writing homework and material a teacher had written himself to support character learning (see Robinson, 2012).

Only school F listed that they had a scheme of work independent of textbooks for Years 7 and 8. Their scheme of work is built around themes rather than topics. The theme they use is based on Shaz Lawrence's 'opening a hotel in China' scheme of work which can be found on her website: www. creativechinese.com.

Exam boards and average results

The schools entered students for the following exam boards: AQA GCSE Mandarin, Edexcel GCSE, AS and A-level Mandarin, as well as IB Mandarin (unclear which level). For GCSE, the average grades were all A or A*. For a number of schools where students scored very highly at GCSE (A or A*), the average mark at AS was just grade C.

This corroborates Zhang and Li's argument that pupils do not achieve exam grades similar to what they would obtain for European languages, and therefore they find learning Mandarin Chinese less rewarding (2010: 92). Conversely, students at all twelve schools scored highly in their GCSE examinations. This demonstrates that the reform of the GCSE has made the qualification more accessible to learners; however, since it is still based on the French model, it does not deal with the 'prominent linguistic characters of Chinese' (Zhang and Li, 2010: 92). Indeed, the speaking and writing controlled assessments have made it easier for students to achieve higher exam grades, but they take up considerable curriculum time and only require students to memorize and regurgitate language.

Survey results
Introducing characters and Pinyin
Most of the teachers in this survey introduce characters and Pinyin at the same time – immediately. The three teachers that began with Pinyin stressed that they introduced characters very quickly afterwards, or introduced a few characters while focussing predominantly on Pinyin:

> There is more focus on Pinyin at the beginning of Year 7, but we introduce a couple of characters at the same time just to let them have a taste of characters and to keep up the interest level. The focus gradually moves over to focus on the characters once we start to learn the textbook *Jìn bù*.

At school K, characters and Pinyin are introduced at the same time, but students study Pinyin more systematically at a later stage:

> Pinyin on top of characters right from the start. After three months I devote time specifically for Pinyin. By then, I found that they often have figured out how to pronounce Chinese characters using Pinyin and their previous phonological knowledge, then I just highlight those special sounds or differences for them to remember.

Despite introducing the two systems at the same time, some teachers carefully choose textbooks that do not print Pinyin over the top of characters, 'otherwise their eyes never go towards the characters and they rely totally on Pinyin'. However, a solid foundation in Pinyin is not underestimated, due to the essential role knowledge of it plays when typing Chinese using a keyboard. At school F, strategies such as requiring students to guess the Pinyin spelling of new vocabulary introduced to them orally are used to build this foundation. Overall, it was found that Pinyin is used predominantly at early stages of learning to teach classroom transactional language and is utilized in lessons that focus more on listening and speaking skills. All teachers try to limit the use of Pinyin over the top or underneath characters as much as possible, to reduce learners' reliance on it for literacy in Chinese.

As for how teachers introduce characters, the term 'radicals' appears in almost every open answer, closely followed by 'strokes'. A few teachers describe how they first teach basic strokes, then radicals, simple pictograph characters, and then the whole character. Teachers mention another strategy for helping students remember characters, namely looking at them as pictures and making up stories about the characters, in addition to mnemonics for stroke order. There are two methods that stand apart, however. One of the methods has been promoted by the US teacher trainer, Shaz Lawrence, at UK Chinese conferences in the past: to begin by only teaching radicals. At school F, students begin the first six weeks of their Mandarin study by learning 20 key radicals, so that they embark on their language study with the ability to break down characters into their component parts. Students at school K start by studying whole character forms, but they are trained right from the start how to analyse characters by breaking them down into their semantic and phonetic components. This analysis of characters is encouraged throughout their study of Mandarin. This teaching method is informed by the teacher's previous masters and doctoral research on how Chinese children learn Chinese characters.

Stroke order

All teachers in this survey have introduced stroke order right from the onset of teaching (predominantly the rules: top to bottom, left to right) but they differ in their opinion of the importance of stroke order in helping pupils acquire Chinese characters. Three teachers were keen to stress that, although they introduce stroke order, they do not require that students adhere to the rules strictly. One teacher only mentions stroke order when introducing new characters, and another only requires students to learn the stroke order of certain characters. Further research into which characters teachers deem students should learn the stroke order for would be interesting.

Whether or not to highlight the importance of stroke order in teaching and assessment is an area that divides the teachers. Four teachers have answered that they do highlight stroke order in their teaching and assessment. One school has commented that they always highlight the importance of stroke order in their teaching, but do not include it in their assessment. Does this not send mixed messages to students about the value of spending extra time learning characters with the correct stroke order?

Three teachers have responded that they include stroke order in their teaching and assessment when they feel they are able to do so, and four teachers have said that they do not highlight stroke order in their teaching and assessment.

Teachers are divided equally between those that believe stroke order is necessary (four) and those that deem stroke order to be unnecessary (four) for school-age learners of Chinese as a foreign language (see Table 2.3).

Table 2.3: Teacher opinions on whether learning stroke order is necessary (in no particular order)

1	Yes. I have taught Chinese and Japanese this way for over 19 years. I prefer them to be as accurate as possible; however, I do not hit the roof if they are incorrect, but gently guide them back to what is correct.
2	No. Some students will look at the characters as a picture. As long as they can produce the character, even by 'drawing', the purpose of communication is fulfilled.
3	Stroke order helps students to remember how to write characters correctly, but I don't think it is necessary to test stroke order in exams.
4	I think it is good, but sadly does not seem to work too well.
5	No, not for the qualifications we offer. But I think it helps students to remember characters.
6	Absolutely! … they don't need to learn to write that many characters, because they can be functionally literate in Chinese using a computer for input, but if they don't get stroke order right from the start it hampers them later. Also, I've noticed that even computer dictionaries like the ones on iPads often depend on stroke order for recognition of the character you are inputting.
7	Yes, not in the beginning but important in the future.
8	Yes.
9	Doesn't really matter.
10	No.
11	I just tell them the principles. As long as the final result – the characters are correct, I don't think it makes much difference for stroke order. In fact, for more practical reasons, we don't have time to go through the stroke order of each individual character.
12	N/A

Interestingly, two teachers believed that stroke order aids students in memorizing characters, but they do not think it is necessary to include stroke order in external examinations. Contrary to the beliefs of the two teachers above, a third teacher believed that learning stroke order would aid students, but that teaching stroke order had not been successful amongst their learners. A final teacher points out that, despite the fact that most learners will not functionally need to write characters in their careers due to the computer, newer mobile technology makes researching new characters even easier because of hand-writing recognition. Students who are unable to write with correct stroke order will be hampered in using this technology for their independent study.

Teaching and learning radicals

The next question teachers were asked was whether or not recognizing radicals helps students to infer the meanings of new characters. Over 80 per cent of the teachers answered with a resounding yes (e.g. 'absolutely, vital, definitely!') One teacher answered more precisely, differentiating between phonetic and semantic radicals and stating that yes, semantic radicals can help students infer the meaning of new characters. Another teacher remarked that radicals only *marginally* help *certain* students to infer the meaning of characters, yet they admitted that more research needs to be conducted in this area.

A teacher who answered yes to the above question included a caveat. Frustrated with what they see as too much focus on simple characters, they write:

> Yes. But I think the stress on the pictorial aspect of characters is a complete waste of time. I think it is important students understand when the radical has a sound and that when it is distorted the phonic is provided by another character. It is important that they can recognize the radical when it is distorted. It is important that they can find where the radical is when looking at a new unfamiliar character.

How then do teachers incorporate the teaching of radicals in their lessons? Some teachers adopt a systematic approach whereas others cover radicals when they appear in characters throughout the course. With the systematic approach, teachers introduce students first to strokes, then radicals, and finally to characters. One reason given in favour of this approach is that it helps to raise students' interest and curiosity. Students were given hand-outs with the list of radicals and explanations of their meaning and how to write them. Then constant repetition is needed throughout the learning process to draw students' attention to radicals as they appear in new characters. One school has devised a set number of radicals to be learnt during the first term of *ab initio* courses in Year 7, 60 radicals. However, for *ab initio* learners in the same school in Year 9, students learn the radicals as they are covered in the textbooks. Indeed, follow-up research is required to determine the rationale behind these differing methods. One can deduce that the school views the introduction of radicals first as more of a novelty, though for entrant learners in Year 9, due to time constraints, a foundation in radicals is not deemed necessary.

However, only two teachers go beyond the study of the most frequently occurring radicals and radicals that appear in vocabulary in textbooks. These teachers attempt to develop an approach that increases students' orthographic awareness of the system of Chinese characters:

> Radicals are explained both when they are individual characters or as components within characters. Students are encouraged to spot those frequently appearing components, analysing the meanings and sounds and make associations between characters. Students enjoy doing this exercise and find both logical and non-logical associations interesting!

Teaching and learning characters

One of the underlying themes in the Chinese as a second language literature and public debate about teaching Chinese in English-speaking secondary schools is the mismatch between the rote-learning method, which many Chinese teachers are accustomed to, and active student approaches to learning that are encouraged in Western classrooms (Medwell *et al.*, 2012; Orton, 2008; 2011). The Chinese method of instruction is usually described as heavily didactic and involves students writing and memorizing many lines of Chinese characters. On the other hand, students in Western classrooms are encouraged to think critically, analyse and challenge information, and, most of all, to be creative. It is the final point that many Chinese teachers profess they have a lack of. Nonetheless, in reality nothing is quite so black and white. To find out what methods teachers of Chinese are using to aid students in UK classrooms to learn Chinese characters, the author listed fourteen strategies and asked teachers to tick which strategies they deploy with their learners. The strategies provided were inspired by the author's experience at school, strategies witnessed in UK classrooms whilst working as an assistant and student teacher, as well as methods suggested in TCFL literature (e.g. Everson, 2009; Scrimgeour, 2011; Xiao, 2009). See Figure 2.4 for an overview of these strategies.

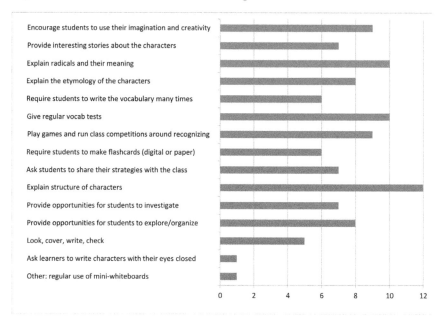

Figure 2.4: Strategies teachers employ to help students remember characters (listed by number of teachers in survey using each strategy)

As the graph demonstrates, the teachers in this survey use a variety of methods and strategies to help their learners acquire Chinese characters. Not surprisingly, every teacher explained the structure of characters to their students; however, not all allowed opportunities for students to investigate and explore components of Chinese characters. The three most popular methods are consistent with more traditional Chinese approaches to teaching and learning: didactic approaches (teacher telling students about characters and radicals and students taking notes) and regular vocabulary tests (students write characters they learnt that week from memory). However, the problem with these approaches is that they rely heavily on short-term memory. Taking notes in class is a passive mode of learning, and, since students' brains are not challenged, they are less likely to remember the content of the lesson.

For the learners in this survey though, the didactic and passive approaches are balanced out with more interactive and creative approaches aimed at challenging and engaging the learners. These approaches include: allowing students to use their imagination and creativity to create stories about characters, games and class competitions to identify characters.

Although creating stories about what they think characters look like are fun and engaging, it still perpetuates the idea that characters are unrelated and need individual acquisition (Scrimgeour, 2011; Xing, 2006: 111). Some of the ways to encourage orthographic awareness include giving learners the opportunities to explore and investigate characters on their own (Scrimgeour, 2011). Almost two thirds of the teachers ticked the box to show that they include these opportunities in their teaching.

In response to a further question about whether teachers use any other strategies or games to help students' character acquisition, it became apparent that one teacher did provide students with opportunities to build characters from their component parts (matching left to right and top to bottom components). However, the majority of strategies and games were less concerned with intra-character relationships than with how to build characters to make words, verb–object phrases, and sentences.

The next question was what learners' need to know about characters to succeed in their language learning and examinations. Two teachers did not provide any response. Five teachers responded by explicitly stating learners need to know that characters are formed of radicals. Of those five teachers, three stated that phonetic radicals should be taught to help associate sound and meaning. They state the need for students to 'make sense of characters' and 'figure out the logic of the system' since, although the system has its irregularities, the process itself reinforces memory. Another teacher does not mention phonetic or semantic radicals, but suggests the need for students to find similarities and patterns between characters. These statements add further weight to Zhang (2009) and Scrimgeour's (2011) argument for what character instruction should look like. A further two teachers highlighted the importance of the sound–meaning connection, but overlooked the phonetic radicals. They highlighted the importance of enhancing the 'artificial' link between the Pinyin pronunciation and the character graph. One of the ways to do this is to integrate more ICT in learning. Two teachers stressed the importance of typing in Chinese for functional and linguistic reasons, which supports research findings of the Computer Chinese (CC) approach (e.g. Xu and Jen 2005b; Zhang, 2009: 86–7). Similarly, another teacher is of the opinion that learners need to develop a much wider reading vocabulary and should be told which characters they need to be able to read and which ones they need to write. This is a strategy adopted by many teachers who realize the expectation that students should memorize excessive numbers of characters is unrealistic (Everson, 1998: 101).

According to the teachers in this survey, the most cited challenge affecting the teaching and learning of Chinese characters in their schools is time pressure and lack of available curriculum time. Indeed, the majority of teachers noted that the most effective method of teaching characters is to offer as much exposure as possible through a sustained and varied 'little and often' approach that incorporates lots of games. A second challenge listed by a couple of the teachers is the students' unwillingness to work hard in order to memorize the characters; students' own linguistic ability is also a factor mentioned. Finally, helping learners establish the relationship between character sound and meaning was also cited as a significant challenge by one teacher.

Conclusion

Even though Pinyin Romanization is not the topic of this paper, it is nonetheless intrinsically linked to the recognition and production of Chinese characters. All of the teachers in this survey introduce Pinyin Romanization at the earliest stages of learning alongside characters. However, with the exception of lessons focussing on speaking, teachers try to remove Pinyin at the earliest possible convenience to force learners to read the characters rather than relying on Pinyin for pronunciation and meaning. Teachers choose textbooks and resources that do not have Pinyin alongside the characters.

Teachers' opinions on the pedagogical advantages of stroke order for writing characters is an entirely different matter: they are equally divided between those that believe writing with stroke order was advantageous and those who do not think it is significant. The most significant split in opinion lies with the issue of stroke order and character memorization. Two native-speaker Chinese teachers believe that writing with correct stroke order aids character recall. However, a British teacher vehemently opposed this belief: '... they [native-speaker Chinese teachers] stress the stroke order when in fact at this level mastering this aspect of writing Chinese adds little to either understanding the characters or remembering them'.

Most of the textbooks used by schools in this survey (e.g. *Chinese Made Easy, Easy Steps to Chinese*) mainly portray characters as simply an assemblage of strokes, with random information about semantic radicals. *Jìn bù* has made inroads to improving character instruction by including a section devoted to characters at the end of every chapter, though it still runs as a separate strand to the characters covered in each topic. The workbooks provide more information, such as etymology and mnemonics to help memorize characters, but these activities are usually set as tasks to complete individually outside the classroom. None of the current resources provide adequate information or exercises to build up learners' metalinguistic knowledge of Chinese characters.

Teachers believe that for learners to master Chinese characters they should be able to recognize, deconstruct, and construct characters from radicals. Helping learners to attach sound to the characters was also an area that was highlighted. Almost half of the teachers surveyed believe the phonetic radicals should be taught to learners. This demonstrates that our teachers have identified important pedagogical aspects of successful character instruction: it is the resources that need to be further developed in line with these views.

There are a few important measures that need to be taken to improve character instruction in schools further, ensure quality instruction is maintained across schools, and build CFL pedagogy for school-age learners in the UK and abroad. First, a comprehensive online network needs to be established where professional development webinars disseminating research and best practice can be shared among all teachers. This network should include forums and areas to share resources. It should provide examples of excellent exercises and activities that can inspire other teachers and provide momentum for approaching character instruction more systematically. Second, schools should work with universities and other partners to conduct research into character instruction in schools. Third, based on resources, discussions, and research produced from the aforementioned channels, new interactive resources should be produced that address specific linguistic challenges of character learning. The resources should focus on functional units of Chinese characters, with particular attention to phonetic characters that have thus far been largely ignored. Online and mobile resources are a promising avenue to develop. This is because of the positive pedagogical and functional effects of computer input for recognition, differentiation, and sound associations for Chinese characters and for engaging ways to practise hand-writing characters on mobile tablets (Zhang, 2009). Educators should not underestimate the power of technology in language learning, after all technology in CFL teaching is not just a language tool but a language skill (Xu and Jen, 2005a, 2005b; Zhang, 2002). As Scrimgeour (2011) contends, we need to give learners the tools and skills to be able to understand why characters are constructed and pronounced the way they are, instead of committing each character to memory. Only in this way can they build transferrable skills that will enable them to handle authentic texts and thereby become independent and autonomous learners.

Follow-up interviews with the teachers in this survey, classroom observations, student questionnaires, and interviews would provide more information to confirm the findings of this paper and offer a wider perspective into the approaches and effectiveness of character instruction in schools in the UK.

PRACTICAL IDEAS

- For each unit, make a list of characters that students need to read and a list of characters that they need to write.
- Identify key semantic and phonetic radicals in the new unit and ask students to provide examples of previously learnt characters that include the same semantic/phonetic components. This could be a good class starter activity as well.
- List some characters with semantic radicals that students have previously studied and also list the English definitions. Ask students to match the Chinese character with the correct English definition.
- Character differentiation: Provide students passages in Pinyin only and ask them to type the text in Chinese characters.
- Character differentiation: Provide passages in Chinese characters with deliberate mistakes and ask students to identify the incorrect characters and then provide the correct characters.
- Character differentiation: PowerPoint Game. Place two similar-looking characters next to each other on a slide and label them A and B with the English translation below. Ask students to write down whether the English matches character A or B. Make this activity fast-paced.
- Metalinguistic training: Create word search games with characters containing the same phonetic components and ask students to find all the characters that contain the same phonetic component. This will enable students to realize that the phonetic components can be found at the top/bottom/right/left-hand side of characters, further enhancing their knowledge of character construction.
- Game: Spot the odd one out. On a PowerPoint slide or worksheet create groups of characters. They could be grouped according to theme (e.g. daily activities), stroke order (all characters are six strokes), semantic/phonetic radicals, character composition (all characters can be broken down into right and left). Place an anomalous character in each group and ask students to identify which is the odd one out and why.

> • Assessment: In unit tests or quizzes include sections that test knowledge of character formation. For instance, you could list a few characters, ask students to circle semantic/phonetic components, then ask them to write down the semantic meaning/ or the pronunciation in Pinyin.

References

Carr, M. (1981) 'Pedagogy, radicals, and grapho-semantic fields'. *Journal of the Chinese Language Teachers Association*, 16 (3), 51–66.

Carruthers, K. (ed.) (2009) *Edexcel GCSE Chinese*. Harlow: Pearson.

Carruthers, K. (ed.) (2010) *Jìn bù1* 进步. Harlow: Pearson.

Carruthers, K. (ed.) (2011) *Jìn bù2* 进步. Harlow: Pearson.

Chu, C. (2004) 'A reflection on traditional approaches to Chinese character teaching and learning'. In Yao, T., Chu, C., Wang, Y., Xu, H. and Hayden, J. (eds) *Studies on Chinese Instructional Materials and Pedagogy*. Beijing: Beijing Language University Press, 240–57.

DeFrancis, J. (1984) *The Chinese Language: Fact and fantasy*. Honolulu: University of Hawaii Press.

Everson, M.E. (1998) 'Word recognition among learners of Chinese as a foreign language: Investigating the relationship between naming and knowing'. *Modern Language Journal*, 82 (2), 194–204.

Everson, M.E. (2009) 'Literacy development in Chinese as a foreign language'. In Everson, M.E. and Xiao, Y. (eds) *Teaching Chinese as a Foreign Language: Theories and applications*. Boston: Cheng and Tsui, 97–111.

Fredlein, P.A. (2001) *Nǐ Hǎo*. Boston: Chang & Tsui Company.

Hayes, E.B. (1987) 'The relationship between Chinese character complexity and character recognition'. *Journal of the Chinese Language Teachers Association*, 22 (2), 45–57.

Huang, J. (2000) *Students' Major Difficulties in Learning Mandarin Chinese as an Additional Language and Their Coping Strategies* (ERIC ED440-537). Online. http://files.eric.ed.gov/fulltext/ED440537.pdf (accessed 4 October 2017).

Huang, P.R. (黄沛荣) (2003) 《汉字教学的理论与实践》 [Theory and practice of Chinese character teaching and learning]. Taipei: Lexue Shuju.

Ke, C. (1996) 'An empirical study on the relationship between Chinese character recognition and production'. *Modern Language Journal*, 80 (3), 340–49.

Ke, C. (1998) 'Effects of strategies on the learning of Chinese characters among foreign language students'. *Journal of the Chinese Language Teachers Association*, 33 (2), 93–112.

Liu, G.-Q. and Lo Bianco, J. (2007) 'Teaching Chinese, teaching in Chinese, and teaching the Chinese'. *Language Policy*, 6 (1), 95–117.

Lǔ, B.S. (吕必松) (ed.) (1999) 《汉字与汉字教学研究论文集》 [Chinese characters and characters teaching]. Beijing: Beijing University Press.

Medwell, J., Richardson, K. and Li, L. (2012) 'Working together to train tomorrow's teachers of Chinese'. *Scottish Languages Review*, 25, 39–46.

Orton, J. (2008) *Chinese Language Education in Australian Schools*. Melbourne: University of Melbourne.

Orton, J. (2011) 'Educating Chinese language teachers: Some fundamentals'. In Tsung, L. and Cruickshank, K. (eds) *Teaching and Learning Chinese in Global Contexts: Multimodality and literacy in the new media age*. London: Continuum, 151–64.

Robinson, K. (2012) *A Systematic Introduction to Reading and Writing Chinese*. Morrisville, NC: Lulu Press.

Samimy, K.K. and Lee, Y. (1997) 'Beliefs about language learning: Perspectives of first-year Chinese learners and their instructors'. *Journal of the Chinese Teachers Association*, 32 (1), 40–60.

Scrimgeour, A. (2008) 'Seen from the learner's perspective: Engaging students meaningfully in learning about and learning how to use the Chinese writing system'. Asia Education Foundation Chinese Language Forum 2008, Melbourne.

Scrimgeour, A. (2011) 'Issues and approaches to literacy development in Chinese second language classrooms'. In Tsung, L. and Cruickshank, K. (eds) *Teaching and Learning Chinese in Global Contexts: Multimodality and literacy in the new media age*. London: Continuum, 197–212.

Shen, H.H. (2005) 'An investigation of Chinese-character learning strategies among non-native speakers of Chinese'. *System*, 33 (1), 49–68.

Tate, M., Wang, L., Zhao, R. X., Liu, J., Li, X., Burch, Y., Lau, C., Liang, Q., Shi, Y. and Zeng, J (2009) *Edexcel Chinese for A2*. London: Hodder education.

Xiao, Y. (2009) 'Teaching Chinese orthography and discourse: Knowledge and pedagogy'. In Everson, M.E. and Xiao, Y. (eds) *Teaching Chinese as a Foreign Language: Theories and applications*. Boston: Cheng and Tsui, 113–30.

Xing, J.Z. (2006) *Teaching and Learning Chinese as a Foreign Language: A pedagogical grammar*. Hong Kong: Hong Kong University Press.

Xu, P. and Jen, T. (2005a) 汉字教学与电脑科技 [Chinese characters and computer technology]. Taiwan: Jinglian Publishing Press.

Xu, P. and Jen, T. (2005b) '"Penless" Chinese language learning: A computer-assisted approach'. *Journal of the Chinese Language Teachers Association*, 40 (2), 25–42.

Yang, J. (2000) 'Orthographic effect on word recognition by learners of Chinese as a foreign language'. *Journal of the Chinese Language Teachers Association*, 35 (2), 1–18.

Yu, B., Zhu, X., Carruthers, K. (2010) *Jìn bù1 进步一*. Harlow: Pearson.

Zhang, G.X. and Li, L.M. (2010) 'Chinese language teaching in the UK: Present and future'. *Language Learning Journal*, 38 (1), 87–97.

Zhang, X. (2006) *Chinese for A level*. London: Cypress Book Co.

Zhang, X. and Heppell, K. (2008) *Chinese for AS*. London: Cypress Book Co.

Zhang, Z.S. (2002) '"Writing" characters using computer'. In He, W., Wu, H. and Wang, C. (eds) *International Research on Teaching Chinese as a Foreign Language*. Journal of Nanjing University, Higher Education Research Institute, Nanjing University.

Zhang, Z.S. (2009) 'Myth, reality and character instruction in the 21st century'. *Journal of the Chinese Language Teachers Association*, 44 (1), 69–89.

Zhao, Y. (2013) 'Chinese characters: What do you know and how do we teach?'. 10th Annual Chinese Conference, 'Securing Excellence: Reaching for a Global Perspective with Mandarin Chinese', Institute of Education, London, 17–18 May 2013.

Zhu, X. and Bin, Y. and Carruthers, K. (2011) *Jìn bù2* 进步二. Harlow: Pearson.

Chapter 3

Teaching Mandarin characters to foreign language learners in secondary schools in England

A case study of two Mandarin lessons in a private school and a state school

Xu Qian

Introduction

This chapter focuses on Mandarin teaching and learning, especially Chinese character teaching in European countries and particularly in Britain.

Moys (1990, in Bovair and Bovair, 1992: 16) argues that, although British people are lucky to speak a language that is used and required globally, it is still necessary for English-speaking children to start learning another language or even more languages 'within their national curriculum entitlement', in order to enable the next generation 'to understand and be understood by their interlocutors from abroad'. As a result, the Department of Education and Science (DES and Welsh Office, 1988) validated the 'diversification of the modern foreign language curriculum' (Edwards, 2001: 253). The 1995 White Paper on Teaching and Learning referenced by Extra and Yağmur (2012: 14) urged that every citizen 'should learn two European languages'. Instructed by the Nuffield Languages Inquiry (2000), foreign language teaching in the UK has started from younger ages up to secondary school pupils. In secondary schools in England, education is offered to children aged between 11 and 16 or even 18 years old. The aim of language teaching in secondary schools is to extend the knowledge of foreign languages that has been taught in primary schools and further build the pupils' ability to communicate with speakers of foreign languages in different social contexts such as employment, travelling, education, etc. About 95 per cent of secondary schools are comprehensive schools, which design their courses to abide with the national curriculum. As for private schools, they can choose and design their own curriculum (Czerniawski,

2011). In 2002, the EU Council claimed that its goal was to maintain linguistic diversity and to encourage multilingualism, because it was believed that an individual who could master more than one language would possess more than one opportunity in education, economy and culture. Edwards (2001: 254) emphasizes that 'bilingualism has always been desirable amongst the social elite' and takes an example of the ability to read and write Latin as a sign of being well educated. The main foreign languages taught in the United Kingdom as a member of the European Union were French and German, but when schools gained the freedom to teach world languages other than those two, languages with strong cultural features became popular, such as Chinese Mandarin.

A study on Mandarin learning in the UK carried out by the National Centre for Languages has shown that 60 per cent of the participant schools offer Mandarin courses, and the largest population of Mandarin learners in secondary schools are Year 9 and 10 (CiLT, 2007: 9). Extra and Yağmur (2012) state that for secondary schools, the overall percentage of students taking a General Certificate of Secondary Education (GCSE) examination in a language dropped drastically from 78 per cent in 2001 to 43 per cent in 2011. The decline was greatest in French and German, but other foreign languages such as Spanish and Chinese[1] have become increasingly popular among students.

The reason for the popularity of Chinese among pupils can be concluded to be as follows: on the one hand, for native Chinese speakers, teaching and learning Mandarin preserve both the language and the culture of China, especially for those who have Chinese backgrounds but are living overseas; on the other hand, non-native Chinese learners choose Mandarin for various reasons such as 'academic and study', 'employment', and 'social interaction' (Cruickshank and Tsung, 2011: 214). Apart from personal interest, the growing economic and cultural power of China should not be neglected. For instance, China has become a new international market for Britain. Offering a 'well-educated multilingual workforce', London is 'an increasingly important centre both for pan-European customer service centres and the coordination of geographically dispersed operations in marketing, sales, human resources, finance and information technology' (Land, 2000, in Edwards, 2001: 253). As a result, the strong need for language diversity, especially the need for Mandarin, has grown dramatically.

With the growing number of Confucius Institutes established in British universities along with the sub-model of Confucius Classrooms in secondary schools, it is of enormous significance to find out how Mandarin is taught in the Institutes and Classrooms worldwide. There is extensive research on Mandarin teaching and learning, but it is far from enough to cover every possible context. The study in this paper was carried out in two Confucius Classrooms of two types of secondary schools in the UK. I observed two Chinese lessons in a private school and a state school respectively and mainly focused on exploring how Mandarin teachers interpret the challenge of Mandarin character identification as well as the strategies applied in Chinese character teaching in bilingual classrooms where Mandarin is taught as a modern foreign language mainly in English.

Language teaching and learning in classroom contexts

It is believed that citizens in Britain have 'less exposure to the authentic use of other languages than do learners of English globally' (Carrier, 2012: 77). Everybody, including immigrants and visitors, tends to speak English in Britain. As a result, foreign language learning usually takes place in classroom contexts. Communicative language teaching (CLT) is regarded as 'the current perspective on modern foreign language (MFL) teaching' and an 'eclectic assortment of traditional and novel approaches based on the tenet of the development in pupils of an ability to communicate in the target language'. The present-practise-produce (PPP) model is widely applied in the process of CLT. At first, the structure and form of the target language are introduced through teacher presentation, and then, with activities and exercises, learners internalize the target language (Pachler *et al.*, 2009: 58). This kind of model conforms to the process of acquiring a second/foreign language, which usually involves the following procedure: input–output–feedback–intake. Input 'provides language-specific information which interacts with whatever innate structure an individual … brings to the language learning situation' (Gass, 2003: 225). Through interaction and negotiation, learners produce output. It is a good opportunity for learners to get feedback for their production (Swain, 1985), to '"notice the holes" in the present state of their language knowledge' (Thornbury, 2006: 48), and 'move from the semantic, open-ended nondeterministic, strategic processing prevalent in comprehension to the complete grammatical processing needed for accurate production' (Swain, 1995: 128). Eventually, the 'successfully and completely processed' input becomes 'part of the internal presentation' and can be considered as intake (Hatch, 1983: 81).

Though language learners are expected to 'produce and comprehend language effortlessly and fluently' (Whong, 2011: 95), teachers should be aware of the time that the learners need in order to 'familiarise', 'assimilate and accommodate' the knowledge (Pachler *et al.*, 2009: 69). Language teachers adopt various teaching strategies, on the one hand to facilitate the input and intake of the language, on the other hand to help students conquer the potential difficulties in learning foreign languages. If difficulties are neglected, they are likely to hinder progress.

Difficulties in Mandarin learning: Character recognition

Chinese is a special language that differs from European languages. Zhou and Marslen-Wilson (1997: 5) state that Mandarin is a 'morphologically limited language which has virtually no inflectional or derivational processes in word formation'. The majority of Chinese words are monomorphemic, monosyllabic, or disyllabic compounds. The written script consists of characters rather than letters. This important feature distinguishes Mandarin from Indo-European languages and is a huge challenge for pupils who learn Mandarin as a foreign language (Shen, 2005). Compared with 'phonographic writing where each letter of the alphabet encodes a phoneme', Chinese characters are 'logographic' and 'simultaneously encod[e] sounds and meaning at the level of the syllable' (Sun, 2006: 101–2). As a result, writing Chinese characters seems like drawing to learners whose native languages use alphabets. It is, nevertheless, crucial to associate the meanings with the structures of the 'drawings' to facilitate character learning.

Generally, a Chinese character consists of two elements: a stroke and a radical. Strokes make up radicals and radicals make up characters. Thus, a stroke is the basis of the configuration of radicals and consequently of characters (Shen, 2005). There are approximate 30 types of strokes, but five major ones are horizontal strokes (一), vertical strokes (|), left-descending strokes (ノ), right-descending strokes (﹨) and bending strokes (⟅); the rest of the strokes are variants of those five. Nonetheless, it is still hard to formulate a universal rule for the number of strokes that form a radical and which radical should be used to form a character, because strokes also form characters at times and characters can be categorized into four types according to their structure.

Considering the massive quantity of characters, Chinese characters are further classified into four categories: 1) xiàngxíng (pictographic) 2) zhǐshì (ideographic) 3) huìyì (compound indicative) and 4) xíngshēng (phonetic–semantic compound) (Shen, 2005: 133–4). Xiàngxíng characters make up approximately 5 per cent of all Chinese characters, while xíngshēng characters more than 80 per cent. Nevertheless, xiàngxíng characters still play a vital role in the formation of Chinese characters because they are often used as components of other characters and function as either radicals or phonetic components. Table 3.1 further explains the four categories with examples.

Table 3.1: Four types of Chinese characters

Type	Explanation	Example
xiàngxíng (pictographic)	It imitates the appearance of the item that a character represents.	刀 means 'knife'. It imitates the shape of a knife, as seen below.
zhǐshì (ideographic)	It usually consists of a xiàngxíng character plus one or more strokes.	刃 consists of a variant of left-descending stroke and the xiàngxíng character 刀 (knife). The stroke indicates the position of the knife, which is at the edge. Thus, 刃 means 'the blade'.
huìyì (compound indicative)	It combines two or more radicals to represent a new character. The new character usually expresses the meaning of the combination.	忍: As explained above, 刃 is 'the blade'. 心 at the bottom means 'heart'. When a 'blade' is put on a 'heart', it makes people feel pain and torture. Thus, 忍 means 'to bear something unpleasant at heart for a long period of time'.
xíngshēng (phonetic–semantic compound)	It consists of both semantic and phonetic components in one character.	病 (bing [4]) means 'disease'. The semantic component is '疒', which means 'sick and uncomfortable'. 丙(bing[3]) serves as the phonetic element and has the same sound as 病 (bing [4]) regardless of their tones.

Compound characters are a common but complex type. They usually consist of radicals and phonetic components. A radical is 'the semantic component of characters' and 'signal[s] the meaning of a given character' (Xing, 2006: 107). Phonetic components usually give clues to the pronunciation of characters. A phonetic component can also be considered a radical, but in order to avoid confusion I adopt Xing's (2006) terminology for this paper, with 'radical' used for meaning and 'phonetic component' for pronunciation. Chen (1999: 141) uses different terminology to talk about radicals and phonetic components; he notes that there are about 1,300 components that serve as 'phonetic determinatives' and 250 as 'semantic determinatives'; in contrast to 'kana in Japanese, or letters in Finnish or English', there is a much larger number of phonetic components in Chinese. What makes the characters more complicated is that only 26 per cent of the common compound characters have the pronunciation implied by their phonetic components and not all radicals represent the expected meanings precisely. Moreover, when phonetic components serve as radicals, they do not have their original function any more. This also causes potential character recognition difficulties for learners of Chinese. Nonetheless, it is clear that teaching radicals and phonetic components facilitates the process of Mandarin character learning, one prime reason being that they indicate the meaning and sound of Chinese characters. Xing (2006: 107) discusses that Chinese language practitioners have agreed that the goal of teaching characters is 'associated with the three properties of characters: sound, meaning and form', and the ability to pronounce, read, and write the characters is closely interrelated with the learners' knowledge of the three properties. The other important reason for teaching radicals and phonetic components is that they are references for consulting dictionaries. Learners who have studied Chinese for more than a year are supposed to read and write more characters. They will inevitably come across new characters that need to be looked up in dictionaries, since the latter are widely used tools for checking meaning, grammar, collocation, etc. when learning a language (Atkins and Varantola, 1997). Characters are arranged by radicals and number of strokes as well as Pinyin in Chinese dictionaries. Thus, if learners are familiar with strokes and radicals, it will be much easier for them to refer to the dictionary (Xing, 2006).

What makes Chinese characters even more complex is that there are different versions of Chinese characters, i.e. simplified and traditional versions, used in different areas of China. In this study, I will solely highlight the recognition of simplified Chinese characters, because it is this version that is taught in both observed lessons and most widely used in mainland China.

Research methodology

1. Participants

I observed two British secondary schools, one state and one private. Both schools are near central London and have offered Mandarin courses over the past few years. Prior to conducting the research, permission to visit and make audio recordings was given by the heads of both schools. The observed teachers were fully informed of the purpose of my research. The field notes, recordings, and transcripts were kept confidential in line with recommended social research practice (Bryman, 2012: 136).

THE PRIVATE SCHOOL

The private school is an independent school with one of the highest reputations in the UK. Due to its admission requirements and high tuition fees, most pupils are from upper-class backgrounds. All the applicants take pre-tests and entrance examinations. Pupils are required to learn two foreign languages, choosing from Mandarin, German, French and Spanish. Language lessons take place in a modern languages centre away from the main school buildings. The Confucius Classroom Programme was established in 2009. Three years later, the Confucius Classroom moved to a newly-built Mandarin centre next to the modern languages centre. The Mandarin centre is strongly reminiscent of Chinese architecture, with a red Chinese arch and traditional Chinese totems at the entrance, a small red arch bridge, and bungalows with red roof tiles as in Mandarin classrooms. There are four full-time and a few part-time Mandarin teachers. All of them are native-speaker Chinese. The Mandarin lesson I observed was delivered by a 29-year-old teacher from north China. She had obtained her master's degree in London and was completing her PGCE Mandarin placement in that school. The lesson I observed was her first lesson in that Year 10 class. There were two girls and nine boys, all of whom appeared to be white British. They had been learning Mandarin for a year and were learning another European language as their other foreign language.

THE STATE SCHOOL

The state school is a co-educational secondary school, providing education to both male and female teenagers aged 11–19. It accepts pupils from both prosperous and deprived families around the borough and is obliged to offer free school meals. The policies for modern foreign language learning are differentiated for monolingual and bilingual pupils. The bilinguals are required to learn two foreign languages, that is, one European language, either Spanish or French, and Mandarin. The monolinguals only learn Spanish or French as their foreign language. The Mandarin lessons take place in a Mandarin classroom in the main building, decorated with Chinese patterns and students' Mandarin works.

From my observation, there was a smaller number of Mandarin staff than in the private school. The Mandarin teacher is from Taiwan and has a Taiwanese accent. She started her teaching career in Taiwan, but, in her late

20s, she moved to England with her British husband. Then she continued her teaching career as a Mandarin teacher in various British schools. She is the core Mandarin teacher in the state school and working closely with the head of the Mandarin department. The class I observed was a Year 9 class with eight girls and ten boys. The pupils were mixed in both races and abilities. The teacher mentioned that some of the pupils in that class came from well-educated families with high social status. Their parents showed huge enthusiasm and encouraged their children to learn Mandarin. The teacher and pupils were under high GCSE exam pressure, and the teacher continually related her teaching content to the examination throughout the lesson.

2. Methods

This empirical study is based on qualitative methods: observations along with field notes and transcripts of audio recordings. Qualitative research considers context and setting as crucial factors when analysing the data and drawing up the findings. My research is placed in the context of two Mandarin lessons in classroom settings from two types of secondary schools in England. Dörnyei (2007: 186) evaluates a classroom environment in accordance with two dimensions: 'instructional context' and 'social context'. He believes that, from an instructional perspective, the learning environment is influenced by teachers and their teaching methods, by students and the curriculum, etc. Meanwhile, from a social perspective, the classroom is 'the main social arena for students'. Hence, a classroom is a very complicated venue to observe. As defined by Allwright and Bailey (1991), classroom-based research values both input and output as well as classroom interactions in the process of a lesson. This study is designed to find out how the observed Mandarin teachers interpret the 'linguistic input and output' in a context where the target language was not familiar to the pupils of both secondary schools.

In order to ensure the validity of the qualitative research, I adopted a 'complete observer' role, as my aim was to see how both teachers interpret the challenges of Mandarin teaching in relation to character recognition (Gold, 1958, referenced in Angrosino, 2007: 54). I believe it is best to be completely uninvolved in the lesson and maintain an observer's role, so as not to impact the teachers' decision on what and how to interpret.

To ensure the authenticity of the data, two aspects are to be included in the orthographic transcripts: '*what* was said' and '*how* it was said' (Braun and Clarke, 2013: 162). First, I transcribed what had been said as closely to the original as possible. For example, colloquialisms were all kept to reflect the identity of the speakers. Since neither of my subjects is a native English speaker, grammatical mistakes like 'two character' and 'A look like B' were also kept, because I believe that they reflect the nature of foreign language lessons; though both teachers are bilingual and able to communicate both in the target language and in the students' native language, they nonetheless occasionally make errors. Second, it should be emphasized that, during conversations, interlocutors do not use punctuation. They use pauses, intonation, and stress to express attitudes and emotions. Consequently, punctuation has been added to ensure 'how it was said' is included.

3. Findings and discussion

Liu and Peng (1997: 228) point out that learners 'begin by learning individual characters' when learning Mandarin. In this chapter, I present some vignettes[2] from my observations in both schools to discuss how teachers interpreted the challenge of character recognition in class.

VIGNETTE 1 FOR THE STATE SCHOOL: 末 AND 本

01. Teacher:	Today we have to try to go to future tense. And you obviously learn a new vocabulary related to week. (?) learn 'weekend'. And 'weekend' you have to use 周 (zhōu). 周 (zhōu) means a cycle and 末 (mò), guess what 末 (mò) mean?
02. Student A:	Does it mean 'end'?
03. Teacher:	'End', so 周末 means 'weekend', OK? So 周 by itself means 'a week', means 'week' or means 'a circle' but here 周末 means 'weekend' xxx
04. Student A:	That looks like 'Japan'. (The written text of 'Japan' in Chinese is 日本.)
05. Teacher:	Japan? It is like that (writing the characters '日本' on board). So sun, root, OK? And 末 (mo[4]) is like this, that is the tree. It's actually quite interesting. A tree, ok, at the end of the tree (?) the root of the tree that means your root, your base. And 末 look like this. OK, it's also a tree but it's kind of at the end of the tree, here, so the stroke is here. It means it's the end of tree but if I put this underneath here, that means, the root, to go deeper than, you know, it's not the tree that you see, it's the root and that means end of the tree. Does it make sense to you?

06. Students: Yea.

07. Teacher: So Chinese character are very interesting coz that means end of tree, that means root of the tree, ok, means root of something.

The confusion was caused by two characters which have the same type and number of strokes: '末' and '本' (see line 04 and 05). Both of the characters have five strokes, i.e. two horizontal strokes一 (one is longer and the other is relatively shorter), one vertical stroke丨, one left-descending stroke丿, and one right-descending stroke乀. The only difference between '末' and '本' is the position of the shorter horizontal stroke. The reason that the teacher mentioned a 'tree' was that both of the characters originate from the character 木 ('tree' or 'wood'). '木' is a xiàngxíng character representing the appearance of a tree (see Figure 3.1). The strokes丿and 乀 are put together to imitate the root of the tree (丿乀). '十' stands for its trunk and branches. '末' and '本' are zhǐshì characters, as they are made up of a xiàngxíng character (木) plus one more stroke (一). The stroke 一 indicates the position of the tree. For '末', the stroke 一 is placed above the stump and root (丿乀) but under the branches (十). Thus, '末' is used to mean 'the end of a stem' and 'the extremity of something'. For '本', its short stroke is placed underneath the root (丿乀) and the character means 'the very basic and fundamental part of something'. The teacher helped the pupils memorize the characters and facilitated character recognition by explaining the background to how these three similar characters (木, 本, 末) were developed and formed.

Figure 3.1: The transformation of '木' from ancient to modern Chinese

VIGNETTE 2 FOR THE STATE SCHOOL: 早

01. Teacher: It's 早 (zǎo). What does 早 mean? (...) It's a picture. It's a picture. Do you remember? I drew this several times. Ian?

02. Student A: The sun-rising.

03. Teacher: Sun-rising on top of the ...

04. Student A: Horizon.

05. Teacher: It's not horizon. It's on top of the **stick**. OK? It looks like a stick, isn't it? So it's, it's early morning about six to eight or sometimes you can say, somebody say six to ten.

Another similar moment happened when the teacher was introducing the time phrases for past tense. When she was asking for the expression of 'early morning', the students had some difficulty recognizing the character '早' written on the whiteboard. 早 means 'early' and 'morning' in different contexts. It is an indicative character with two radicals (日 and 十). 日 means 'the sun'. '十' is originally written as '甲', which indicates 'a growing seed coming out of the earth with its breaking seed coat on the top'. Gradually, '甲' is simplified into '十'. '早' illustrates the scene of the sun rising above the horizon at dawn. When explaining '早', the teacher separated it into two radicals (日 and 十) and visualized the character as a picture. '早' is a high-frequency Chinese character and radical, so it was identified by the learners very quickly. As for the radical at the bottom (十), the teacher did not mention the original character and its transformation in order to reduce confusion; instead, she described it as 'a stick' for the students to memorize (in line 05). She simplified and visualized the character by using drawings.

VIGNETTE 3 FOR THE STATE SCHOOL: 午

01. Teacher: That is pm.

02. Students: [pm.

03. Teacher: What do you think that is? (Pointing to 午)

04. Students: Is that the noon? [From noon …

05. Teacher: Noon. That kinds of means noon. Remember we say what does this little flick mean to you?

06. Student A: The moon.

07. Teacher: It's not a moon. Won't be the moon. xxx Say again. That is a little **birdy**. OK. Remember my bird here. Oh, I have to draw it well so you can see. **Bird rest on top of the tree or a stick.** It's a noon time because the sun is too bitter. OK. So, that, remind yourself that is the little birdy. So that itself means noon.

This is an interesting moment where the teacher used imagination and a story to help the pupils recognize the character. '午' means 'midday' in modern Mandarin but it is related to 'horse and bridle' in classical Chinese, indicating 'middle' and 'straight', as the stroke ノ at the top represents the head of a horse and 十 is its body. The shorter horizontal stroke (一) stands for the bridle. When the bridle is pulled, the horse stands straight in a nice manner. Later, it came to mean 'noon'. The teacher did not explain that complicated history because she believes that it would cause more confusion. Instead, she employed the figure of a bird as a metaphor for the stroke ノ and a tree/stick for 干 (in line 07).

VIGNETTE 4 FOR THE PRIVATE SCHOOL: 踢 AND 打

01. Teacher: Football, play football, play football. So on the side, you can check here, grammar 'to play', so thirty seconds, read through, tell me the difference between 'play', 打 (dǎ) and 踢 (tī), OK? What's the difference? xxx

02. Student A: When we say to 'kick' (?), when we say 'to play', we touch it with our hand.

03. Teacher: Yes, so the radical here. What radical is it, Amy? What radical is this?

(The teacher writes the Chinese characters '打' and '踢' on the whiteboard.)

04. Student A: The one on the left is foot and the right is hand.

05. Teacher: Yes, so this is foot radical and here (circled the radicals and draws pictures of foot and hand under the Chinese characters.)

06. Students: Hand.

07. Teacher: Hand. So hand radical. 一二三四 (one, two, three, four), yea, (draws a picture of a hand while counting the number of fingers in Mandarin), so 打 (dǎ) 乒 (pīng) 乓 (pāng) 球 (qiú) (to play ping-pong), you use your hand. 打 (dǎ) 网 (wǎng) 球 (qiú) (to play tennis), you use your hand. 打 (dǎ) 篮 (lán) 球 (qiú) (to play basketball), you use your hand. xxx

08. Teacher: But 踢 (tī) 足 (zú) 球 (qiú) (to play football)，you use your?

09. Students: Foot.

In this vignette, the teacher was teaching expressions for hobbies. There is a salient disparity in the expression 'to play' ball games between English and Mandarin. In English, the same verb is used for 'playing' whatever the ball game, while in Mandarin different verbs are required depending on the type of ball game. Games relating to hands such as basketball are described by '打', which originally means 'to hit'. Games such as football should be described by '踢', which means 'to kick'. Both of the characters are compounds with radicals on the left side. Radicals indicate the meaning of characters. The radical of '打' is '扌', which is developed from the xiàngxíng character '手 (hand)'. Logically, the radical '扌' implies actions related to hands. As for '踢', its radical '⻊' is transformed from the character '足', which means 'foot'. Thus, characters with the radical '⻊' are always associated with 'foot'. The teacher specifically explained these two radicals and used drawings of a foot and a hand to facilitate recognition.

A 'multilevel interactive-activation framework' (see Figure 3.2) was adopted by Taft and Chung (1999). It considers strokes as the basic elements forming radicals; characters are composed of radicals with different functions. For example, compound characters have both radicals and phonetic components (Everson, 1998). The characters cannot be read out until they are forming legitimate structures, because most of the components of characters only have names but no sounds. This is different from English letters. For example, 'ow' can be spelt out by the names of letters (o and w) or read aloud as the diphthong sounds the combination usually forms, /aʊ/ (as in 'cow') or /əʊ/ (as in 'slow'). By contrast, a Chinese radical such as '忄' cannot be pronounced until it is put in a well-formed character, such as '悦' (yue[4] 'happy)'. Once the phonological units and character configuration are introduced, the semantic units of Chinese characters can be noticed and learned. Wu and Liu (1997) confirm that the recognition of characters occurs before phonology is activated. Shu and Anderson (1999) reiterate that pupils will notice the elementary units of both the spoken and written form and start to associate the two together when learning to read in Chinese. Therefore, it is necessary for Mandarin teachers to point out the elements of Chinese characters before and while introducing actual characters.

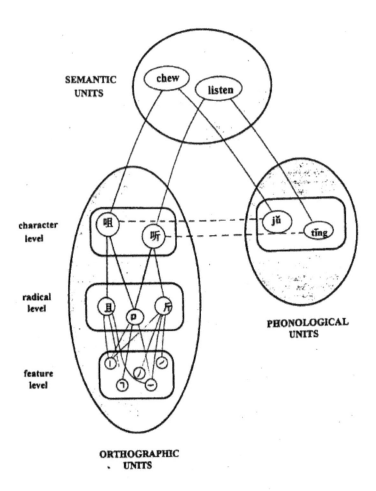

Figure 3.2: Multilevel interactive-activation framework (Taft and Chung, 1999: 245)

Liu (1999: 178) describes Chinese characters as script units and states that 'the association between a character and its familiarity of being used for reading quickly develops'. The 'visual complexity' of memorizing a character also depends on the number of strokes (Lee and Kalyuga, 2011: 1099). For example, '一' and '孁' clearly present different levels of difficulty for memorizing. It is true that characters with fewer strokes are easier to memorize; however, Everson (2009: 103) argues that 'the depth of concept-driven processing for characters' is expanded if Mandarin teachers can provide the background information for characters such as their 'etymological background, information and analysis of their radicals, and examples of the words as used in different contexts'. Lee and Kalyuga (2011) support the view that memorizing the characters by strokes requires more effort than memorizing chunks of characters. Therefore, Mandarin teachers should let learners notice and be aware of the elements composing characters. One of the most effective ways to do this is to separate the characters into different parts and use meaning-based explanations together with drawings and pictures that demonstrate the origins of the components. There were moments in both schools when the teachers used drawings and imagination to facilitate the recognition of characters and they divided the characters into different elements to explain their meanings. The study conducted by Taft and Chung (1999: 247–8) shows that learners with an 'awareness of radicals' recognize characters much faster than those who neglect radicals and strokes because 'analysing a character in terms of its radicals potentially involves deeper processing' and 'the deeper the processing of the stimulus during the learning phase, the better the recall'. Shu and Anderson (1999: 12) believe that 'morphology was of greatest value when the words were conceptually easy' and the acquisition of Chinese characters is facilitated if the pupils 'are able to triangulate different sources of information'. Li and Chen (1997) emphasize the importance of radical components in character recognition. Shen and Ke (2007: 97) support the idea that radicals serve as 'the functional orthographic units in the recognition of Chinese characters' and 'the semantic transparency of a radical in a target character facilitates recognition of that character'. That is why both teachers constantly emphasize the strokes and radicals during their lessons. Additionally, they create imaginary backgrounds for specific character elements to make comprehension and recognition much more effective. In vignette 4, for instance, the teacher clarified the radicals mainly because pupils are more likely to get the correct meaning of the characters if they are familiar with the semantic radicals (see also Feldman and Siok, 1999). Zhou and Marslen-Wilson (1999: 57) emphasize that the orthography of Chinese characters plays a vital role in 'initial lexical access, the effective mapping from orthography to semantics, the automaticity of phonological activation, and the efficient flow of activation from semantics to phonology'. As an example, for '午' from vignette 3, the left-descending stroke on the top ' ノ ' is described as a little bird resting on the tree at noon. This also reflects the pedagogical suggestions regarding character teaching from Xiao (2009: 117–8), that is, '(1) a three-step presentation of new characters, (2) methods to prevent orthographic errors, and (3) corrective measures to treat orthographic errors'. Clearly, all three suggestions emphasize awareness of the linguistic features of Mandarin characters. They all urge Chinese teachers to split the characters into radicals and components, analyse the configurations, and offer visual aids for character recognition.

Furthermore, Wen (2009: 140) encourages the use of visual images for enhancing Mandarin listening and speaking skills because, as she explains, 'visual aids help decrease the load of working memory and thus speed up input processing'. Obviously, this strategy was applied by both teachers to facilitate character recognition (see Figure 3.3).

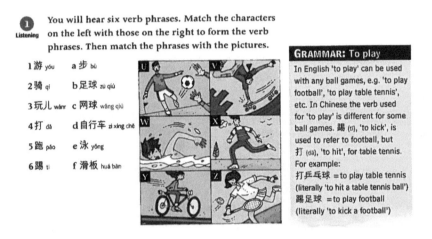

Figure 3.3: Visual aids for listening used by the teacher of the private school, from *Edexcel GCSE Chinese textbook* by Yan *et al.* ©2009. Reprinted with permission from Pearson Education Limited

Conclusion

The central purpose of this study is to explore how Mandarin teachers explain the challenge of Chinese character learning to pupils from an English-speaking background and how they apply the strategies of teaching Chinese characters as a foreign language.

I observed that both Chinese teachers paid special attention to character recognition, which they believe to be one of the major challenges for pupils who use alphabetic languages as their first language. The strategies used by both teachers were effective and salient, at least in the context of the observed schools. The primary method for reading practice in Mandarin used by both teachers was to separate Chinese characters into small elements such as strokes and radicals and then explain the different parts of the characters using stories and drawings. This made pupils interested in the unique configuration of Chinese written texts, which is completely different from the word formation of alphabetic languages. Information on the different character-forming elements also helped pupils from both schools understand the characters better.

The different contexts of the observed schools should also be noted. For example, from my observation, though all the pupils of the private school appeared to be white British students, they had more opportunities to be immersed in a learning environment with salient Chinese cultural characteristics and to consult native Mandarin teachers in the school. They also had more chances to visit China, because there were often exchange activities between the private school and its partner school in China. Such factors can motivate pupils to learn Mandarin, because they are intrigued by their personal experience. As for the state school, the Mandarin teacher emphasized the GCSE exam much more often and was much stricter than the teacher from the private school. Partly because of the limited Mandarin staff numbers at the school, the teacher from the state school did not have enough help from other Mandarin teachers. In addition, there was a lot of pressure on the state school teacher due to the high expectations of both parents and the school. Another factor that led to the teacher in the state school being stricter than her counterpart was the quality of her students. The observed state school is one of the top state schools within its borough and the pupils were aware of the importance of the GCSE exam, so they were highly motivated. Most of the pupils were also well behaved as far as I observed; however, the class size for Mandarin lessons in the state school was larger than in the private school, which means that the teacher from the state school had to put more effort into class management.

The study presented a few dominant teaching strategies in both classroom settings, but there are several limitations that indicate the direction for future research. First, the study covers a limited number of observed schools and teachers. Although I conducted my observation in two types of schools, there is not enough evidence to draw any conclusion with regard to which strategy works better than the others. Further studies should be carried out with more Mandarin teachers, covering more types of schools, in order to collect a greater amount of data. Second, though the two schools were of different types, each of them was considered one of the top schools in its area. Further research could be extended to schools with a greater disparity to see whether Mandarin teachers in other types of school interpret the challenges of character recognition in a different way. Thirdly, the Mandarin teachers I observed were both native Chinese speakers. They were fluent speakers of both English and Chinese, but the fact that they acquired their second language under an Asian pedagogy that is different to that in the West (Slethaug, 2007) may have an influence on their teaching strategies and interpretation of second language acquisition. There should be more studies on Mandarin teachers with different backgrounds and experience, even non-native speaker teachers of Chinese, to see how different teachers help learners overcome the difficulties of Chinese character recognition. Fourthly, the study was conducted in an area with substantial resources in the United Kingdom. Future research can be carried out in areas where the popularity of Mandarin and the pedagogy of Mandarin teaching are different from the contexts in this study. Fifthly, the observations only took place in two one-hour lessons. It is hard to summarize the characteristics of teaching within such a short period of time. Further research should be designed with a longer duration of observation. Bearing the limitations of this study in mind, I believe that studies in different contexts and research on Mandarin character teaching strategies are still in enormous demand and would result in Mandarin teachers having a better understanding of teaching Chinese in a classroom setting, and would lead to improved skills in teaching Chinese as a foreign language.

PRACTICAL IDEAS

- Use various strategies when teaching different types of Chinese characters. As Chinese characters are categorized into xiàngxíng, zhǐshì, huìyì, and xíngshēng, teachers ought to vary their teaching methods according to the features of the characters.
- Xiàngxíng characters usually originate from ancient drawings and patterns. It is usually helpful to associate the characters with their origins and history. However, if the backgrounds are too complicated to explain, it is better to simplify or even omit and create better stories to facilitate the learning. Be creative.
- Zhǐshì characters mostly come from xiàngxíng characters with one or more strokes added. Thus, Mandarin teachers may elicit the 'roots' of the zhǐshì characters as well as how the added strokes indicate the meaning, in order to enhance the learners' understanding and recognition.
- Huìyì and xíngshēng characters are more likely to be considered combinations of radicals or semantic and phonetic components. Teachers can first divide the characters into smaller elements and then re-compose them when each part is understood.

- Even though the concepts may sound dull, introduce the concepts of the four character categories to the learners in order to raise their awareness of character formation. This will help learners to get prepared for different types of characters and adjust their learning styles.
- Emphasize the elements of characters instead of every individual stroke. It might be useful to teach each stroke of a xiàngxíng character with a small number of strokes; however, it would be more effective to teach the components in terms of a huìyì or xíngshēng character.
- Encourage students to use Chinese dictionaries. It is a practical way to get access to Chinese strokes and radicals because strokes and radicals are key retrieval tools when consulting a dictionary.
- Teach characters with similar forms together. For example, the teacher can bring up '本', '末' and '未' at the same time, so that students will learn them in a systematized way.
- Use visual aids and colour coding. These can accelerate the speed of character recognition. For example, the teacher could always colour code the radical 氵 in blue, because 氵 means water and the colour blue can easily remind learners of its meaning.

Notes

[1] This study mainly focuses on the teaching of Mandarin rather than other varieties of Chinese, and I shall use Mandarin, Putonghua and Chinese interchangeably, even though they may be used to embody different concepts in other research.

[2] Notes on transcription:

Emphasis: **bold italics**	Overlapping: [
Unclear on audio recording: (?)	Omitted: xxx
Pause (one dot is one second of pause): (.)	Translation of the vernacular: *(italics)*

References

Allwright, D. and Bailey, K.M. (1991) *Focus on the Language Classroom: An introduction to classroom research for language teachers*. Cambridge: Cambridge University Press.

Angrosino, M. (2007) *Doing Ethnographic and Observational Research*. London: SAGE Publications.

Atkins, B.T.S. and Varantola, K. (1997) 'Monitoring dictionary use'. *International Journal of Lexicography*, 10 (1), 1–45.

Bovair, K. and Bovair, M. (1992) *Modern Languages for All*. London: Kogan Page.

Braun, V. and Clarke, V. (2013) *Successful Qualitative Research: A practical guide for beginners*. London: SAGE Publications.

Bryman, A. (2012) *Social Research Methods*. 4th ed. Oxford: Oxford University Press.

Carrier, M. (2012) 'Overview on multilingual education in the United Kingdom'. In Stickel, G. and Carrier, M. (eds) *Language Education in Creating a Multilingual Europe: Contributions to the Annual Conference 2011 of EFNIL in London* (Duisburg Papers on Research in Language and Culture 94). Frankfurt: Peter Lang, 77–80.

Chen, P. (1999) *Modern Chinese: History and sociolinguistics*. Cambridge: Cambridge University Press.

CiLT (2007) *Mandarin Language Learning. Research Study* Research Report No DCSF-RW019). *Online.* http://dera.ioe.ac.uk/6645/1/DCSF-RW019.pdf (accessed 10 November 2017).

Cruickshank, K. and Tsung, L. (2011) 'Teaching and learning Chinese: A research agenda'. In Tsung, L. and Cruickshank, K. (eds) *Teaching and Learning Chinese in Global Contexts: Multimodality and literacy in the new media age*. London: Continuum, 213–24.

Czerniawski, G. (2011) *Emerging Teachers and Globalisation*. London: Routledge.

DES (Department of Education and Science) and Welsh Office (1988) *Modern Languages in the School Curriculum: A statement of policy*. London: HMSO.

Dörnyei, Z. (2007) *Research Methods in Applied Linguistics: Quantitative, qualitative, and mixed methodologies*. Oxford: Oxford University Press.

Edwards, V. (2001) 'Community languages in the United Kingdom'. In Extra, G. and Gorter, D. (eds) *The Other Languages of Europe: Demographic, sociolinguistic and educational perspectives* (Multilingual Matters 118). Clevedon: Multilingual Matters, 243–60.

Everson, M.E. (1998) 'Word recognition among learners of Chinese as a foreign language: Investigating the relationship between naming and knowing'. *Modern Language Journal*, 82 (2), 194–204.

Everson, M.E. (2009) 'Literacy development in Chinese as a foreign language'. In Everson, M.E. and Xiao, Y. (eds) *Teaching Chinese as a Foreign Language: Theories and applications*. Boston: Cheng and Tsui, 97–111.

Extra, G. and Yağmur, K. (eds) (2012) *Language Rich Europe: Trends in policies and practices for multilingualism in Europe*. Cambridge: Cambridge University Press. Online. www.teachingenglish.org.uk/sites/teacheng/files/LRE_English_version_final_01.pdf (accessed 4 October 2017).

Feldman, L.B. and Siok, W.W.T. (1999) 'Semantic radicals in phonetic compounds: Implications for visual character recognition in Chinese'. In Wang, J., Inhoff, A.W. and Chen, H.-C. (eds) *Reading Chinese Script: A cognitive analysis*. Mahwah, NJ: Lawrence Erlbaum Associates, 19–36.

Gass, S.M. (2003) 'Input and interaction'. In Doughty, C.J. and Long, M.H. (eds) *The Handbook of Second Language Acquisition*. Oxford: Blackwell, 224–55.

Hatch, E. (1983) 'Simplified input and second language acquisition'. In Andersen, R.W. (ed.) *Pidginization and Creolization as Language Acquisition*. Rowley, MA: Newbury House Publishers, 64–86.

Lee, C.H. and Kalyuga, S. (2011) 'Effectiveness of different pinyin presentation formats in learning Chinese characters: A cognitive load perspective'. *Language Learning*, 61 (4), 1099–118.

Li, H. and Chen, H.-C. (1997) 'Processing of radicals in Chinese character recognition'. In Chen, H.-C. (ed.) *Cognitive Processing of Chinese and Related Asian Languages*. Hong Kong: Chinese University Press, 141–60.

Liu, I. (1999) 'Character and word recognition in Chinese'. In Wang, J., Inhoff, A.W. and Chen, H.-C. (eds) *Reading Chinese Script: A cognitive analysis*. Mahwah, NJ: Lawrence Erlbaum Associates, 173–88.

Liu, Y. and Peng, D. (1997) 'Meaning access of Chinese compounds and its time course'. In Chen, H.-C. (ed.) *Cognitive Processing of Chinese and Related Asian Languages*. Hong Kong: Chinese University Press, 219–32.

The Nuffield Languages Inquiry (2000) *Languages: the next generation*. London: The Nuffield Foundation.

Pachler, N., Barnes, A. and Field, K. (2009) *Learning to Teach Modern Foreign Languages in the Secondary School: A companion to school experience*. 3rd ed. London: Routledge.

Shen, H.H. (2005) 'An investigation of Chinese-character learning strategies among non-native speakers of Chinese'. *System*, 33 (1), 49–68.

Shen, H.H. and Ke, C. (2007) 'Radical awareness and word acquisition among nonnative learners of Chinese'. *Modern Language Journal*, 91 (1), 97–111.

Shu, H. and Anderson, R.C. (1999) 'Learning to read Chinese: The development of metalinguistic awareness'. In Wang, J., Inhoff, A.W. and Chen, H.-C. (eds) *Reading Chinese Script: A cognitive analysis*. Mahwah, NJ: Lawrence Erlbaum Associates, 1–18.

Slethaug, G.E. (2007) *Teaching Abroad: International education and the cross-cultural classroom*. Hong Kong: Hong Kong University Press.

Sun, C. (2006) *Chinese: A linguistic introduction*. Cambridge: Cambridge University Press.

Swain, M. (1985) 'Communicative competence: Some roles of comprehensible input and comprehensible output in its development'. In Gass, S.M. and Madden, C.G. (eds) *Input in Second Language Acquisition*. Rowley, MA: Newbury House Publishers, 235–53.

Swain, M. (1995) 'Three functions of output in second language learning'. In Cook, G. and Seidlhofer, B. (eds) *Principle and Practice in Applied Linguistics: Studies in honour of H.G. Widdowson*. Oxford: Oxford University Press, 125–44.

Taft, M. and Chung, K. (1999) 'Using radicals in teaching Chinese characters to second language learners'. *Psychologia*, 42, 243–51.

Thornbury, S. (2006) *An A–Z of ELT: A dictionary of terms and concepts used in English language teaching*. Oxford: Macmillan Education.

Wen, X. (2009) 'Teaching listening and speaking: An interactive approach'. In Everson, M.E. and Xiao, Y. (eds) *Teaching Chinese as a Foreign Language: Theories and applications*. Boston: Cheng and Tsui, 131–50.

Whong, M. (2011) *Language Teaching: Linguistic theory in practice*. Edinburgh: Edinburgh University Press.

Wu, J.-T. and Liu, I.-M. (1997) 'Phonological activation in pronouncing characters'. In Chen, H.-C. (ed.) *Cognitive Processing of Chinese and Related Asian Languages*. Hong Kong: Chinese University Press, 47–64.

Xiao, Y. (2009) 'Teaching Chinese orthography and discourse: Knowledge and pedagogy'. In Everson, M.E. and Xiao, Y. (eds) *Teaching Chinese as a Foreign Language: Theories and applications*. Boston: Cheng and Tsui, 113–30.

Xing, J.Z. (2006) *Teaching and Learning Chinese as a Foreign Language: A pedagogical grammar*. Hong Kong: Hong Kong University Press.

Yan, H., Liu, L., Tate, M., Wang, L., Bin, Y. and Zhu, X. (2009) *Edexcel GCSE Chinese textbook*. Harlow: Pearson.

Zhou, X. and Marslen-Wilson, W. (1997) 'The abstractness of phonological representation in the Chinese mental lexicon'. In Chen, H.-C. (ed.) *Cognitive Processing of Chinese and Related Asian Languages*. Hong Kong: Chinese University Press, 3–26.

Zhou, X. and Marslen-Wilson, W. (1999) 'Sublexical processing in reading Chinese'. In Wang, J., Inhoff, A.W. and Chen, H.-C. (eds) *Reading Chinese Script: A cognitive analysis*. Mahwah, NJ: Lawrence Erlbaum Associates, 37–64.

Chapter 4

Literature in Chinese language teaching and learning supported by the use of the internet and digital resources

Fotini Diamantidaki

Introduction

Over the last twenty years, foreign language teaching and learning has taken on a new dimension thanks to the application of new technologies in the classroom and the development of the internet. The internet as a resource has two salient attributes: it is a vast source of information and can be a source of interactivity, if used correctly by the teacher. The latter confirms the very persuasive argument of Thomas *et al.* (2012) that technology alone cannot improve the delivery of knowledge: simply having access to a computer and the internet cannot make a teacher teach better. However, with judicious use and careful planning, access to technology can make life in the foreign language classroom a little bit more interesting, especially if its use is underpinned by appropriate language pedagogy. It would be ideal if both aspects, information and interactivity, were combined during the planning and teaching process in order to promote effective learning. The discussion that follows will try to make that case.

Unlike the dynamic environment that can be created with the use of the internet in the classroom and the excitement that this can bring to the learner, the use of literature has not lately experienced a similarly warm reception in foreign language teaching and learning. Conversely, it has been gradually abandoned due to the view that literature is too difficult or not even a necessary component of foreign language teaching (Diamantidaki, 2010). Instead, more instrumental functions of the language with so-called communicative value have been favoured to the detriment of the use of literature.

Changes to the national curriculum in England, however, have encouraged educators to believe that literature can regain its place in the languages classroom and eventually have an impact on children's learning. In 2013, the Department for Education (DfE) in London published a new programme of study for KS3 which clearly stated that all pupils should:

- understand and respond to spoken and written language from a variety of authentic sources
- discover and develop an appreciation of a range of writing in the language studied
- read and show comprehension of original and adapted materials from a range of different sources
- read literary texts in the language (such as stories, songs, poems and letters) to stimulate ideas, develop creative expression, and expand understanding of the language and culture.

The entire process starts at key stage (KS) 2 (7–11years), so that by the end of KS3 (11–14 years), pupils are expected 'to understand and communicate personal and factual information that goes beyond their immediate needs and interests, developing and justifying points of view in speech and writing, with increased spontaneity, independence and accuracy. It should also provide suitable preparation for further study.' (DfE, 2013: 2) 'The teaching should enable pupils to express their ideas and thoughts in another language and to understand and respond to its speakers, both in speech and in writing. It should also provide opportunities for them to communicate for practical purposes, learn new ways of thinking, and read great literature in the original language.' (DfE, 2013: 1)

In light of the above, this chapter proposes that the use of literature supported by the use of the internet and digital resources is of great potential in foreign language teaching, with the hope that the suggested combination (literature–digital resources) will motivate teachers and eventually learners to improve reading skills and develop linguistic proficiency (Ellis and Shintani, 2014). To acquire a foreign language, the learner needs to be exposed to some sort of input, which will allow him or her to appreciate the complexity of the language taught, going beyond learning rules and isolated items of vocabulary (Krashen, 2004).

Context
In a Chinese as a foreign language (CFL) classroom in English schools, there are several impediments to implementing reading in general (without yet

considering the literary element) as a task and as part of a lesson. This is partly due to learners having very little exposure to reading, either in their L1 or the target language (TL) and 'thus [finding] the effort of reading widely for general understanding difficult and unrewarding. Such readers adopt a word-by-word processing strategy which makes it very difficult for them to read for pleasure.' (Ellis and Shintani, 2014: 172) This raises issues, since it involves teaching reading as a skill during foreign language lessons. Such a task is rarely implemented during lessons, as the focus is mainly on new words and structures and on producing sentences in the TL. Input is mainly given through the present–practise–produce model (PPP), which incorporates opportunities for controlled production in the TL (Ellis and Shintani, 2014) and through the very structured question and answer model, as described below:

a. The teacher presents new vocabulary; practise through choral and individual repetition.
b. The teacher asks the students yes/no questions.
c. The teacher asks the students either/or questions.
d. The teacher asks the students: 'What is it?'

Such a process does not always leave room for more meaningful interaction to take place, nor does it successfully build confidence in getting the students to read longer passages. The teacher is lucky if the students leave the lesson knowing a structure or a sentence. Time is also an issue, as the teacher meets the students a few times each week for no longer than an hour, as is locating the appropriate resources for the level and topic that needs teaching. Considering this context, literature can be considered a tool rather than an end (Hişmanoğlu, 2005) for modern foreign language teaching and learning; it is a tool that helps develop reading skills and linguistic proficiency (Ellis and Shintani, 2014).

Why should we teach literature in the foreign language classroom?

One of the reasons for integrating literature is that it is real language produced by a real writer for a real audience and designed to convey a real message: this characterizes literature as authentic material as discussed by Morrow (1979). However, Widdowson (2003; see also 1978) as presented in Ellis and Shintani (2014) conceives of authenticity not as a property that resides in a text itself, but more like a process of authentication. 'Authentic', therefore, is used for the 'specific ways in which language is made communicatively appropriate to context' (93). He continues by arguing persuasively that it is 'people who make a text real by realizing it as discourse, that is to say by relating to specific contexts of communal cultural values and attitudes' (98). Hence, a literary text is not relevant only to the era when it was written: its message is transferable across eras, it evolves and can be adapted to other contexts, in Widdowson's words, which leads us to the next reason for integrating literary texts in the foreign language classroom, namely cultural enrichment.

Literature can help readers understand the lifestyle of the country of the language they are studying. It is possible to do so with radio and newspapers, but literature is a more intimate approach. For example, even if the characters in a novel are fictitious, a literary text can provide a living context in which characters from different social backgrounds associate with the reality of the reader. Readers can explore the thoughts, feelings, habits and customs, beliefs and fears of a population living in a particular era, and start making links with their own reality.

Another aspect of reading a literary text is that readers gain a lot of vocabulary and can enrich their lexical knowledge. As Collie and Slater (1987: 5) argue, '[t]he compressed quality of much literary language produces unexpected density of meaning'. Literature provides a rich context in which elements of the lexicon or syntax can be highlighted during the teaching process. A first reading can also help the reader become familiar with the different styles of language, see the variety of possible structures, and understand new meanings of words and phrases using context and personal interpretation. A more detailed reading of a text may allow students to make assumptions about the meaning of the linguistic elements and deduce the meaning of a text as a whole. The overall aim in this process is for the learner to achieve 'foreign language competence' (Thom, 2008: 121) through 'a dynamic, student-centred approach' (Hişmanoğlu, 2005: 57).

Finally, literature motivates learners by engaging their imagination and their creativity and by generating emotions. This can capture the learners' interest and create an atmosphere in which students learn how to use the vocabulary and structures taught in a less mechanical way. Using literature may be more motivating than role plays or working from texts that have been made for pedagogical purposes and are not therefore authentic. However, it is crucial that the text is chosen according to the learners' level of knowledge and on the topic being taught.

How to integrate literature into the curriculum

In the first instance when Chinese literature is mentioned to teachers and pupils within a classroom setting in England, the reaction may be one of doubt, hesitation, and acute anxiety about the accessibility of literary language for students. One suggestion for integrating literature within the foreign language classroom is to use literary texts with the same linguistic material that needs to be taught in a lesson, such as the family, seasons, education or clothing. I therefore suggest that a literary text can be integrated as part of the teaching materials used during the teaching process and not included as a one-off task. Choosing appropriate texts for specific topics – a pre-defined set of topics that schools have to cover for GCSE in any language – will allow the pupils to develop more complex skills in reading within the particular topic area, see the language in context and undistorted, and, with the right guidance, go beyond the survival stage of communication and 'ultimately increase their reading proficiency' (McKay, 1982: 529).

I would like to illustrate this point by showing some Chinese literature and suggesting that, if a literary work is integrated within a topic, it becomes automatically more real, relevant to the curriculum, and, most importantly, easier to teach.

The reasons for using Chinese to demonstrate the use of literature in the classroom are twofold: first, the change in the national curriculum in England means that all foreign languages to be taught are considered equal. Second, Chinese, the teaching of which is increasing in schools, albeit from a low base, gives an opportunity to look at the transferability of pedagogy between European languages and Chinese with a view to finding similarities and differences in the approach of reading strategies across languages. Hence, this paper aims to assert, through its theoretical framework and application, that the implementation of literature teaching in the classroom is indeed transferable and, with some adaptation, is applicable to any context of foreign language teaching and learning where the internet is also accessible.

We know that 'learning to read is a complex, multifaceted process and even more so in a second language' (Park *et al.*, 2013: 268); therefore, it is of paramount importance that the teacher knows the literature of the target language and has the ability to plan a lesson which addresses the pupils' linguistic and cultural needs. A combination of engaging and interactive student-led activities is also a key aspect of my suggestion.

A selection of poems for the Chinese classroom, which have been selected for use in KS5 (16–18 years), is presented in Table 4.1. The actual poems are available for reference on the 21st century Chinese Poetry website.

Table 4.1: A selection of poems for the Chinese classroom

Poem title	Poet's name	Topic
Parting Before Daybreak	An Qi	Young people
Ferry	Bei Xiaohuang	Young people
Filling in the Blanks	Chen Guiliang	Family
January (or an Evening of Reading)	Chen Yanqiang	Work and leisure
The Wall	Gao Pengcheng	Education
The Shepherd	Jin Qiufeng	Family, the environment
Seductive Wind	Li Shangyu	Media
Wednesday Afternoon Tea	Liu Yali	Work and leisure
Ow, Mama	Song Yu	Family
A Pair of Chopsticks	Zhang Shaobao	Family

Many of the learners in KS5 are working towards an examination whose stated aims in the specification (CIE, 2014) are '[t]o develop insights into the culture and civilization of countries where Chinese is spoken; and to encourage positive attitudes to language learning and a sympathetic approach to other cultures and civilizations'. Well-chosen poems can further these aims, whilst at the same time making reference to the overarching topic of the specification.

The use of the internet and digital technologies in the Chinese as a foreign language classroom

As mentioned earlier, using a computer does not automatically make a teacher teach better, but there is a truth in the claim that the internet and digital technologies (IDTs) can enhance learning if underpinned by appropriate pedagogy. Assuming that IDTs have a dual role to play – that of information conveyance and interactivity – can their integration completely redefine existing approaches to language learning and therefore encourage new classroom practices? Or do IDTs simply enhance existing good practices developed by teachers? (Evans: 2009b)

Evans (2009b) aims to answer these questions by implementing the use of information and communications technology (ICT) in the foreign language classroom through exposure to authentic links and authentic cross-communication projects. Mitchell (2009: 32–59) suggests creative and innovative ways of using the internet productively to aid language comprehension through the use of text. However, the use of texts as language-learning aids is primarily guided by experienced teachers, and the internet mainly plays the role of information resource. Subsequent chapters in Evans (2009b) present more interactive approaches to ICT use, either adopted by teachers or explored as part of projects. One of these approaches is active learning through computer mediated communication (CMC) between 14–16-year-old pupils in England learning a foreign language and pupils of a similar age in target language countries. Computer mediated communication has allowed students from every continent to interact in the target language using different kinds and different levels of discourse. In this way, pupils are able to peer scaffold their own learning (Evans, 2009a: 110). During the same process, elements of cross-cultural interactions amongst pupils were observed and elements of code switching took place naturally, meaning that pupils were able to switch every time they felt uncomfortable. (Evans, 2009a: 115).

Al-Seghayer (2001) compared EFL students' vocabulary learning and developed a programme that provides users reading a narrative English text with a variety of glosses or annotations for words in the form of printed text, graphics, video and sound, all different modalities that are aimed at aiding comprehension and the learning of unknown words. The research is measured under three conditions: printed text only, printed text and still images, printed text and a video clip. All three conditions aimed to find which of these modalities was the best for word recognition and production. Not surprisingly, using the third mode 'text with a video clip' was the most effective way of learning new vocabulary since, according to Al-Seghayer (2001: 202), 'video builds a better mental image, better created curiosity leading to increased concentration, and embodies an advantageous combination of modalities (vivid or dynamic image, sound, and printed text)'.

Lee and Kalyuga (2011) investigated the effects of simultaneously presenting visual Pinyin and its auditory pronunciation compared to an auditory-only presentation (no Pinyin condition) using relatively more complex learning materials (classical Chinese texts) in a computer-based learning environment. Pinyin is the term used for Romanized phonetic transcription that helps with the pronunciation of Chinese characters. The aim of their study was to present effective techniques for reducing the level of intrinsic cognitive overload when reading Chinese characters in classical texts, bearing in mind that Classical Chinese 'is characterized by using significantly fewer characters for expressing ideas' (Lee and Kalyuga, 2011: 12). They have effectively compared the learning effects of three computer-based presentation techniques where learners see on the screen full Pinyin transcription of Chinese characters, partial Pinyin transcription, and no Pinyin transcription. A full Pinyin condition means that all characters were transcribed with Pinyin and a partial Pinyin condition means that only 'potentially new or key characters were transcribed' (Lee and Kalyuga, 2011: 12). The results, as explained by the authors, 'demonstrated the superiority of the partial pinyin transcription over the other two conditions for the more advanced learners' (Lee and Kalyuga, 2011: 11).

An effective illustration of the study above is the GoChinese website, which is an online Chinese learning platform that makes any level of text in Chinese more accessible for learners. Up to 1,000 characters from any source can be cut and pasted into the platform. I suggest *The Destination* by Anyi Wang (n.d.) for testing the functionality. One click and the text is segmented into words, with or without Pinyin above. Another click and the text can be heard. Hovering the mouse over any word gives the English meaning. There is still the excitement and considerable challenge of working out the meaning at sentence level, but the learner is supported, making literature accessible in a way that would otherwise not be achievable in school. This provides the intellectual stretch that some of the more utilitarian language-learning texts at KS5, where learners spend considerable time looking up characters and deciding on word segmentation, do not.

Winke *et al*. (2010) have conducted a study on the effects of captioning for learners of Arabic, Chinese, Spanish and Russian. More specifically, they investigated how the use of authentic videos via DVD, YouTube, and ViewPoint, with use of captions or without, helped or impeded vocabulary comprehension. All learners took comprehension and vocabulary tests based on the videos. For leaners of Chinese, captioning during the second showing of the video was more effective. The data revealed that learners used captions to 'increase their attention, improve processing, reinforce previous knowledge and analyse language' (Winke *et al*., 2010: 65).

In this section, I have used different studies and online learning platforms to assert that the use of the internet and digital technologies in CFL learning can be a useful and interactive tool to enhance vocabulary acquisition, increase learner interactivity, and aid comprehension.

Use of literature and digital technologies in the Chinese as a foreign language classroom

Literature can provide the stimulus and the motivating element for improving reading skills and developing linguistic proficiency (Ellis and

Shintani, 2014) when combining appropriate reading strategies with the use of digital technologies.

An underlying pedagogy needs to be adopted in order to teach the literary source. This can be achieved by applying distinctive steps during the teaching process, which enhances comprehension of the text/poem. The use of digital technologies as a motivating and student-centred tool can enhance the entire teaching and learning process.

In this respect Cummins (2008), Luke and Freebody (1999), and Scarborough (2001) suggest three components of the reading process: word recognition, language comprehension and text interpretation.

WORD RECOGNITION

Either through phonological decoding or sight-reading, word recognition is widely recognized as a vital skill for early reading development (Hoover and Gough, 1990; Joshi and Aaron, 2000; McBride-Chang and Kail, 2002; Ziegler and Goswami, 2005, cited in Park *et al.*, 2013: 269). Without it, it is impossible to start the process of understanding what is being read. This is particularly relevant in the case of CFL learning, as the general teaching input is mainly done by teaching characters in the first instance, without always providing a text where pupils can see all the characters in context so as to start making sense of the language they are learning.

Word recognition in Chinese is of paramount importance, as decoding characters is key to the production of meaning at a later stage. If learners do not know the words or characters, they cannot make sense of the text they are trying to read. Phonetic translation in Pinyin can help overcome the initial cognitive barrier. The internet is both an invaluable source of information about and direct access to primary literary sources that would otherwise be inaccessible to MFL learners. In the CFL context, it is particularly useful for accessing texts such as Tang poetry in classical Chinese. Wang Wei's poem (Wei, n.d.) is an excellent example of this. It can be used by learners to create a literary translation of their own based on the literal translation:

鹿 柴　　　　　Lù Chái

空 山 不 见 人　　Kōng shān bú jiàn rén

但 闻 人 语 响　　Dàn wén rén yǔ xiǎng

返 景 入 深 林　　Fǎn jǐng rù shēn lín

复 照 青 苔 上　　Fù zhào qīng tái shàng

Empty hill not see person	Hills are empty, no man is seen
Yet hear person voice sound	Yet the sound of people's voices is heard
Return scene enter deep forest	Light is cast into the deep forest
Duplicate light green moss on	And shines again on green moss.

(Wei, n.d.)

When reading Chinese poems, the learner has to focus immediately on the characters and elucidate which characters might go together to form words: the poems are almost puzzles that need to be decoded. Characters carry meaning: the more sophisticated the poems, the more complex the layers of meaning.

In order to quicken the process of word cognition, 'a number of studies suggest that technology-supported automaticity training can facilitate faster lexical access during reading' (Park *et al.* 2013: 269). Park *et al.* adduce studies by Fukkink *et al.* (2005), Li (2010), and Tozcu and Coady (2004) in support of this assertion. This idea was illustrated in the previous section with the discussion of the GoChinese.net platform, which allows faster character access through a multisensory approach where learners can listen, read and recognize the words and characters (through the use of translation and/or Pinyin).

LANGUAGE COMPREHENSION

Once the first obstacle, word recognition, is overcome, the next stage when reading a text is to achieve comprehension. In the CFL classroom, a combination of computer-assisted language learning (CALL) and effective application of reading strategies can allow learners to understand what they are reading. In this respect, there has been extensive research into different 'types of multimedia used in vocabulary learning studies'. Park *et al.* (2013: 269) discuss studies on a wide variety of media ranging 'from electronic dictionaries [...] to short readings' and which work at different levels, from sentence-level translation to word-level basic translation, (Gettys *et al.*,

2001; Grace, 1998). They also discuss the effect of multimedia glosses (for example graphics, videos, or audio) versus textual translations (Abraham, 2008; Al-Seghayer, 2001; Yoshii and Flaitz, 2002).

Comprehension is also promoted through well-planned lessons based on effective reading strategies that enhance the teacher's methodology and questioning. In this regard, Jones (2001) suggests clear steps for teaching reading in the language classroom. I have adapted them for Chinese poems:

With the source visible/audible

1. Identify what you have understood – read and listen for the gist: what characters did you read that you recognized; what did you understand?
2. What words did you read/hear that you recognized?
3. Practise and expand – read/listen again: can you add anything else to your list? What else did you understand? How did you guess the meaning of the unfamiliar characters or words? Did you use radicals or components of characters with which you were already familiar to make a guess at pronunciation and meaning? (If listening, did you try writing the character/word down in Pinyin? How will you go about finding out what the remaining unknown characters/words mean?)

Away from the source

Use the language you have read in combination with the vocabulary you already know to discuss the topic area with other learners.

In the light of Jones's adapted strategies, the Mandarin Chinese poem reader must rely mostly on identifying what the poem has to offer, what characters can be recognized, and how the reader has interpreted the characters according to the specific context of the poem.

Moving away from the poem and discussing the topic area with others is the next stage for Chinese, because the learner is less likely to move straight away to reproduction in written form: this is due to the complexity of writing the characters and the fact that the pronunciation of a Chinese character does not give a learner much indication of how to write it. A suggestion might be that if the learners are familiar with specific characters, using a computer and typing the characters to create a poem might turn out to be a very rewarding task for learners without them having to remember how to write the characters by hand.

Fotini Diamantidaki

TEXT INTERPRETATION

When moving away from the text or source, as discussed by Jones (2001), what learners find most challenging is to go beyond the comprehension stage, create new meanings, and eventually offer their own interpretation on the text. Kitajima (2002), cited in Park *et al.* (2013: 270), suggests that computer-assisted reading materials could help learners improve their higher-order interpretation skills by embedding prompts in digital texts, leading to students applying reading strategies. Further, Kitajima suggests that this is achieved through a process of recognizing organizational patterns within the text, such as themes and word patterns.

Conclusion

Approaches to teaching and learning foreign languages constantly evolve, depending, in large measure, on prevailing fashions of thought. The current focus is not just on the teacher–learner relationship: a much more integrated approach is sought, one in which multimedia plays a significant role in motivating and facilitating language and literature teaching and learning, particularly since the internet and digital technologies play such a key role in the life of young learners today. This paper has argued in favour of using literature and digital resources in the language classroom to motivate foreign language learners. The use of digital resources can assist the process of learning and make learners increasingly conscious of their own learning, and therefore gradually increase their independence.

PRACTICAL IDEAS
- Introduction to literature needs to be gradual. Before seeking meaning, learners must have understood the vocabulary first, which motivates them to spend time on understanding the text.
- Establish a framework for guided reading and graded comprehension:
  o Level 1: understand the basics: who, with whom, what, where.
  o Level 2: explore the themes and images of the text/poem.
  o Level 3: guide and allow independent interpretation of meaning.
- Different kinds of vocabulary activities can be organized to help towards a gradual understanding of the literary source. Pupils can:
  o Replace the words: replace the adjectives with a set of other possible adjectives.
  o Change the tense.
  o Describe characters: match adjectives with characters, which can lead to a writing activity.
  o Act a part/role/scene or mime (think of emotions and personality).

References

21st century Chinese Poetry (n.d.) *Selected Poems*. Online. http://modernchinesepoetry.com/poems.php (accessed 2 January 2018).

Abraham, L.B. (2008) 'Computer-mediated glosses in second language reading comprehension and vocabulary learning: A meta-analysis'. *Computer Assisted Language Learning*, 21 (3), 199–226.

Al-Seghayer, K. (2001) 'The effect of multimedia annotation modes on L2 vocabulary acquisition: A comparative study'. *Language Learning and Technology*, 5 (1), 202–32.

CIE (Cambridge International Examinations) (2014) Cambridge international examinations, Chinese Mandarin. Online. www.cambridgeinternational.org/programmes-and-qualifications/cambridge-igcse-chinese-mandarin-foreign-language-0547 (accessed 9 November 2017).

Collie, J. and Slater S. (1987) *Literature in the Language Classroom: A resource book of ideas and activities*. Cambridge: Cambridge University Press.

Cummins, J. (2008) 'Technology, literacy, and young second language learners: Designing educational futures'. In Parker, L.L. (ed.) *Technology-Mediated Learning Environments for Young English Learners: Connections in and out of school*. New York: Lawrence Erlbaum Associates, 61–98.

DfE (Department for Education) (2013) *Languages Programmes of Study: Key Stage 3: National Curriculum in England*. London: Department for Education. Online. www.gov.uk/government/uploads/system/uploads/attachment_data/file/239083/SECONDARY_national_curriculum_-_Languages.pdf (accessed 10 February 2015).

Diamantidaki, F. (2010) 'Les (nouvelles) technologies de l'information et de la communication et la didactique de la littérature en FLE'. In Diamantidaki, F. *Internet et documents littéraires: Un moyen d'enseigner la langue*. Lille: Éditions Universitaire Européens, 63–89.

Ellis, R. and Shintani, N. (2014) *Exploring Language Pedagogy through Second Language Acquisition Research*. London: Routledge.

Evans, M. (2009a) 'Engaging pupils in bilingual, cross-cultural online discourse'. In Evans, M.J. (ed.) *Foreign-Language Learning with Digital Technology*. London: Continuum, 104–29.

Evans M. (ed.) (2009b) *Foreign-Language Learning with Digital Technology*. London: Continuum.

Fukkink, R.G., Hulstijn, J. and Simis, A. (2005) 'Does training in second-language word recognition skills affect reading comprehension? An experimental study'. *Modern Language Journal*, 89 (1), 54–75.

Gettys, S., Imhof, L.A. and Kautz, J.O. (2001) 'Computer-assisted reading: The effect of glossing format on comprehension and vocabulary retention'. *Foreign Language Annals*, 34 (2), 91–99

GoChinese (2014) Online. www.gochinese.net/goChinese (accessed 9 November 2014).

Grace, C.A. (1998) 'Retention of word meanings inferred from context and sentence-level translations: Implications for the design of beginning-level CALL software'. *Modern Language Journal*, 82 (4), 533–44.

Hişmanoğlu, M. (2005) 'Teaching English through literature'. *Journal of Language and Linguistic Studies*, 1 (1), 53–66.

Hoover, W.A. and Gough, P.B. (1990) 'The simple view of reading'. *Reading and Writing*, 2 (2), 127–60.

Jones, B. (2001) *Developing Learning Strategies* (Advanced Pathfinder 2). London: Centre for Information on Language Teaching and Research.

Joshi, R.M. and Aaron, P.G. (2000) 'The component model of reading: Simple view of reading made a little more complex'. *Reading Psychology*, 21 (2), 85–97.

Kitajima, R. (2002) 'Enhancing higher order interpretation skills for Japanese reading'. *CALICO Journal*, 19 (3), 571–81.

Krashen, S. (2004) 'The case of narrow reading'. *Language Magazine*, 3 (5), 17–19.

Lee, C.H. and Kalyuga, S. (2011) 'Effectiveness of on-screen pinyin in learning Chinese: An expertise reversal for multimedia redundancy effect'. *Computers in Human Behavior*, 27 (1), 11–15.

Li, J. (2010) 'Learning vocabulary via computer-assisted scaffolding for text processing'. *Computer Assisted Language Learning*, 23 (3), 253–75.

Luke, A. and Freebody, P. (1999) 'A map of possible practices: Further notes on the four resources model'. *Practically Primary*, 4 (2), 5–8.

McBride-Chang, C. and Kail, R.V. (2002) 'Cross-cultural similarities in the predictors of reading acquisition'. *Child Development*, 73 (5), 1392–407.

McKay, S. (1982) 'Literature in the ESL classroom'. *TESOL Quarterly*, 16 (4), 529–36.

Mitchell, I. (2009) 'The potential of the internet as a language-learning tool'. In Evans, M.J. (ed.) *Foreign-Language Learning with Digital Technology*. London: Continuum, 32–59.

Morrow, K. (1979) 'Communicative language testing: Revolution or evolution?'. In Brumfit, C.J. and Johnson, K. (eds) *The Communicative Approach to Language Teaching*. Oxford: Oxford University Press, 143–57.

Park, Y., Zheng, B., Lawrence, J. and Warschauer, M. (2012) 'Technology-enhanced reading environments'. In Thomas, M., Reinders, H. and Warschauer, M. (eds) *Contemporary Computer-Assisted Language Learning*. London: Bloomsbury Academic, 267–85.

Scarborough, H.S. (2001) 'Connecting early language and literacy to later reading (dis)abilities: Evidence, theory, and practice'. In Neuman, S.B. and Dickinson, D.K. (eds) *Handbook of Early Literacy Research*. New York: Guilford Press, 97–110.

Thom, N.T.T. (2008) 'Using literary texts in language teaching'. *VNU Journal of Science: Foreign Languages*, 24, 120–6.

Thomas, M., Reinders, H. and Warschauer, M. (eds) (2012) *Contemporary Computer-Assisted Language Learning*. London: Bloomsbury Academic.

Tozcu, A. and Coady, J. (2004) 'Successful learning of frequent vocabulary through CALL also benefits reading comprehension and speed'. *Computer Assisted Language Learning*, 17 (5), 473–95.

Wang, A. (n.d.) 本次列车终点 *(The Destination)*. Online. http://www.mypcera.com/book/2003new/da/w/wanganyi/001/001.htm (accessed 2 January 2018).

Wei, W. (n.d.) *Deer enclosure*. Online. www.chinese-poems.com/deer.html (accessed 4 October 2017).

Widdowson, H.G. (1978) *Teaching Language as Communication*. Oxford: Oxford University Press.

Widdowson, H.G. (2003) *Defining Issues in English Language Teaching*. Oxford: Oxford University Press.

Winke, P., Gass, S. and Sydorenko, T. (2010) 'The effects of captioning videos used for foreign language listening activities'. *Language Learning and Technology*, 14 (1), 65–86.

Yoshii, M. and Flaitz, J. (2002) 'Second language incidental vocabulary retention: The effect of text and picture annotation types'. *CALICO Journal*, 20 (1), 33–58.

Ziegler, J.C. and Goswami, U. (2005) 'Reading acquisition, developmental dyslexia, and skilled reading across languages: A psycholinguistic grain size theory'. *Psychological Bulletin*, 131 (1), 3–29.

Part Two

Action research and
teaching Chinese in schools

2

Chapter 5

Chinese teachers as researchers

Using research as a tool to improve practice

Lin Pan, Rob Neal, Paul Tyskerud and Katharine Carruthers

Introduction

This chapter takes as its point of departure the stance that modern foreign language teachers should consider being involved in research to explore their classrooms. This would enable them to have a better understanding of their students' learning and their own teaching, and it would also contribute to their professional development. Language teachers play a central role in their classrooms since they monitor learning and evaluate their students' day-by-day performance and progress. To this end, it is crucial that teachers develop a range of skills in planning, monitoring, and evaluating their own professional activities and the results of the teacher–student interaction. Research has increasingly become both a useful skill that teachers can include in their professional repertoire and an interesting and meaningful journey on which to embark. By 'research skills' for modern foreign language teachers, we do not mean scholarly theoretical knowledge of the literature or empirical research skills conventionally deployed in traditional academic research. We believe that it is important and necessary for language teachers to have a range of specific research skills for exploring and solving immediate problems in their own classrooms and institutions (Walker, 1985; Nunan, 1993; Mertler, 2014). In this chapter, we advocate doing action research in language classrooms because it allows teaching practitioners to reach a more personal goal when investigating the teaching and learning in their own classrooms (Freeman and Richards, 1993) and it gives teachers a voice in decision-making and control over their environment and professional lives.

Action research presupposes certain skills and knowledge needed for classroom research. In particular, teachers need to be able to conceptualize their practice clearly in a fair way, be aware of issues amenable to action research, and they need some basic skills in data collection and analysis (Burns, 1999). As suggested by Walker (1985), these skills include 1) the ability to monitor and describe both their own and their pupils' activities and behaviours, 2) the ability to evaluate their practice, performance, and policy in teaching and administration, 3) the ability to provide evidence and analysis of the school's programme for management purposes, and 4) the ability to modify or change their behaviours on the basis of their understanding of classroom settings. These abilities can be developed through action research projects. In this chapter, we will explain in detail how to develop the skills for action research and share with you two case studies of how two teachers of Mandarin Chinese, after some training, have deployed their action research skills in understanding their students and classrooms.

While advocating action research in language classrooms, we admit that language teachers have no obvious incentive to do research. For one thing, teachers usually find that they do not have time to do research as academics do, as they have full teaching schedules and any research which they do is not usually acknowledged or rewarded; for another, it is not particularly easy for teachers to find the resources, support, or facilities needed for research, such as books or articles from the literature, or people who can offer advice about methods for collecting and analysing data. Hence, many teachers have been discouraged from doing research. However, what we propose in this chapter is that action research is a powerful form of teacher development, because the classroom enquiry and self-reflection that it entails are important components of the professional growth of teachers. It provides a sound source for pedagogical planning and action and enables teachers to frame the local decisions of the classroom within broader educational, institutional, and theoretical considerations. It 'reinvigorates classroom teaching, leads to positive change in the classroom, and raises the teachers' awareness of the complexities of their work' (Burns, 2010: 7). Action research is a source of teacher empowerment.

Using action research as a tool to improve classroom practice

The origin of action research can be traced back to the late 19th century (McKernan, 1996). In the early part of the 20th century, John Dewey, one of the progressive educators of that time, challenged the orthodox scientific research methods. His ideas were democratic in nature, as he argued for demystifying the approaches towards educational research derived from the natural sciences and advocated that researchers, practitioners, and those involved in the educational community should be engaged in educational enquiry collectively in order to confront common educational problems (Burns, 2010). In recent times, the approaches of action research are essentially participatory, in that they are conducted by and with members of the actual community under study (Bailey, 1998) in naturally occurring settings, primarily using methods common to qualitative research (Nunan, 1992; McKernan, 1996; Phillips and Carr, 2014), such as observing and recording events and behaviours. It can be said that 'the findings and insights that are gained through action research are driven primarily by the data collected by the participants within their specific teaching situations, rather than by theories proposed through investigations which are external to the teaching context, but which many attempt to generalize to that context' (Burns, 1999: 24).

Action research is a process of reflective practice, where the teachers are the researchers (Burns, 1999; 2010). The teachers reflect on their teaching by taking a questioning and problematizing stance towards their teaching. They take an area where they feel it could be done better and intervene in a deliberate way in the problematic situation in order to develop new ideas and alternatives and bring about changes and, even better, improvements in practice. Hence, 'the linking of the terms "action" and "research" highlights the essential feature of the method: trying out ideas in practice as a means of improvement and as a means of increasing knowledge about the curriculum, teaching and learning. The result is improvement in what happens in the classroom and school, and better articulation and justification of the educational rationale of what goes on.' (Nunan, 1993: 2). In Nunan's words, action research provides a way of working that links ideas and practice into one whole: ideas-in-actions. (Nunan, 1993: 5). In action research, a teacher becomes an investigator or explorer of his or her personal teaching context, while at the same time being one of the participants in it (Burns, 2010). It should be noted that the improvements that happen due to action research are based on data that an action researcher collects systematically, and that the changes made in the teaching situation arise from solid data rather than from mere assumptions about what the teaching should be like. To summarize, action research can be characterized in the following ways (Burns, 2010; Mills, 2014):

1. It is contextual, small-scale and localized: it identifies and investigates problems within a specific situation.
2. It is evaluative and reflective, as it aims to bring about change and improvement in practice.

3. It is participatory, as it provides for collaborative investigation by teams of colleagues, practitioners and researchers.
4. Changes in practice are based on the collection of information or data that provides the impetus for change.

Action research suffers from a lack of prestige compared with more established forms of language education research, as it is less based on formal experiments. However, it has its unique strengths. First, it addresses issues that are of immediate concern to practitioners. Second, the results can be promoted and disseminated via workshops, staff meetings, or papers for other teachers working in similar situations. Furthermore, teachers improve their teaching by being involved in a genuine research process of data collection, analysis and interpretation, which contrasts with intuitive reflection. In addition, unlike traditional research, which tends to leave the implementation of research to the practitioners, in action research putting findings into practice is an integral part of the research process (Burns, 1999: 25). This process empowers the teacher-researchers by reaffirming their professional judgement and encouraging involvement in decision-making with respect to curriculum design and policy in school and perhaps beyond.

Steps in action research

According to Kemmis and McTaggart (1988; see also Burns 1999; 2010), leading figures in the field, action research occurs through a dynamic and complementary process, which involves four broad phases in a cycle of research: planning, action, observation and reflection. First, in the planning phase, a teaching practitioner identifies a problem or issue and develops a plan of action: he or she should consider specific possible improvements to teaching and learning. Second, the teacher acts to implement the plan. This implementation process is usually carefully planned, involving some deliberate interventions in the teaching situations, and it often takes a period of time. Third, the teacher observes systematically the effects of the critically informed action in the context in which it occurs. This phase involves documenting the context, actions and opinions of those involved. It is a data collection phase where the teacher-researcher collects information about what is happening. And finally, he or she reflects on, evaluates and describes the effects of the action to understand the issue that has been explored. Planning, action, observation and reflection form the first cycle of action research. But the cycle may become a continuing, or iterative, spiral of cycles that recur until the action researcher has achieved a satisfactory outcome. This model of action research is illustrated by the diagram in Figure 5.1, which shows its iterative or recursive nature.

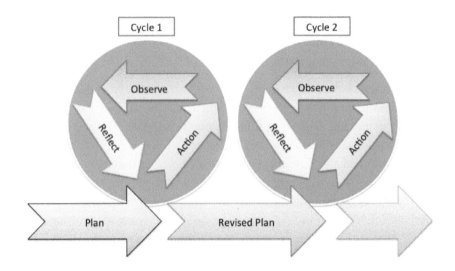

Figure 5.1: Action research cycles (Adapted from Kemmis and McTaggard, 1988: 11–4)

Though Kemmis and McTaggart's model was proposed in the late 1980s, it is probably the best known and is still the most representative model of action research. However, there are critiques of their model and theories. The criticism is mainly centred on their assumption of a fixed sequence of procedures that are self-contained and on the contention that the model overlooks the complexity of the action research process. For example, McNiff (1988, 2014) advocates a more flexible approach that allows action researchers to be creative and spontaneous in conducting their action research projects. That is, the teacher-researchers can have their own theorizing and steps tailored to their own needs or their students' needs regarding teaching and the classroom instead of rigidly following the steps that are illustrated above. In a similar vein, although we advocate Kemmis and McTaggart's model as presenting a clear overall picture of action research, we acknowledge that it involves many interwoven aspects: 'exploring, identifying, planning, collecting information, analysing and reflecting, hypothesizing and speculating, intervening, observing, reporting, writing and presenting' (Burns, 1999: 35). These processes and features are not necessarily clearly delineated and separate points in the research, but all of them play important roles. To illustrate in more concrete terms how to do action research, the next section is dedicated to two case studies of actual classroom situations in schools in England. Mandarin Chinese language teachers identified a problematic area in their teaching and intervened with positive changes.

Both teacher-researchers attended a one-day workshop on how to do action research organized by the UCL Institute of Education Confucius Institute. During the two months that followed, they applied the techniques to which they had been introduced in their classrooms to address their teaching concerns, and as a result they have also contributed to this collection in chapters 6 and 7 respectively. In this chapter, both case studies are presented following the planning, action, observation and reflection cycle. In chapters 6 and 7, each project is analysed in detail by the teachers themselves doing action research in their classrooms, applying the principles.

Case study 1: The intelligibility of Anglophone young beginner learners of Mandarin Chinese in England

Rob, the teacher researcher, found that tone, or the use of pitch differences 'to distinguish the dictionary meaning of words' (Collins and Mees, 2008: 133), is generally considered to be particularly problematic for Anglophone learners and has consequently been the focus of the majority of research into Chinese as a foreign language (CFL) pronunciation studies (Xing, 2006; Ke, 2012). While various reasons have been put forward to explain why Anglophone learners tend to struggle with tones, ranging from interference of English intonation patterns (White, 1981; Chen, 1997) to the inherent unfamiliarity of native English speakers with tones (McGinnis, 1997; Winke, 2007), it is by no means clear how important standard tones are for communication. Hence, set within the context of teaching and learning Chinese at a comprehensive secondary school in the north of England, the aim of this action research project is not to question whether tones are difficult for Anglophone learners, but to make some preliminary investigations into which specific areas of the L2 speech signal mislead L1 Chinese listeners. By working at the syllable level and engaging closely with the construct of intelligibility, it will be argued that there is a danger of placing 'perfect' tones on a pedestal at the expense of equally significant pronunciation priorities for the beginner Anglophone learner of Chinese, such as initials and finals.

Planning: From 'nativeness' to 'intelligibility'

Much of the CFL pronunciation research remains heavily influenced by the 'nativeness' principle, which holds that 'it is both possible and desirable to achieve native-like pronunciation in a foreign language' (Levis, 2005: 370). For example, Shen (1989), Miracle (1989), Chen (1997), Winke (2007), Tao and Guo (2008) and Zhang (2010) all use native speakers to rate the L2 Chinese participants' tonal productions as 'correct' or 'incorrect.' Partly as a result of such research, three native-speaker Chinese teachers were deployed to rate the tonal productions of students, yet Rob was struck by the high levels of subjectivity involved in judging the acceptability of the tones (Neal, 2014). In this research project, therefore, the decision was taken to move away from a simplistic focus on whether students' tones were 'correct' or 'incorrect' according to L1 Chinese raters, to a wider focus on intelligibility, defined as 'the extent to which the listener can understand the speaker's intended words' (Zielinski, 2008: 70). As well as being able to test whether intended meanings could still be understood despite non-standard tones, this new emphasis on intelligibility would allow the researcher to begin to draw up more robust pronunciation priorities by focusing primarily on those areas of speech that led to breakdowns in communication (Derwing and Munro, 2005: 385).

Action

Originally, role plays were recorded on digital voice recorders in which five students were asked simple questions about their lives in Mandarin Chinese. The role plays featured topics already covered in class (e.g. hobbies, food and drink) and lasted around 90 seconds. At the time of the recordings, all students had been studying Chinese for six months and were either 14 or 15 years old. None of them had had any previous experience of learning a tonal language and they were all L1 English speakers. Working independently and with full access to written transcripts of the students' role plays, three L1 Chinese raters were asked to listen to the audio files and code each character as acceptable or unacceptable in terms of tonal production according to Chao's (1968) system of tone values. Two of the raters were Chinese teachers at the same school as the students, although the other rater had had virtually no previous exposure to L1 English speakers of Chinese. In order to increase the reliability of the study, only tones coded as acceptable by all three raters were used to calculate each student's overall tonal acceptability rating.

For the follow-up, sections of the audio files taken from the learners' role plays were sent via email to five students at a senior high school in Beijing. Given that familiarity with a topic and non-native accents are likely to promote comprehension (Gass and Varonis, 1984), raters were used who would not be overly familiar with the accents of L1 beginner English learners of Chinese or the *Jìn bù* textbook students had been following (Bin *et al.*, 2010). Each rater was asked to listen to the audio file only once and transcribe what they thought they had heard in Chinese characters. Following Derwing and Munro (1997), each transcript was then used to calculate an intelligibility score based on the number of characters the rater could successfully transcribe. For example, if a rater successfully transcribed 80 characters out of a possible 100, then the student would be awarded an intelligibility rating of 80 per cent. The overall intelligibility rating for each L1 English student, based on an average score of the five Beijing high school raters, was then compared with the students' original tonal accuracy scores from previous research.

Particular attention was paid to the areas where the raters had transcribed a different character from what the speaker had intended to say. Knowledge of the speakers' original intentions was based on familiarity with the students' L2 Chinese accents and 'insider knowledge' of the language covered in class and produced for homework. The source of the breakdown in intelligibility was categorized as either being a result of the tone, or the initial consonant of the syllable or the final part of the syllable deviating from the standard form, or a combination of two or all three of the factors. For example, if the rater transcribed 是 shì (be) when the student had intended to say 十 shí (ten), then the breakdown would be traced directly to tone. However, if the rater transcribed 猫 māo (cat) when the student had attempted to say 妈 mǎ (mother), then both tone and the final would be implicated as contributing to the misunderstanding.

Observational findings

The corpus of speech produced by the five participants totalled 412 characters. It was immediately apparent that all five participants obtained much higher intelligibility ratings than tonal accuracy ratings (see Figure 5.2).

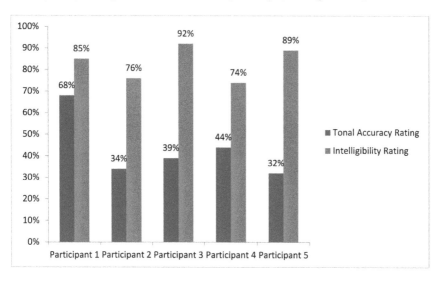

Figure 5.2: Comparing participants' tonal accuracy and intelligibility ratings

This appears to lend support to the claim that L1 Chinese speakers may well be 'able to understand intended meanings regardless of incorrect tones, simply based on the discourse context' (Duff *et al.*, 2013: 49). However, there should be no room for complacency. It is unlikely that participants 2 and 4 for example, with intelligibility rates of 76 and 74 per cent respectively, are making much sense at all and are certainly a very long way from 'a comfortably intelligible pronunciation' (Abercrombie, 1949: 120, as quoted in Derwing and Munro, 2005: 384), which seems to be a reasonable goal of pronunciation instruction.

Given concerns about the limitations of this actions research project, it is difficult to be certain about the specific causes of the intelligibility breakdowns. Nevertheless, it seems reasonable to conclude that the participants' pronunciation problems run far deeper than non-standard tones (see Figure 5.3).

For example, while 15 per cent of all the intelligibility breakdowns can be traced directly to tone, 13 per cent of the breakdowns can be linked directly to finals. Although there are no examples of intelligibility problems being caused solely by initials, 52 per cent of the breakdowns implicate non-standard initials as a contributory factor. Moreover, the most frequent cause of breakdown occurs when the tone, initial and final are all different from the target pronunciation (23 per cent), suggesting that in these cases, the real cause of the problem is inadequate lexical knowledge as much as non-standard pronunciation.

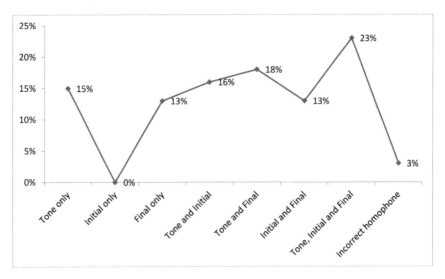

Figure 5.3: Causes of combined breakdowns in intelligibility (n = 62)

Reflection

While much of the previous research into CFL pronunciation has focused mainly on tones, the findings here suggest that more emphasis should be placed on initials and finals in the classroom alongside tones. A good place to start would arguably be with a renewed focus on the Romanized orthography known as Pinyin, which has become the standard transcription of Mandarin Chinese words (Lin, 2007: 7). Rushing to launch into teaching characters, teaching Pinyin properly may have been neglected with negative consequences for the students' intelligibility. However, as it is widely known, a focus on Pinyin can easily lead into an over-reliance on using the Latin alphabet to represent Chinese sounds, which could in turn slow down character learning in the long term. A sensible trade-off would be for more research into establishing precisely which initials and finals are most important for intelligibility rather than spending valuable teaching time on all the sounds of Pinyin. The data sets used in this research project however, have been far too small to begin to answer this question.

A key issue related to teaching pronunciation is the extent to which it can be picked up implicitly or whether explicit instruction is necessary (Derwing and Munro, 2014). Initially assuming that students could simply acquire an acceptable Chinese accent through frequent exposure to Chinese in the classroom is in line with communicative language teaching (CLT), which emphasizes authentic use of language and sees repetition and corrective feedback as disruptive to communication (Derwing and Munro, 2014: 38). However, the evidence from this study suggests that without explicit correction, learners are showing evidence of fossilized speech patterns (ibid.: 38). For example, alongside the two instances of incorrect homophones, raters often had problems transcribing students' Chinese names, with none of them being able to transcribe participant 4 or participant 5's Chinese names successfully. This is despite the fact that all the learners were frequently exposed to accurate pronunciation of their own Chinese names, both from the teacher and other L1 Chinese teachers during lessons. A renewed focus on pronunciation will need to be handled sensitively and without demotivating or scaring some learners by being overly strict in the classroom. However, the alternative approach of ignoring pronunciation issues is potentially even more confidence-sapping for learners in the long run, for if they find that they cannot make the limited Chinese they know intelligible to others, they will surely lose motivation quickly (Zielinski and Yates, 2014: 75). The challenge, therefore, is to teach pronunciation in ways that are 'systematic, [...] non-threatening, engaging, and confidence-building' (75).

Case study 2: An investigation into the most effective strategies for beginner Anglophone learners to read and write Chinese characters

Paul, the teacher researcher, understands that rote learning, storytelling and making reference to radicals are three of the most commonly used strategies recommended by teachers to assist learners in learning to read and write Chinese characters (McGinnis, 1999; Shen, 2005). In Paul's teaching practice, he has constantly wondered what strategies for learning pupils themselves believe to be most effective for supporting them to learn to read and write Chinese characters. Besides investigating this issue, he has also hoped to make his research findings more generalizable in order to fill a current void in research into how Anglophone learners learn Mandarin and what they find most difficult about learning the language. A further goal of the investigation was to gauge ten teachers' opinions of the most effective strategies and assess whether their perceptions match those of the learners. In his study, a sample group of 42 beginner learners of Mandarin Chinese from two UK secondary schools completed two questionnaires prior to and post intervention period (a period in which pupils gained a deeper understanding of the three strategies mentioned above). Results showed rote learning for writing to be the most favoured strategy by both pupils and teachers. Rote learning was also favoured by pupils for reading, whereas teachers preferred the use of radicals.

Planning: What works best for Anglophone learners?

Rote learning is the method Paul used when learning how to read and write Chinese characters and is the method that has been favoured historically by native-speaker Chinese teachers of native-speaking Chinese pupils (McGinnis, 1999). Storytelling involves telling a story about an individual Chinese character in the hope that the story and the character will be recalled later (Shen, 2005). An example may be describing to pupils that the character for 'good' (好) in Chinese consists of the character for 'woman' (女) combined with the character for 'child' (子). By combining the two we gain insights into the Chinese psyche: that the idea of a female (女) with a child (子) is good (好). Understanding and making reference to radicals (the part of the character that can offer a learner clues about the meaning of the character) appears to appeal to pupils because they only need to recall some of the character and not the whole character if they can recall which radical is in the character (Shen, 2005). For example, the verb 'to eat' (吃) in Chinese contains the radical for mouth (口). If a learner can recall that they eat with their mouth and therefore the character for 'eat' contains the radical for mouth, this may help them to recall and reproduce that character more easily.

There is a severe shortage of evidence relating to the strategies that primary or secondary school learners of Mandarin Chinese use, as the majority of research has been conducted into university students' strategy selection (Shen, 2005; Sung and Wu, 2011). The scarcity of academic literature and increase in curriculum provision of Mandarin Chinese in secondary and primary schools in the UK confirms an important need for further evidence to support teachers in using the most appropriate strategies for learning Mandarin Chinese and to support pupils in adopting the most effective strategies. Although research into the most effective learning strategies used by learners of Roman alphabet-based languages offer useful insights (Krashen, 1981; Oxford, 1990), one cannot draw easy comparisons or firm conclusions from their findings when considering a character-based language (Scrimgeour, 2011). Whether or not language learning strategies are innate, as some evidence has suggested (Chomsky, 1986), and therefore arguably transferable to different types of languages, would be interesting to investigate further. Additionally, it is important to consider how large the impact of motivation is (Crow, 1986) or whether the process of writing is a deeper and therefore more difficult process (Corson, 1995). It may also be the case that learners of different ability levels use different strategies (Everson and Ke, 1997; Chang 2010).

The teachers' and pupils' questionnaires were specifically designed to address the five key objectives of the research project. The questions in the questionnaire were then cross-referenced with these objectives with the aim of ensuring that they would provide data relevant to the objectives. In order to enable comparison between teachers' and pupils' perceptions, the questionnaires had to be very similar. A list of the objectives of the investigation, expressed as questions, can be seen below:

1) Which learning strategies do pupils perceive to be the most effective for learning to read and write Chinese characters?
2) Which learning strategies do teachers perceive to be the most effective to enable their pupils to learn to read and write Chinese characters?
3) Does teaching pupils about the three seemingly most effective learning strategies impact on their perceptions of the most effective learning strategies?

4) Is there a difference between teachers' and pupils' perceptions of the most effective learning strategies?
5) Is there a difference between the perceptions of pupils in a selective school compared to a non-selective school?

A diagram of the data collection cycle can be seen in Figure 5.4:

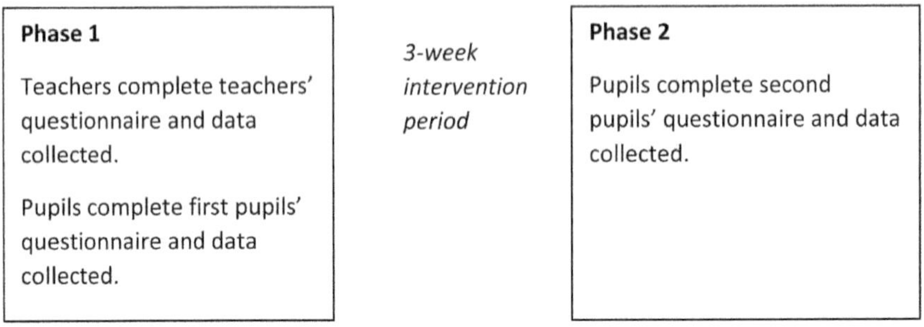

Phase 1	*3-week intervention period*	**Phase 2**
Teachers complete teachers' questionnaire and data collected. Pupils complete first pupils' questionnaire and data collected.		Pupils complete second pupils' questionnaire and data collected.

Figure 5.4: Data collection cycle

Action

Following a Mandarin teachers' action research group meeting at the Institute of Education in London in March 2014, Paul became aware that two colleagues were also interested in investigating pupils' perceptions of the most effective learning strategies for learning to read and write Chinese characters. Having shared his research project objectives with them, the two colleagues were keen to support the investigation by contributing to the collection of data. One colleague therefore carried out some of the data collection within her school in Sheffield. The other colleague supported the collection of some of the data relating to teachers' perceptions by contacting a number of her colleagues whom she knew would be interested in contributing to this research.

The sample groups were selected using specific criteria. It was essential that participants in the pupils group were in their first year of learning Mandarin and studying at a school in the UK. It was also important that participants in the teachers group were working either part- or full-time as Mandarin teachers in UK schools. The 28 pupils from the selective grammar school were Paul's Year 8 Mandarin class, who began learning Mandarin in September 2013. The 14 pupils from the non-selective comprehensive school were the pupils of Paul's colleague's Mandarin class, who began learning Mandarin at the same time. Data was analysed by converting raw data into percentages to give a clearer idea of what proportion of the pupil and teacher cohorts preferred the respective methods of learning to read and write Chinese characters. It was agreed that Paul would first share findings with his two colleagues and following that, they would have the opportunity to inform their pupils or colleagues of the findings. The research results were later presented at a national Mandarin teacher's conference.

Observational findings

Which learning strategies do Anglophone pupils perceive to be the most effective for learning to read and write Chinese characters?

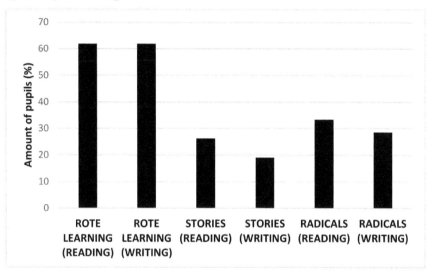

Figure 5.5: Percentage of pupils who, post-intervention, rated a strategy either 'often' or 'all the time' the most effective

As can be seen clearly in Figure 5.5, the percentage of pupils who perceived rote learning to be the most effective strategy for both reading and writing either 'often' or 'all the time' in the post-intervention questionnaire was significantly higher than that for any other strategy. The fact that the percentage of pupils who perceived rote learning to be most effective for reading (61.9 per cent) was nearly double that of pupils who perceived radicals (33.3 per cent) to be most effective, and the percentage for writing (61.9 per cent) was over double that of pupils who perceived use of radicals to be most effective (28.6 per cent), is quite a telling result. Use of radicals was perceived to be the second most effective strategy for both reading and writing Chinese characters and the use of stories for both skills (reading: 26.2 per cent; writing: 19 per cent) was perceived to be the third most effective strategy.

Is there a difference between teachers' and pupils' perceptions of the most effective learning strategies?

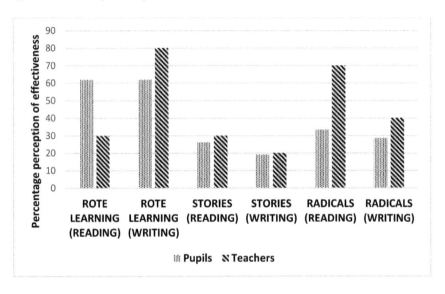

Figure 5.6: Comparison of the perception of strategy effectiveness between the post-intervention pupils' and teachers' questionnaires

As Figure 5.6 illustrates, there were mixed levels of agreement between pupils and teachers when responding to how effective they perceived a strategy to be. The largest percentage difference in reported perception between teachers and pupils concerns the use of radicals for learning to read Chinese characters, with 36.6 per cent more teachers than pupils perceiving the strategy to be, often or all of the time, the most effective. Although the percentage difference is over one third and therefore appears large, it is important to recall that the sample size of the teachers group is very small and therefore 30 per cent of the teachers sample only equates to three people. The second largest difference in perception between the pupils group and the teachers group of the most effective strategy related to the use of rote learning for reading, where 31.9 per cent more pupils than teachers found the strategy to be, often or all the time, the most effective. Despite the small sample size of the teachers group, the large difference in the perception of the effectiveness the two learning strategies could be interpreted as concerning. It is, however, conceivable that, owing to their limited exposure and experience of learning the language, pupils' perception of the most effective strategy may be subject to change over time. Nevertheless, it would be advisable for teachers to address this large difference in the perception of these two strategies' effectiveness and explore what is at its root.

Reflections

The results are discussed here in terms of implications for practice:

1. ROTE LEARNING FOR WRITING

Teachers and pupils from both schools were unanimous in their perception that rote learning was the most effective strategy for learning how to write Chinese characters. The first key implication of this unanimous result is that teachers could ensure that sufficient lesson time is dedicated to discussing it and supporting pupils in the effective adoption of this strategy. Teachers could not only spend time convincing pupils of the benefits of this strategy, but also prove to them that, if they are willing to adopt this strategy, they could reap the rewards of their efforts in terms of developing their writing skills. It could be argued that, if pupils are taught how to utilize rote learning as a strategy effectively, and if they experience the benefits of the strategy, this would resolve many of their Mandarin Chinese language learning concerns. It must be noted that the perception as reported in the present investigation relates to beginner learners of the language and that this strategy may not be perceived as most effective by either intermediate or advanced learners. In addition, this research only concerns pupils' and teachers' perception of the most effective strategies and it cannot be claimed that the perceived most effective strategies are necessarily the best strategies. To suggest a strategy is the best, as opposed to perceived as the most effective, would require a much deeper investigation into the cognitive processes associated with each skill, which was not the aim of the present investigation.

2. DIFFERENCES BETWEEN PUPIL AND TEACHER PERCEPTION OF THE MOST EFFECTIVE STRATEGIES

The differences observed between pupils' and teachers' perceptions of the most effective strategies for certain skills relating to learning Chinese have important implications for teaching practice. The most noteworthy discrepancy between pupil and teacher perception relates to the use of radicals for reading. One should be mindful of pupils' relative lack of confidence in the effectiveness of radicals for reading compared with rote learning. Teachers should consider why this might be. It is possible that this discrepancy exists because radicals become more useful for learners who have reached an intermediate or advanced level of Mandarin Chinese: teachers are advanced learners of the language, whereas the pupils were beginners at the time this research was conducted. Nonetheless, it is the teachers' role to teach learning strategies that are most suited to their pupils' level of expertise, hence teachers should adapt their teaching to their pupils' level.

3. PUPILS FROM DIFFERENT TYPES OF SCHOOLS MAY PREFER DIFFERENT STRATEGIES

The third and final implication for practice of the present investigation relates to the differing perception of pupils from a non-selective mixed school compared with pupils from a selective grammar school regarding certain skills. Like the observed differences between pupils' and teachers' perceptions, the main point of contention for pupils from the two different schools was the effectiveness of rote learning and radicals for reading. In both cases, there were considerable differences in perceived effectiveness. The implication of this finding on teaching practice is that teachers of Mandarin should be aware that different pupils perceive different strategies to be most effective. Classroom activities, homework activities, and assessments should therefore be designed to cater for these differences in perception. Furthermore, a range of strategies should be presented early on in the course of learning the language, so that pupils can select the one that they find most effective.

Discussion

We hope that the two action research projects conducted by teachers of Mandarin Chinese illustrated above have illustrated the kind of professional concerns that may motivate action research enquiries and ways of reporting them. We also hope to make clear that there is no one-size-fits-all pattern in action research. Teachers, in their projects, can research whatever issues interest them using various suitable methods and reporting their research in ways that often differ from more formalized academic research.

In Rob's project, he was initially interested in understanding the intelligibility of his students' spoken Chinese. By analysing the intelligibility breakdowns that emerged from the transcriptions of five Chinese high school students, he realized and argued that he needed to pay more attention to pronunciation issues in the classroom, with an increased focus on initials and finals alongside tones. Furthermore, he has conceptualized action research as a journey in which original research questions lead to more important ones. When reflecting on his project, he acknowledged that he is now moving away from a narrow focus on tones to identifying problems likely to interfere with intelligibility. The next phase of the journey will be to investigate whether a more explicit focus on tones, initials and finals in the classroom can actually lead to more accurate pronunciation. Rob recognizes that this action research project has directed him towards further research cycles. In Paul's project, he pointed out that, on a personal level, the investigation has instilled in him the importance of always being aware that different pupils may find different learning strategies more effective, although some strategies appear more popular than others. Strategy selection should be presented as key in the early part of any Mandarin Chinese curriculum and should be reviewed at regular intervals throughout the course of a pupil's learning. He further contends that it is likely that more and more British pupils will learn Mandarin Chinese in British schools in future alongside the traditional European languages, and he hopes that his investigation may contribute to addressing some of the problems that pupils could encounter. Though each project is unique and uses different research methods, both emerge from the teachers' feelings of needing to improve or change their practice and to tackle problems in their teaching context. What is more significant is that their action research raises new areas or questions that may take them and the other teacher-researchers into further fields of investigation (Burns, 1999).

We hope this chapter has served its aim of encouraging teachers of Mandarin Chinese and teachers of modern foreign languages in general to carry out their own small-scale action research projects, as it is practical and teacher-friendly and can be used widely in the initial and continuing professional learning of language teachers. It is a way of improving teaching practice, as we can see from the two projects illustrated in this chapter. More importantly, we also see that the significance of doing action research for language teachers is that they can generate pedagogical theories. In the current MFL classroom, teachers are still seen as 'expert practitioners', not as 'expert knowers' in that 'many teachers see their practice as informed by common sense or practical wisdom and they talk about practice as activity, rather than as considered, committed and purposeful action' (McNiff and Whitehead, 2005; McNiff, 2013; 2014): teachers are often described as implementers of practice but not theorists of practice (McNiff and Whitehead, 2005; McNiff, 2013; 2014). This is where action research comes in. It can help teachers improve their practice, and it can also help them see their practice as a form of practical theorizing. Practice and theory are interrelated and should always inform each other. The authors of this chapter have therefore advocated that language teachers should be the decision-makers: they need to have a say in what counts as theory, curriculum and policy for language teaching. To do so, they need to take the initiative and be the creators and promoters of new theory and new pedagogy. Action research is a valuable tool for them to realize this goal. By doing so, teachers of Mandarin Chinese and other modern foreign languages will broaden the platform for sharing their work, engage in more professional discussion and debate on classroom research, and more importantly, help contribute towards foreign language pedagogy and policies, thereby ensuring that MFL teaching becomes properly embedded within school curricula.

Practical ideas

Below is a diagram showing steps involved in action research. Stages 1 and 2 are to identify and specify your area of concern. In Stage 1, the teachers usually define the purpose of their action research by asking themselves these questions: What is going on in my classes that is causing my concern? Why am I starting this action research project? Then you identify an issue that you would like to learn more about. For example: 'Some of the students are very silent and seem never to want to answer my questions or participate in activities.' In this case, it is suggested that you do some research about learner motivation and 'tips on activities design', which will inform you about what the other teachers and scholars say about second language learners in their language acquisition. In Stage 2, you turn the issue you want to investigate into a more specific question for action research. Ask yourself, 'how can I narrow down the issue under investigation to make it manageable within a specific time frame?' To continue with the example above, more specific questions may either focus on the learners' motivation: 'how do I improve students' learning motivation in classroom activities?' or on the learning activity design: 'what activities can make students more active in classrooms?'

Stages 3 and 4 are to design data collection methods and match your data collection methods with what you want to find out. First ask 'how am I going to conduct the research?' or 'what data-collecting methods will I need, and why?' There are many different methods for collecting data in classrooms. Burns (1999: 79) gives a few examples of observational or non-observational approaches to data collection. Methods of collecting observational data include keeping notes of classroom happenings; writing diaries about feelings, interactions and activities; keeping audio or video recording of classroom interactions; and drawing maps, diagrams or layouts of teacher–student interactions. Non-observational methods include interviews, discussions, questionnaires and surveys; and collecting life/career histories or documents and policies. The teacher needs to choose the best and what appear to be the most revealing research methods, and to collect data in the classroom. Before collecting data, it is important to gain consent, i.e. permission for conducting research from your senior management team and from your participants (and if they are below 18, gain written permission from their parents).

In Stage 5, you are going to analyse data and disseminate it to attract opinions and make an impact. At the analysis stage, go through your data for broad patterns, ideas and trends that seem to address or answer your questions. You can develop tables, charts or sets of quotes to display in a concise form. Then think deeply about what the data are saying by reflecting beyond the immediate surface details and by reflecting again on your research questions (Burns, 2010). Then write down what you have found and participate in conversations, peer dialogues, workshops and school visits to share your research results with other teachers, scholars and policymakers.

While being aware that what we have presented is not exhaustive, we hope that we have provided you with some thoughts and advice on how to do action research by yourself. We hope that teachers will become 'expert knowers' who will be able to implement considered, committed and purposeful action in their classrooms. When they become theorists of practice via action research, they will be able to improve their own practice and have a real say in their professional practice generally.

Action research steps

Stage 1
Decide on an area of practice that you want to
investigate, and research what literature already exists in
this area.

Stage 2
Determine your objectives from the area of practice that
you would like to research and where a gap in research
knowledge exists.

Stage 3
Decide what data you need to collect to address
your objectives and what research tools will be most
appropriate to achieve this.

Stage 4
Design the data collection materials and conduct the
data collection pre- and post-intervention period.

Stage 5
Analyse the data and evaluate its usefulness. Disseminate
useful findings to interested parties. Implement useful
findings into practice. Reflect on what further research
could be done.

References

Bailey, K.M. (1998) 'Approaches to empirical research in instructional settings'. In Byrnes, H. (ed.) *Perspectives in Research and Scholarship in Second Language Learning*. New York: The Modern Language Association of America, 75–104.

Bin, Y., Zhu, X., and Carruthers, K. (2010) *Jìn bù 1 进步一*. Harlow: Heinemann.

Burns, A. (1999) *Collaborative Action Research for English Language Teachers*. Cambridge: Cambridge University Press.

Burns, A. (2010) *Doing Action Research in English Language Teaching: A guide for practitioners*. New York: Routledge.

Chang, C. (2010) 'See how they read: An investigation into the cognitive and metacognitive strategies of nonnative readers of Chinese'. In Everson, M.E. and Shen, H.H. (eds) *Research Among Learners of Chinese as a Foreign Language* (Chinese Language Teachers Association Monograph 4). Honolulu: National Foreign Language Resource Center, 93–116.

Chao, Y.R. (1968) *A Grammar of Spoken Chinese*. Berkeley: University of California Press.

Chen, Q. (1997) 'Toward a sequential approach for tonal error analysis'. *Journal of the Chinese Language Teachers Association*, 32 (1), 21–39.

Chomsky, N. (1986) *Knowledge of Language: Its nature, origin, and use*. New York: Praeger.

Collins, B. and Mees, I.M. (2008) *Practical Phonetics and Phonology: A resource book for students*. 2nd ed. London: Routledge.

Corson, D. (1995) *Using English Words*. Dordrecht: Kluwer.

Crow, J.T. (1986) 'Receptive vocabulary acquisition for reading comprehension'. *Modern Language Journal*, 70 (3), 242–50.

Derwing, T.M. and Munro, M.J. (1997) 'Accent, intelligibility, and comprehensibility: Evidence from four L1s'. *Studies in Second Language Acquisition*, 19 (1), 1–16.

Derwing, T.M. and Munro, M.J. (2005) 'Second language accent and pronunciation teaching: A research-based approach'. *TESOL Quarterly*, 39 (3), 379–97.

Derwing, T.M. and Munro, M.J. (2014) 'Myth 1: Once you have been speaking a second language for years, it's too late to change your pronunciation'. In Grant, L. (ed.) *Pronunciation Myths: Applying second language research to classroom teaching*. Ann Arbor: University of Michigan Press, 34–55.

Duff, P., Anderson, T., Ilnyckyj, R., VanGaya, E., Wang, R.T. and Yates, E. (2013) *Learning Chinese: Linguistic, sociocultural, and narrative perspectives*. Berlin: De Gruyter.

Everson, M.E. and Ke, C. (1997) 'An inquiry into the reading strategies of intermediate and advanced learners of Chinese as a foreign language'. *Journal of the Chinese Language Teachers Association*, 32 (1), 1–22.

Freeman, D. and Richards, J.C. (1993) 'Conceptions of teaching and the education of second language teachers'. *TESOL Quarterly*, 27 (2), 193–216.

Gass, S. and Varonis, E.M. (1984) 'The effect of familiarity on the comprehensibility of nonnative speech'. *Language Learning*, 34 (1), 65–89.

Ke, C. (2012) 'Research in second language acquisition of Chinese: Where we are, where we are going'. *Journal of the Chinese Language Teachers Association*, 47 (3), 43–113.

Kemmis, S. and McTaggart, R. (eds) (1988) *The Action Research Planner*. 3rd ed. Victoria: Deakin University.

Krashen, S.D. (1981) *Second Language Acquisition and Second Language Learning*. Oxford: Pergamon Press.

Levis, J.M. (2005) 'Changing contexts and shifting paradigms in pronunciation teaching'. *TESOL Quarterly*, 39 (3), 369–77.

Lin, Y.-H. (2007) *The Sounds of Chinese*. Cambridge: Cambridge University Press.

McGinnis, S. (1997) 'Tonal spelling versus diacritics for teaching pronunciation of Mandarin Chinese'. *Modern Language Journal*, 81 (2), 228–36.

McGinnis, S. (1999) 'Student goals and approaches'. In Chu, M. (ed.) *Mapping the Course of the Chinese Language Field* (Chinese Language Teachers Association Monograph 3). Kalamazoo, MI: Chinese Language Teachers Association, 151–88.

McKernan, J. (1996) *Curriculum Action Research: A handbook of methods and resources for the reflective practitioner*. 2nd ed. London: Kogan Page.

McNiff, J. (1988) *Action Research: Principles and practice*. London: Routledge.

McNiff, J. (2013) *Action Research: Principles and practice*. 3rd ed. London: Routledge.

McNiff, J. (2014) *Writing and Doing Action Research*. London: SAGE Publications.

McNiff, J. and Whitehead, J. (2005) *Action Research for Teachers: A practical guide*. London: David Fulton.

Mertler, C.A. (2014) *Action Research: Improving schools and empowering educators*. 4th ed. Thousand Oaks, CA: SAGE Publications.

Mills, G.E. (2014) *Action Research: A guide for the teacher researcher*. Harlow: Pearson Education.

Miracle, W. (1989) 'Tone production of American students of Chinese: A preliminary acoustic study'. *Journal of the Chinese Language Teachers Association*, 24 (3), 49–65.

Neal, R. (2014) 'Teaching and learning Mandarin tones in an English secondary school'. *Scottish Languages Review*, 27, 9–20.

Nunan, D. (1992) *Research Methods in Language Learning*. Cambridge: Cambridge University Press.

Nunan, D. (1993) 'Action research in language education'. In Edge, J. and Richards, K. (eds) *Teachers Develop Teachers Research: Papers on classroom research and teacher development*. Oxford: Heinemann, 39–50.

Oxford, R.L. (1990) *Language Learning Strategies: What every teacher should know*. New York: Newbury House.

Phillips, D.K. and Carr, K. (2014) *Becoming a Teacher through Action Research: Process, context, and self-study*. 3rd ed. New York: Routledge.

Scrimgeour, A. (2011) 'Issues and approaches to literacy development in Chinese second language classrooms'. In Tsung, L. and Cruickshank, K. (eds) *Teaching and Learning Chinese in Global Contexts: Multimodality and literacy in the new media age*. London: Continuum, 197–212.

Shen, H.H. (2005) 'An investigation of Chinese-character learning strategies among non-native speakers of Chinese'. *System,* 33 (1), 49–68.

Shen, X.S. (1989) 'Toward a register approach in teaching Mandarin tones'. *Journal of the Chinese Language Teachers Association*, 24 (3), 27–47.

Sung, K.-Y. and Wu, H.-P. (2011) 'Factors influencing the learning of Chinese characters'. *International Journal of Bilingual Education and Bilingualism*, 14 (6), 683–700.

Tao, L. and Guo, L. (2008) 'Learning Chinese tones: A developmental account'. *Journal of the Chinese Language Teachers Association*, 43 (2), 17–46.

Walker, R. (1985) *Doing Research: A handbook for teachers.* London: Methuen.

White, C. (1981) 'Tonal pronunciation errors and interference from English intonation'. *Journal of the Chinese Language Teachers Association*, 16 (2), 27–56.

Winke, P.M. (2007) 'Tuning into tones: The effect of L1 background on L2 Chinese learners' tonal production'. *Journal of the Chinese Language Teachers Association*, 42 (3), 21–55.

Xing, J.Z. (2006) *Teaching and Learning Chinese as a Foreign Language: A pedagogical grammar.* Hong Kong: Hong Kong University Press.

Zielinski, B.W. (2008) 'The listener: No longer the silent partner in reduced intelligibility'. *System*, 36 (1), 69–84.

Zielinski, B. and Yates, L. (2014) 'Myth 2: Pronunciation instruction is not appropriate for beginning-level learners'. In Grant, L. (ed.) *Pronunciation Myths: Applying second language research to classroom teaching.* Ann Arbor: University of Michigan Press, 56–79.

Zhang, H. (2010) 'Phonological universals and tonal acquisition'. *Journal of the Chinese Language Teachers Association*, 45 (1), 39–65.

Chapter 6

Investigating the intelligibility of Anglophone young beginner learners of Mandarin Chinese

Rob Neal

Introduction

Despite the explosion of interest in teaching and learning Mandarin Chinese as a foreign language (CFL) across the world (Xing, 2006; Tsung and Cruickshank, 2011), its position in the UK school curriculum remains precarious, both at the primary and secondary school level (Board and Tinsley, 2014: 8). Obstacles to further development include a continued focus on European languages such as French, German and Spanish (British Council, 2013), a lack of qualified and experienced teachers of Mandarin Chinese (Ofsted, 2008), and a dearth of research into teaching and learning Chinese as a foreign language (Zhang and Li, 2010). One constructive way forward is the creation of a 'specifically Chinese pedagogy' (Orton, 2011: 159) that takes into account the unique challenges of learning Chinese as a foreign language. Tone, or the use of pitch differences 'to distinguish the dictionary meaning of words' (Collins and Mees, 2013: 133), is generally considered to be particularly problematic for Anglophone learners and has consequently been the focus of the majority of research into CFL pronunciation studies (Xing, 2006; Ke, 2012). Set within the context of teaching and learning Chinese at a comprehensive secondary school in the north of England, the aim of this action research project is not to question whether tones are difficult for Anglophone learners, but to make some preliminary investigations into which specific areas of the L2 speech signal mislead L1 Chinese listeners. By working at the syllable level and engaging closely with the construct of intelligibility, it will be argued that there is a danger of placing 'perfect' tones on a pedestal at the expense of equally, if not more significant, pronunciation priorities for the beginner Anglophone learner of Chinese such as initials and finals.

Action research as a journey: From tones to intelligibility

In a recent research project, I examined the tonal production of five of my own students and their ability to notice and self-correct their tonal errors after six months of Chinese study (Neal, 2014). With four of the five participants scoring less than 50 per cent in terms of overall tonal accuracy rates and all students displaying a general inability to notice or correct their tonal errors during a stimulated recall interview, my conclusion that students need to pay more attention to tones appears to be self-evident. Although I argue that there was some evidence of universal phonological constraints in participants' data sets (Zhang, 2010), as well as signs of interference from English intonation patterns (White, 1981; Chen, 1997), the most convincing explanation for participants' difficulties in producing accurate tones appears to be their inherent unfamiliarity with tones (McGinnis, 1997; Winke, 2007). In terms of action research, I feel that I have successfully diagnosed the problem of why my students tend to struggle with tones. The logical next step was to plan some pedagogical interventions along the lines of raising students' tonal awareness and giving them a deeper understanding of the formal tonal system before their faulty tones fossilized and proved resistant to change.

Nevertheless, nagging doubts persisted about the value of such an approach. This was partly a result of personal bias stemming from my own experience of learning Chinese as a beginner. Traipsing around the streets of Beijing on my way to and from lessons, I would listen to recorded conversations repeatedly and commit them to memory, blissfully unaware of how the Mandarin tonal system actually worked. Although I did not realize it at the time, such a focus on small 'intonation units' (Tao and Guo, 2008: 35) has a number of advantages for the beginning learner, as it lessens the cognitive load of having to concentrate on every tone at the individual syllable level as well as being a source of 'high frequency formulaic chunks' (Duff *et al.*, 2013: 48). I also feared that over-emphasizing tones in the classroom, while raising learners' tonal awareness, may unwittingly destroy their confidence. For example, Roma, an adult Mandarin learner based in Canada, decided that after her Chinese teacher repeatedly corrected her tonal production, her future strategy regarding tones was 'simply to ignore them' (ibid.: 48). But perhaps the biggest reason for not stressing tones stemmed from uncertainty whether standard tones were actually that important for communication, vividly expressed by one of my students during a stimulated recall interview:

> If I was just walking past someone and I haven't got much time, I'm just passing, I might just say 'ni hao' other than like putting a lot of like emphasis on it. Otherwise they might be gone by the time like I say it or whatever. And like if it's easier, like if I'm doing a long sentence and I don't want to forget it, I'll like do it in flat tone 'cos like even though it might mean different things in different tones, I think they'll still understand the context.

These comments certainly resonated with my own experiences when travelling around China away from the safety of the language classroom in Beijing. Ultimately, did it really matter if L2 speakers of Chinese had non-standard tones as long as they could be readily understood? More importantly, there was every possibility that when my students used their Chinese in genuinely communicative settings – whether with a waiter from Anhui at a Chinese restaurant in England, or with a market trader in Shanghai during a summer camp – both interlocutors would effectively be speaking in a second language with somewhat non-standard tones. I consequently decided to revisit sections of students' production data and move away from a simplistic focus on whether tones were 'correct' or 'incorrect' according to L1 Chinese raters, to a wider focus on intelligibility, defined as 'the extent to which the listener can understand the speaker's intended words' (Zielinski, 2008: 70). As well as being able to test whether intended meanings could still be understood despite non-standard tones, this new focus on intelligibility would allow me to begin to draw up more robust pronunciation priorities by focusing primarily on those areas of speech that led to breakdowns in communication (Derwing and Munro, 2005: 385).

Procedure

I had originally recorded role plays on digital voice recorders in which I asked five of my students simple questions about their lives in Mandarin Chinese. The role plays featured topics already covered in class (e.g. hobbies, food and drink) and lasted around 90 seconds. At the time of the recordings, all students had been studying Chinese for six months and were either 14 or 15 years old. None of them had had any previous experience of learning a tonal language and they were all L1 English speakers. Working independently and with full access to written transcripts of the students' role plays, three L1 Chinese raters were asked to listen to the audio files and code each character as acceptable or unacceptable in terms of tonal production according to Chao's (1968) system of tone values. Two of the raters were Chinese teachers at the same school as the students, although the other rater had had virtually no previous exposure to L1 English speakers of Chinese. In order to increase the reliability of the study, only tones coded as acceptable by all three raters were used to calculate each student's overall tonal acceptability rating. Short and weak neutral tones were not included in the analyses.

For this follow-up project, the audio files taken from the learners' role plays were sent via email to five students at a senior high school in Beijing. Given that familiarity with a topic and non-native accents are likely to promote comprehension (Gass and Varonis, 1984), I was keen to use raters who would not be overly familiar with the accents of L1 beginner English learners of Chinese or the *Jìn bù* textbook my students had been following (Bin *et al.*, 2010). Nevertheless, I recognize that the role plays covered similar ground, so there was a risk that the students who were rated later would have artificially high levels of intelligibility. Each rater was asked to listen to the audio file only once and transcribe what they thought they had heard in Chinese characters. Following Derwing and Munro (1997), each transcript was then used to calculate an intelligibility score based on the number of characters the rater could successfully transcribe. For example, if a rater successfully transcribed 80 characters out of a possible 100, then the student would be awarded an intelligibility rating of 80 per cent. The overall intelligibility rating for each L1 English student, based on an average score of the five Beijing high school raters, was then compared with the students' original tonal accuracy scores from my previous research.

Particular attention was paid to the areas where the raters had transcribed a different character from what the speaker had intended to say. Knowledge of the speakers' original intentions was based on my familiarity with the students' L2 Chinese accents and 'insider knowledge' of the language covered in class and produced for homework. The source of the breakdown in intelligibility was categorized as either being a result of the tone, or the initial consonant of the syllable, or the final part of the syllable deviating from the standard form, or a combination of two or all three of the factors. For example, if the rater transcribed 是 shì (be) when the student had intended to say 十 shí (ten), then the breakdown would be traced directly to tone. However, if the rater transcribed 猫 māo (cat) when the student had attempted to say 妈 mā (mother), then both tone and the final would be implicated as contributing to the misunderstanding. Any examples of raters transcribing the wrong homophone (i.e. when syllables share identical tones, initials, and finals, but have different characters with different meanings) were also noted.

I decided to work entirely at the syllable level, because each Chinese character is one syllable in length and generally carries a tone, as well as an initial and a final. Many words in modern Chinese and around 95 per cent of morphemes are monosyllabic (Lin, 2007: 5), so the syllable appears to be a particularly important unit for listeners when they are analysing a piece of spoken input. Nevertheless, I recognize that listeners will also make use of other cues when recognizing words in the speech signal, including the lexical chunk and the general context, as well as the role played by grammar and intonation (Field, 2008). In other words, a purely phonetic approach to intelligibility at the syllable level is clearly not enough and some breakdowns in intelligibility will lack a straightforward phonetic explanation (Munro, 2011: 10). Moreover, there may well have been instances of raters transcribing characters inaccurately for reasons unrelated to the original speech production such as 'distraction by an earlier non-standard production, memory difficulties, spelling difficulties [and] unexpected word use' (Zielinski, 2006: 26). To gain a deeper insight into the causes of the breakdowns in understanding, it would have been necessary to interview the raters (Zielinski, 2008), but this was beyond the scope of this research project.

Results and analyses

The corpus of speech produced by the five participants totalled 412 characters. In light of the small data sets, I did not conduct any inferential statistical tests of difference with each learner conceptualized as a separate 'unit of analysis' (Merriam, 2009: 41). I make no claims that my findings are representative of the whole class of 18 learners, although after considering each learner separately, I subsequently endeavour to pull together common themes and draw some pedagogical implications.

Participant 1

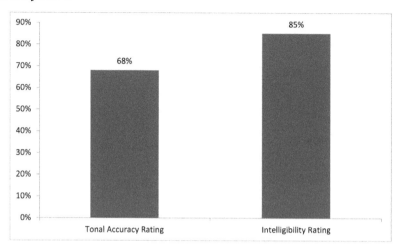

Figure 6.1: Comparing tonal accuracy with intelligibility: Participant 1

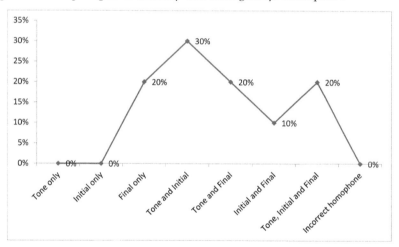

Figure 6.2: Causes of breakdown in intelligibility for participant 1 (n = 10)

Participant 1's intelligibility rating, at 85 per cent, is clearly higher than his tonal accuracy rating of 68 per cent. Tone is not implicated as the main source of the communication breakdown in any of the ten examples that arose from the five transcriptions. However, tone contributes to seven of the breakdowns (70 per cent). There are two examples of finals being the main cause of a breakdown in intelligibility (20 per cent); they also contribute to five other breakdowns (50 per cent). Non-standard initials contribute to a communication breakdown on six occasions (60 per cent), although there are no examples of initials being the main source of the breakdown.

Participant 2

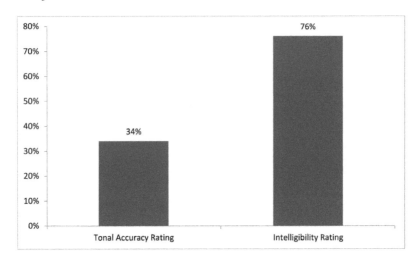

Figure 6.3: Comparing tonal accuracy with intelligibility: Participant 2

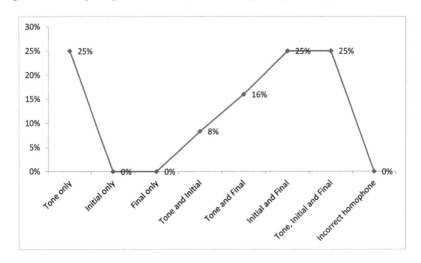

Figure 6.4: Causes of breakdown in intelligibility for participant 2 (n = 12)

Participant 2's intelligibility rating of 76 per cent is much higher than her tonal accuracy rating of 34 per cent. Three of the 12 breakdowns in intelligibility (25 per cent) appear to be caused specifically by problems with the tone, for example, 跳 tiào (jump) as opposed to 条 tiáo (measure word), with tone also contributing to all the other breakdowns of intelligibility. Initials and finals contribute to seven (58 per cent) and eight (67 per cent) of the breakdowns respectively, with no examples of initials or finals being the main cause of the communication breakdown.

Participant 3

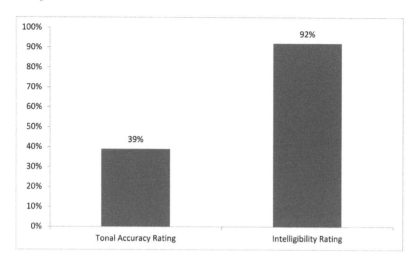

Figure 6.5: Comparing tonal accuracy with intelligibility: Participant 3

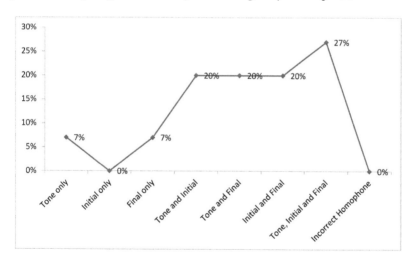

Figure 6.6: Causes of breakdown in intelligibility for participant 3 (n = 15)

There is also a huge difference between Participant 3's tonal accuracy rate of 39 per cent and his intelligibility rating of 92 per cent. One of the 15 breakdowns in intelligibility (7 per cent) can be traced directly to tone: 喝 hē (drink) and 和 hé (and). There is also one example of a final being the main cause of the breakdown in intelligibility: 杨 yáng (surname) as opposed to 姚 yáo (surname), with no examples of initials being the main cause of the breakdown. Tone, initials, and finals all contribute to 10 of the 15 communication breakdowns (67 per cent).

Participant 4

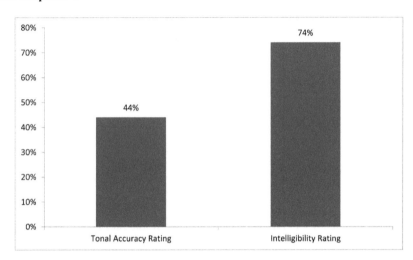

Figure 6.7: Comparing tonal accuracy with intelligibility: Participant 4

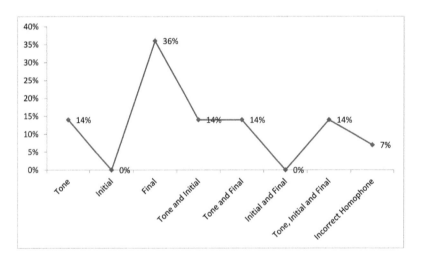

Figure 6.8: Causes of breakdown in intelligibility for participant 4 (n = 14)

Participant 4 also obtains a much higher intelligibility rating (74 per cent) than her tonal accuracy rating (44 per cent). Two of the 14 intelligibility breakdowns (14 per cent) can be traced directly to problems with tone: 水 shuǐ (water) as opposed to 睡 shùi (sleep) and 有 yǒu (have) instead of 游 yóu (swim). Tone also contributes to six other breakdowns (43 per cent). There are no examples of initials being the main cause of a communication breakdown, although initials contribute to four of the 14 breakdowns (29 per cent). There are five examples of intelligibility problems being caused specifically by finals, for example, 出 chū (go out) instead of 吃 chī (eat), with finals also contributing to four other breakdowns (29 per cent). There is also one example of an incorrect homophone: 伯 bó instead of 博 bó, for part of a name.

Participant 5

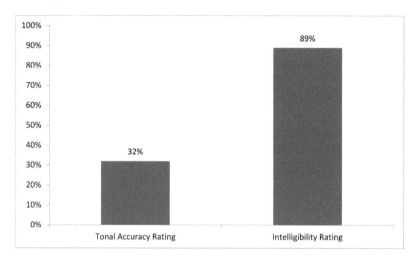

Figure 6.9: Comparing tonal accuracy with intelligibility: Participant 5

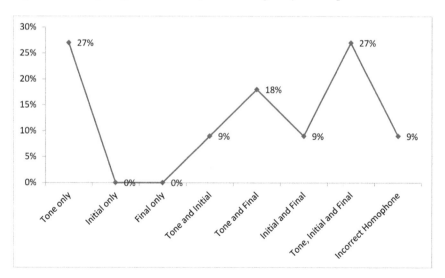

Figure 6.10: Causes of breakdown in intelligibility for participant 5 (n = 11)

Participant 5 also obtains a much higher intelligibility rating (89 per cent) compared with her tonal accuracy rating (32 per cent). Three of the 11 breakdowns in intelligibility (27 per cent) can be traced directly to tone, for example, 午 wǔ (noon) instead of 物 wù (thing), with tone contributing to six other breakdowns (55 per cent). Initials contribute to five of the breakdowns (45 per cent) and finals to six of the breakdowns (55 per cent), although there are no examples of initials or finals being the main cause of the communication breakdown. There is also one instance of an incorrect homophone causing confusion as part of a name: 宇 yǔ as opposed to 雨 yǔ.

Emerging themes and issues

It is immediately apparent that all five participants obtain much higher intelligibility ratings than tonal accuracy ratings (see Figure 6.11). This appears to lend support to the claim that L1 Chinese speakers may well be 'able to understand intended meanings regardless of incorrect tones, simply based on the discourse context' (Duff *et al.*, 2013: 49). However, there should be no room for complacency. Even participant 3, who, with an intelligibility rating of 92 per cent notched the highest score, basically still only has nine out of every ten syllables understood. This would undoubtedly prove to be very heavy work for a listener who, if forced to work too hard to construct meaning, is likely to give up even trying to understand the speaker (Lippi-Green, 1997). It is unlikely that participants 2 and 4, with intelligibility rates of 76 and 74 per cent respectively, are making much sense at all and are certainly a very long way from 'a comfortably intelligible pronunciation' (Abercrombie, 1949: 120 as quoted in Derwing and Munro, 2005: 384), which seems to be a reasonable goal of pronunciation instruction.

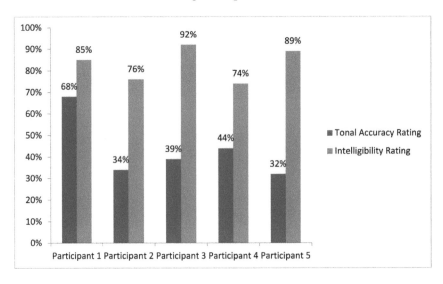

Figure 6.11: Comparing participants' tonal accuracy and intelligibility ratings

Given concerns about the somewhat simplistic research design already noted, it is difficult to be certain about the specific causes of the intelligibility breakdowns. Nevertheless, it seems reasonable to conclude that the participants' pronunciation problems run far deeper than non-standard tones (see Figure 6.12). For example, while 15 per cent of all the intelligibility breakdowns can be traced directly to tone, 13 per cent of the breakdowns can be linked directly to finals. Although there are no examples of intelligibility problems being caused solely by initials, 52 per cent of the breakdowns implicate non-standard initials as a contributory factor. Moreover, the most frequent cause of breakdown occurs when the tone, initial and final are all different from the target pronunciation (23 per cent), suggesting that in these cases, the real cause of the problem is inadequate lexical knowledge as much as non-standard pronunciation.

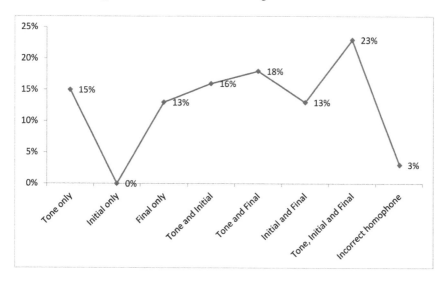

Figure 6.12: Causes of combined breakdowns in intelligibility (n = 62)

Pedagogical implications

In this final section, I attempt to draw some pedagogical implications from my research findings. I appreciate that I cannot generalize from my findings to the wider student population and shall be making claims about L2 Chinese pronunciation only in relation to this group of students. Nevertheless, I hope that other Mandarin teachers in Anglophone settings will weigh up the extent to which these pedagogical suggestions resonate with their own teaching contexts. Perhaps most importantly, I need to recognize that I may have 'overtly or subtly dismiss[ed] a variety of pronunciation issues as unimportant' (Foote *et al.*, 2016: 12). Since I share an L1 with the vast majority of my students, I have rarely found my students' pronunciation of Chinese to be an obstacle to communication. Yet engaging with the construct of intelligibility showed that it clearly is an issue. Despite a small data set of only 412 characters, there is a combined total of 62 breakdowns in intelligibility based on the five transcriptions.

While much of the previous research into CFL pronunciations has focused mainly on tones, the findings here suggest that I should also be placing more emphasis on initials and finals in the classroom alongside tones. A good place to start would arguably be with a renewed focus on the Romanized orthography known as Pinyin ('sound spelling'), which has become the standard transcription of Mandarin Chinese words (Lin, 2007: 7). In my rush to launch into teaching characters, I may well have neglected the teaching of Pinyin properly, with negative consequences for the students' intelligibility. An advantage of Pinyin is that it makes use of 'distinct diacritical marks [...] placed directly above a syllable to indicate each of the four Mandarin lexical tones' (McGinnis, 1997: 228–9), so that an increased focus on Pinyin should help promote tonal awareness. However, as I know from my own Mandarin Chinese learning journey, a focus on Pinyin can easily lead into an over-reliance on using the Latin alphabet to represent Chinese sounds, which could in turn slow down character learning in the long term. A sensible trade-off would be for more research into establishing precisely which initials and finals are most important for intelligibility rather than spending valuable teaching time on all the sounds of Pinyin.

A key question related to teaching pronunciation is the extent to which it can be picked up implicitly or whether explicit instruction is necessary (Derwing and Munro, 2014). Influenced by my own Chinese language learning experience of living in Beijing, I had initially assumed that students could simply acquire an acceptable Chinese accent through frequent Chinese input in the classroom. Such a view is also in line with communicative language teaching (CLT), which emphasizes authentic use of language and sees repetition and corrective feedback as disruptive to communication (Derwing and Munro, 2014: 38). However, the evidence from this study suggests that without explicit correction, learners are showing evidence of fossilized speech patterns (ibid.: 38). For example, alongside the two examples of incorrect homophones, raters often had problems transcribing students' Chinese names, with none of them being able to transcribe participant 4 or participant 5's Chinese names successfully. This is despite the fact that all the learners were frequently exposed to accurate pronunciation of their Chinese names, both from myself and other L1 Chinese teachers during lessons.

A renewed focus on pronunciation will need to be handled sensitively if I am not going to run the risk of demotivating and scaring some of my learners by being overly strict in the classroom. However, the alternative approach of ignoring pronunciation issues is potentially even more confidence-sapping for learners in the long run, for if they find that they cannot make the limited Chinese they know intelligible to others, they will surely lose motivation quickly (Zielinski and Yates, 2014: 75). On a more positive note, the occasional use of Chinese high school students as 'intelligibility raters' has the potential to be extremely motivating for my students and could be developed as a way of embedding links with a Chinese partner school. English students, in turn, could become 'intelligibility raters' for the Chinese students' L2 English productions. It should also be acknowledged that there is a modest range in the intelligibility ratings. For example, while rater 1 gives participant 4 an intelligibility rating of 53 per cent, the same data is given an intelligibility rating of 84 per cent by rater 2. Such discrepancies in the rating highlight that 'successful communication depends on the abilities and efforts of both speaker and listener' (Munro, 2011: 11). Thus, rather than placing 100 per cent responsibility for intelligibility on the L2 speaker, there should also be an increased emphasis on listener awareness and listener training (Grant, 2014: 13).

Conclusion

In this research project, I have investigated the intelligibility of five of my students' spoken Chinese. By analysing intelligibility breakdowns that emerged from the transcriptions of five Chinese high school students, I have come to the conclusion that I need to pay more attention to pronunciation issues in the classroom, with an increased focus on initials and finals alongside tones. I have conceptualized action research as a journey in which original research questions lead to more important ones: I am now moving away from a narrow focus on tones to identifying problems likely to interfere with intelligibility. While this journey is taking time, effort, and perseverance, it is intellectually stimulating and providing some useful clues about how to be a more effective teacher. The next phase of the journey will be to investigate whether a more explicit focus on tones, initials and finals in the classroom can actually lead to more accurate pronunciation. While I dispute Macaro's (2003) claim that being involved with research does 'not always have to represent an extra workload for the teacher' (Macaro, 2003: 51), I would encourage other Chinese teachers to carry out their own small-scale research projects. By sharing our work and engaging in healthy debate, we can all help contribute towards a CFL pedagogy and thereby ensure that Chinese becomes properly embedded within the UK school curriculum.

PRACTICAL IDEAS

- Teachers don't have time to correct every pronunciation error. The focus should instead be on those errors that most affect intelligibility, such as 'chē' instead of 'chī' or 'shī' instead of 'shì'.
- Students will vary massively in their pronunciation needs, so it is important to assess them individually even if they all share the same L1. The most effective way is to record them speaking Chinese and note any problems that lead to intelligibility breakdowns.
- Help students notice the differences between their own productions and more intelligible utterances. Explain the nature of the pronunciation error in terms that the student can understand. For example, 'can you hear how you are raising your voice at the end of the sentence?' Then provide the students with a model that they can imitate.
- Encourage peer correction in a friendly atmosphere: can learners correct each other's pronunciation errors or at least recognize when there's a problem?
- Give clear advice about how to produce the most difficult target sounds: 'what are you doing with your tongue when you pronounce "sh"?'
- Use technology: does the voice recognition software on your phone understand your spoken Chinese? Practise with both single words and sentences.
- Encourage exposure to authentic spoken Chinese outside the classroom via online videos featuring both L1 Chinese and L2 Chinese speakers.
- Use songs and raps to make pronunciation teaching fun and remind your students that everyone, including L1 Chinese speakers, has some sort of accent.
- Ask students to come up with their own names for each of the tones and don't be afraid to use lots of gestures.
- Spend time pointing out specific differences between Pinyin and English – 'yǒu' is not pronounced like 'you' – otherwise students may assume it sounds just like English which will quickly lead to intelligibility breakdowns.

References

Bin, Y., Zhu, X., and Carruthers, K. (2010) *Jìn bù 1* 进步一. Harlow: Heinemann.

Board, K. and Tinsley, T. (2014) *Language Trends 2013/14: The state of language learning in primary and secondary schools in England.* Reading: CfBT Education Trust. Online. www.britishcouncil.org/sites/default/files/language-trends-survey-2014.pdf (accessed 14 July 2016).

British Council (2013) 'Lack of Mandarin teaching damaging young people's prospects'. British Council press release, 4 February. Online. www.britishcouncil.org/organisation/press/lack-mandarin-teaching (accessed 14 July 2016).

Chao, Y.R. (1968) *A Grammar of Spoken Chinese.* Berkelcy: University of California Press.

Chen, Q. (1997) 'Toward a sequential approach for tonal error analysis'. *Journal of the Chinese Language Teachers Association,* 32 (1), 21–39.

Collins, B. and Mees, I.M. (2013) *Practical Phonetics and Phonology: A resource book for students.* 2nd ed. London: Routledge.

Derwing, T.M. and Munro, M.J. (1997) 'Accent, intelligibility, and comprehensibility: Evidence from four L1s'. *Studies in Second Language Acquisition,* 19 (1), 1–16.

Derwing, T.M. and Munro, M.J. (2005) 'Second language accent and pronunciation teaching: A research-based approach'. *TESOL Quarterly,* 39 (3), 379–97.

Derwing, T.M. and Munro, M.J. (2014) 'Myth 1: Once you have been speaking a second language for years, it's too late to change your pronunciation'. In Grant, L. (ed.) *Pronunciation Myths: Applying second language research to classroom teaching.* Ann Arbor: University of Michigan Press, 34–55.

Duff, P., Anderson, T., Ilnyckyj, R., VanGaya, E., Wang, R.T. and Yates, E. (2013) *Learning Chinese: Linguistic, sociocultural, and narrative perspectives.* Berlin: De Gruyter.

Field, J. (2008) *Listening in the Language Classroom.* Cambridge: Cambridge University Press.

Foote, J.A., Trofimovich, P., Collins, L. and Urzúa, F.S. (2016) 'Pronunciation teaching practices in communicative second language classes'. *Language Learning Journal,* 44 (2), 181–96.

Gass, S. and Varonis, E.M. (1984) 'The effect of familiarity on the comprehensibility of nonnative speech'. *Language Learning,* 34 (1), 65–89.

Grant, L. (2014) 'Prologue to the myths: What teachers need to know'. In Grant, L. (ed.) *Pronunciation Myths: Applying second language research to classroom teaching.* Ann Arbor: University of Michigan Press, 1–33.

Ke, C. (2012) 'Research in second language acquisition of Chinese: Where we are, where we are going'. *Journal of the Chinese Language Teachers Association,* 47 (3), 43–113.

Lin, Y.-H. (2007) *The Sounds of Chinese.* Cambridge: Cambridge University Press.

Lippi-Green, R. (1997) *English with an Accent: Language, ideology, and discrimination in the United States.* London: Routledge.

Macaro, E. (2003) 'Second language teachers as second language classroom researchers'. *Language Learning Journal,* 27 (1), 43–51.

McGinnis, S. (1997) 'Tonal spelling versus diacritics for teaching pronunciation of Mandarin Chinese'. *Modern Language Journal*, 81 (2), 228–36.

Merriam, S.B. (2009) *Qualitative Research: A guide to design and implementation*. San Francisco: Jossey-Bass.

Munro, M.J. (2011) 'Intelligibility: Buzzword or buzzworthy?'. In Levis, J. and LeVelle, K. (eds) *Pronunciation and Intelligibility: Issues in research and practice: Proceedings of the 2nd Pronunciation in Second Language Learning and Teaching Conference, September 2010*. Ames: Iowa State University, 7–16.

Neal, R.J. (2014) 'Teaching and learning mandarin tones in an English secondary school'. *Scottish Languages Review*, 27, 9–20.

Ofsted (Office for Standards in Education) (2008) *Every Language Matters: An evaluation of the extent and impact of initial training to teach a wider range of world languages*. London: Ofsted. Online. http://dera.ioe.ac.uk/8173/ (accessed 14 July 2016).

Orton, J. (2011) 'Educating Chinese language teachers: Some fundamentals'. In Tsung, L. and Cruickshank, K. (eds) *Teaching and Learning Chinese in Global Contexts: Multimodality and literacy in the new media age*. London: Continuum, 151–64.

Tao, L. and Guo, L. (2008) 'Learning Chinese tones: A developmental account'. *Journal of the Chinese Language Teachers Association*, 43 (2), 17–46.

Tsung, L. and Cruickshank, K. (eds) (2011) *Teaching and Learning Chinese in Global Contexts: Multimodality and literacy in the new media age*. London: Continuum.

White, C. (1981) 'Tonal pronunciation errors and interference from English intonation'. *Journal of the Chinese Language Teachers Association*, 16 (2), 27–56.

Winke, P.M. (2007) 'Tuning into tones: The effect of L1 background on L2 Chinese learners' tonal production'. *Journal of the Chinese Language Teachers Association*, 42 (3), 21–55.

Xing, J.Z. (2006) *Teaching and Learning Chinese as a Foreign Language: A pedagogical grammar*. Hong Kong: Hong Kong University Press.

Zhang, G.X. and Li, L.M. (2010) 'Chinese language teaching in the UK: Present and future'. *Language Learning Journal*, 38 (1), 87–97.

Zhang, H. (2010) 'Phonological universals and tonal acquisition'. *Journal of the Chinese Language Teachers Association*, 45 (1), 39–65.

Zielinski, B. (2006) 'The intelligibility cocktail: An interaction between speaker and listener ingredients'. *Prospect*, 21 (1), 22–45.

Zielinski, B. (2008) 'The listener: No longer the silent partner in reduced intelligibility'. *System*, 36 (1), 69–84.

Zielinski, B. and Yates, L. (2014) 'Myth 2: Pronunciation instruction is not appropriate for beginning-level learners'. In Grant, L. (ed.) *Pronunciation Myths: Applying second language research to classroom teaching*. Ann Arbor: University of Michigan Press, 56–79.

Chapter 7

An investigation into the most effective strategies for beginner Anglophone learners to read and write Chinese characters

Paul Tyskerud

Introduction

My experience of teaching Mandarin consists of a PGCE training year at Sheffield University and five subsequent years of teaching Mandarin to secondary school pupils between the ages of 11 and 18 years at a selective grammar school in Kent as well as primary school pupils through outreach programmes. Almost every pupil I have taught over the past five years as the head of Mandarin has had no prior experience of learning Mandarin before arriving at the school. This situation of teaching predominantly beginners has offered me many opportunities to experiment with teaching methods and analyse learning strategies and led me naturally to consider action research as a way of more formally investigating my observations. My observations and reflections during this time have enabled me to build up a strong picture of how I think non-native pupils learn Mandarin best and have of course shaped my approaches to the teaching of the subject. I do, however, still have many unanswered questions, and therefore feel it is necessary to investigate further, using more stringent methods, exactly how pupils feel they best learn to read and write Chinese characters and additionally how teachers feel it is best to teach them.

From my observations of pupils in British schools learning Mandarin over the past six years, and from my own experiences as a non-native learner of Mandarin less than ten years ago, I have adapted to the classroom the action research theories as presented in Chapter 5 in this collection, based on rote learning, storytelling and radicals. I have personally experimented with the best ways to teach and learn Mandarin according to the theories and I will discuss these again briefly here in order to link them to my own practice.

Rote learning is the process by which learners memorize information by repetition. In the case of Chinese characters, it involves continually writing out a character until you can write it from memory. It is the way that I personally learnt how to read and write Chinese characters and is the method that has been favoured historically by native-speaker Chinese teachers of native-speaking Chinese pupils (McGinnis, 1999; Shen, 2005). I have observed this method to be very effective for motivated pupils who very much enjoy learning the language. However, for pupils who have shown little engagement and enjoyment of the language, this has appeared to be a very difficult and unappealing method of learning Mandarin.

Storytelling involves telling a story about an individual Chinese character in the hope that the story and the character will be recalled later. An example may be describing to pupils that the word for 'good' (好) in Chinese consists of the character for 'woman' (女) combined with the character for 'child' (子). By combining the two, we gain insight into the Chinese psyche: that the idea of a female (女) with a child (子) is good (好). This method appears to appeal to a broader range of pupils than rote learning and appears to be less dependent on pupils' levels of engagement (McGinnis, 1999). I have observed pupils who would often struggle with the process of rote learning become more engaged in their learning when given the opportunity to try to recall a character having heard a story about that character. However, it is difficult to prove how well pupils recall the character subsequently.

Understanding radicals, the frequently smaller, condensed part of actual characters that can offer learners clues about characters' meaning, appears to appeal to pupils. A radical is the part of the character that can offer a learner clues about the meaning of the character. It is often a smaller, condensed version of an actual character. Hence, pupils only need to recall some of the character and not the whole character if they can recall which radical is in the character (Shen, 2005). For example, the verb 'to eat' (吃) in Chinese contains the radical for mouth (口). If learners call to mind the connection between eating and mouths, it is easier for them to recall that the character for 'eat' contains the radical for mouth, which may help them to recall and reproduce that character more easily.

Through personal observation and discussions with my other three full-time Mandarin teaching colleagues as well as colleagues from around the UK during national conferences and CPD meetings on teaching and learning Mandarin, the above three methods appear to be most commonly taught by Mandarin teachers. These methods are, however, often instinctively considered by teachers to be helpful, as opposed to being proven by research. Sometimes, these may simply be the methods that the teacher feels helped them most when learning how to read and write Chinese characters. To what extent each of the methods really supports or even potentially hinders pupils in their learning is still very much open to debate, owing to the limited research that has been conducted on the topic. This absence of conclusive evidence has compelled me to investigate further the observations from my own and my colleagues' experience of teaching Mandarin to non-native learners.

The research involving pupils took place in two different schools, a selective grammar school in Kent and a non-selective comprehensive school in Sheffield. Both have at least one full-time Mandarin teacher and have been teaching Mandarin as part of the curriculum for over five years. The two schools were selected to offer a range of perspectives, as findings from only one type of school may have offered somewhat limited opinions on the topic. The teachers were from four different schools in England. All teachers were teaching at least part-time Mandarin at the time of the research.

The research aimed to investigate five aspects of learning strategies associated with learning to read and write Chinese characters. The following five questions summarize the aims of the investigation:

1) Which learning strategies do pupils perceive to be the most effective for learning to read and write Chinese characters?
2) Which learning strategies do teachers perceive to be the most effective for their pupils to learn to read and write Chinese characters?
3) Does teaching pupils about the three seemingly most effective learning strategies influence their perceptions of the most effective learning strategies?
4) Is there a difference between teachers' and pupils' perception of the most effective learning strategies?
5) Is there a difference between the perception of pupils in a selective school compared with a non-selective school?

I have chosen action research because it enables a practical approach to investigation and the focus can always remain on improving my own practice (Bell, 2005) and that of my colleagues. In agreement with Denscombe's (2007) suggestion, my aim is to investigate 'my own practices with a view to altering these in a beneficial way' (124). In order to carry out my action research project effectively, it is necessary firstly to consider exactly what I define as useful or sufficient evidence to warrant changing my practice because of it. The concept of 'warranted assertibility' (Dewey, 1991) in relation to enquiry has existed for over 70 years and is considered by some practitioner-researchers as the standard by which their research outcomes should be judged. Put simply, Dewey states that one can proceed from sufficiently robust evidence to assert what is true. In the case of the action research, assertions can be made based on the data collected, provided that it is sufficiently robust. While a scientific approach in which extraneous variables can be accounted for is clearly unsuitable and given that human behaviour and perception are being investigated, small-scale qualitative and quantitative research can be considered the most appropriate approach for the present investigation (Bell, 2005). Specifically, I will be conducting practical action research, which, as defined by Denscombe (2007: 127), sees it as the researcher's role 'to encourage practical deliberation and self-reflection on the part of the practitioners'. In this case, the 'practitioners' are my colleagues and me.

There will always be proponents and opponents to the many different approaches to conducting research, particularly action research. The observational and 'fuzzier' aspect of action research, specifically in relation to its scientific validity, is often criticized, but I am in agreement with Hargreaves (1996: 13) who states that 'there is much to gain and little to lose in moving as soon as possible to an evidence-based teaching profession'. What I believe is also true is that if teachers feel too much pressure to adhere to a scientific investigative approach in order to achieve better practice, this would only become a barrier to practitioner research due to the time constraints and strains of always trying to achieve scientific validity. The classroom environment is an ever-changing entity, so attempting to achieve laboratory-like conditions to produce scientific conclusions would be both impossible and inappropriate.

Issues of validity, reliability, and robustness

'The key to validation lies in the formulation of the original research aims, objectives and design, through which assessment criteria will be built in' (Heilbronn, 2008: 152). Although not specifically referring to the validity of data, the Heilbronn quote offers researcher-practitioners a reminder of how to ensure that validity is at the core of all that they do whilst conducting action research. For any research practitioner, it is important to be conscious of the potential limitations of the research being conducted and the data being collected.

The importance of validity in the case of the present investigation is accentuated by the fact that if the validity of the data is affected, the findings and consequent conclusions become less generalizable. From my perspective and that of my colleagues, this would essentially make the research less useful. The following quotation summarizes accurately the importance of maintaining an unbiased approach to the design of the research:

> As with all research, when done well, practitioner action research will challenge what we think we know rather than confirm it. This is why it has the potential to help us constantly rethink our practices to create schools that are more educationally sound, caring, and just places for our children and youth. (Anderson and Herr, 2009: 164)

Questionnaires

When discussing selection of the most appropriate data collection methods, Denscombe (2007) states that it should be based on three factors: which method will enable the researcher to gain a clearer picture of the situation, which method will offer an accurate measurement of things, and which method will offer the ability to provide facts and evidence about the subject. In addition, it is thought that the decision should be based on the criterion of usefulness and that all methods have their benefits and drawbacks. Triangulation was a key consideration for me, as I was aware that if I chose only one research method, then the data may be somewhat limited in its usefulness and consequent generalizability. In order to address this, I chose to have three different sample groups, in an attempt to offer a number of perspectives on the topic and three potentially different viewpoints. As a result, where my data may be perceived to be somewhat limited due to using only one data collection method, it could be argued that the broader perspective gained from my three different participant groups somewhat counterbalances this potential problem. The teachers' and pupils' questionnaires were specifically designed to address the five key objectives of the research project as mentioned above. The questions in the questionnaires were then cross-referenced with these objectives, which were set out as questions, with the aim of ensuring that they provide data relevant to the objectives. In order to enable comparison between the teachers' and pupils' perception, the questionnaires had to be very similar.

Qualitative and quantitative data

Both qualitative and quantitative data were collected during the course of the research project. Quantitative data included pupils' rating on Likert scale questionnaires on how easy or difficult they found the four skills of reading, writing, listening and speaking as well as their rating of how effective they found the three learning strategies for reading and writing Chinese characters. Qualitative data were also gathered when asking pupils if there were any other reasons than those stated in the questionnaire for why they believed a certain skill to be difficult. This combination of quantitative and qualitative data enabled a fuller picture of pupils' and teachers' perception on the topics in question (Klein, 2012).

It is always necessary to consider the relative benefits and drawbacks of the two different types of data and what they can offer the researcher in terms of generalizable assertions. Klein (2012: 172) states that '[i]n the field of education, more and more emphasis is being placed on evidence-based and data-based decision making'. In particular, quantitative data has become increasingly relied upon to justify decisions ranging from policy change to curriculum choices, and there appears to be a sense within the profession that if quantitative data cannot be provided, decisions cannot be justified. With this in mind, it was decided in the present investigation to collect predominantly quantitative data, so that when the results are presented to both pupils and teachers, the statistical analyses can offer reassurance to a potentially sceptical audience.

There are disadvantages associated with the use of quantitative data as opposed to qualitative data. Denscombe (2007: 284) states that both 'data overload' and 'quality of data' are two drawbacks associated with analysing this type of data. For this reason, it is hoped that the qualitative data provides a necessary balance to the overall data landscape of the present investigation.

Sample
Who?
The sample base for the present investigation consisted of one group of 42 pupils and a second group of ten teachers. The pupils' group consisted of pupils who study Mandarin at secondary school and all pupils were between the ages of 12 and 15 years. At the time of the investigation, the pupils were all within their first year of learning Mandarin. The pupils were from two different schools, 28 of the pupils were male and studying at a selective all-boys grammar school in Kent at the time of the investigation, 14 of the pupils were male (2) and female (12) pupils studying at a mixed comprehensive school in Sheffield. The teachers' group consisted of male and female teachers who were all in either full-time or part-time roles as Mandarin teachers in schools around the UK. The teachers came from all-boys selective schools, all-girls selective schools, and mixed comprehensive

schools. Some of the schools were academies and some were local authority-run.

How?

Following a Mandarin teachers' action research group meeting at the Institute of Education in London, I became aware that two colleagues whom I had not met before the meeting were also interested in investigating pupils' perception of the most effective learning strategies for learning to read and write Chinese characters. Having shared my research project objectives with them, my two colleagues were keen to support the investigation by contributing to the collection of data. One colleague carried out the data collection within her Sheffield school with her 14 beginner Mandarin pupils. The other colleague supported the collection of data relating to teachers' perception by contacting a number of her colleagues whom she knew would be interested in contributing to this research. I must therefore acknowledge my two colleagues and their support in collecting the data that is used in the investigation.

Pupils' group

The research cycle for the pupils' group involved the completion of two questionnaires, with an intervention period between the two questionnaires. The intervention period involved a three-week period in which both I and my colleague in Sheffield were required to familiarize our pupils with the three previously mentioned learning strategies. The only formal requirement for this intervention period was to use lesson time to introduce the three learning strategies and discuss and consider their effectiveness. It was essential that pupils also had a chance to practise using the three strategies. Prior to the intervention, pupils would complete a pre-interview questionnaire aimed at gauging their perception of the three different strategies. The post-interview questionnaire was administered after the three-week intervention period and was identical to the pre-interview questionnaire. The importance of the intervention period was to address one of the key objectives, namely whether pupils' familiarity with the three strategies changed their perception of those strategies.

Teachers' group

There was no intervention period for the teachers' group because the teachers were already familiar with the three learning strategies. The teachers' questionnaire was designed to address the research question that asked whether the teachers' perception of the three learning strategies differed from the pupils' perception. A diagram of the data collection cycle can be seen in Figure 7.1:

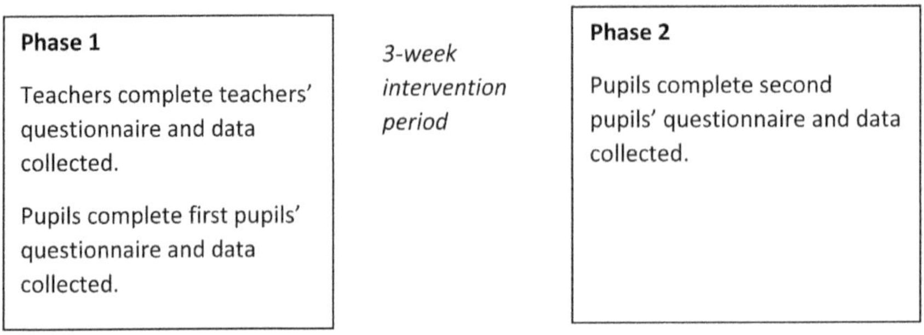

Phase 1		Phase 2
Teachers complete teachers' questionnaire and data collected.	*3-week intervention period*	Pupils complete second pupils' questionnaire and data collected.
Pupils complete first pupils' questionnaire and data collected.		

Figure 7.1: Data collection cycle

In the present investigation, the majority of participants were children, and it was important to ensure at all times that both they and the adult participants were treated as 'sensitive, dignified human beings' (Alderson, 2004: 98). To ensure that my practitioner research investigation was ethically sound, it was necessary to adhere to the recommendations of the British Educational Research Association (BERA, 2011). This was achieved by informing participants of their rights in relation to voluntary informed consent and their right to withdraw at any moment as well as by maintaining the privacy of all information disclosed during the process of the research.

Findings and analysis

Analysis of data can be considered a matter of interpretation, so any two researchers could analyse the same data in two different ways. The data analysis will be discussed in this section with reference to how it is linked to the objectives of the investigation. Firstly though, it is important to note that all data relating to the teachers' questionnaire will be reported as a raw number, for example 6 (out of 10). This is due to the relatively small sample size and the importance of acknowledging the size of this sample, so as not to mislead the reader by implying a percentage that may be interpreted as being a much larger raw number than it actually is. Owing to the larger sample size of the pupils' group, results will be reported in percentages. Where results are being compared between the two sample groups, they will be presented as percentages for ease of comparison, but the sample size of the teachers' group will be acknowledged in these cases, so as not to cause any misinterpretation of the results or misassumptions about the generalizability of results from the sample.

1) Which learning strategies do pupils perceive to be the most effective for learning to read and write Chinese characters?

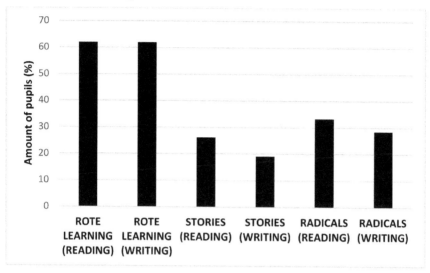

Figure 7.2: Percentage of pupils who, post-intervention, rated a strategy either 'often' or 'all the time' the most effective

As can be seen clearly in Figure 7.2, the percentage of pupils who perceived rote learning to be the most effective strategy for both reading and writing either 'often' or 'all the time' in the post-intervention questionnaire was significantly higher than that for any other strategy. The fact that the percentage of pupils who perceived rote learning to be most effective for reading (61.9 per cent) was nearly double that of pupils who perceived radicals (33.3 per cent) to be most effective, and the percentage for writing (61.9 per cent) was over double that of pupils who perceived use of radicals to be most effective (28.6 per cent), is quite a telling result. Use of radicals was perceived to be the second most effective strategy for both reading and writing Chinese characters and the use of stories for both skills (reading: 26.2 per cent; writing: 19 per cent) was perceived to be the third most effective strategy.

The differences between English words and Chinese characters as well as the similar appearance of Chinese characters to each other were the most significant reasons for pupils finding reading difficult. The difficulty of memorizing how to write a character combined with lack of familiarity with the stroke order accounted for a large proportion of the reasons given for why pupils find writing in Chinese difficult. Little categorization of pupils' additional comments was necessary, as only two pupils from the whole sample specified their own personal reason by choosing to give a further reason for why they answered 'difficult' or 'very 'difficult'.

2) *Which learning strategies do teachers perceive to be the most effective for their pupils to learn to read and write Chinese characters?*

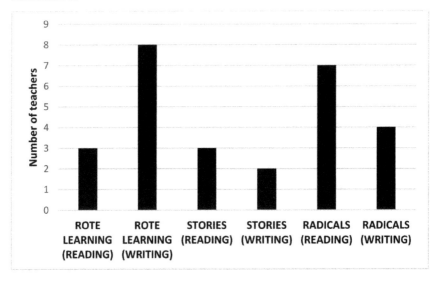

Figure 7.3: Number of teachers who rated a strategy either 'often' or 'all the time' the most effective

Figure 7.3 clearly indicates that 8 of the 10 teachers perceived rote learning to be 'often' or 'all the time' the most effective strategy for their pupils to use for learning to write Chinese characters. Conversely, only 3 of the 10 teachers believed rote learning to be the most effective strategy for pupils learning to read Chinese characters; however, 7 of the 10 teachers believed that using radicals is often or always the most effective strategy. These results clearly indicate that teachers believe that different strategies are more effective for different skills and that no single strategy is the most effective for both reading and writing Chinese characters.

3) Does teaching pupils about the three seemingly most effective learning strategies impact on their perceptions of the most effective learning strategies?

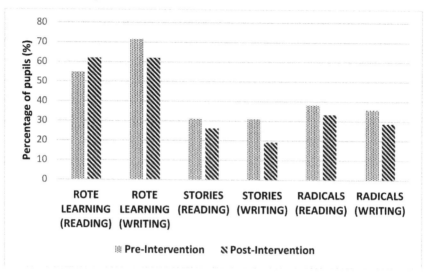

Figure 7.4: Percentage change in pupil perception of the most effective strategy between pre- and post-intervention period

Figure 7.4 shows that pupils' perceptions of all three learning strategies for both the skills of reading and writing did not change hugely between the pre- and post-intervention period. For certain strategies, there were, however, some changes of close to or more than 10 per cent of pupils reporting that they either often or always used a certain strategy. The number of pupils reporting the effectiveness of using stories for learning to write Chinese characters, either often or all the time, decreased by 11.9 per cent between the pre- and post-intervention period. This could suggest that the more pupils were taught about or made familiar with this strategy, the less effective they perceived it to be. In addition, the number of pupils reporting the effectiveness of using rote learning for learning to write Chinese characters either often or always decreased by 9.5 per cent between the pre- and post-intervention period. Although the percentage decreases are relatively low, it could be interpreted that increased knowledge of and familiarity with the strategies has led to pupils questioning their effectiveness.

4) Is there a difference between teachers' and pupils' perception of the most effective learning strategies?

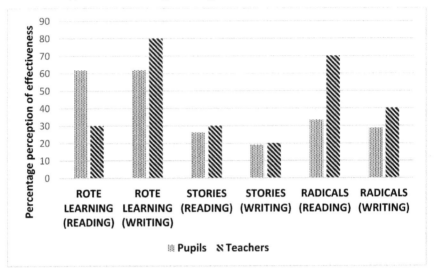

Figure 7.5: Comparison of the perception of strategy effectiveness between the post-intervention pupils' and teachers' questionnaires

As Figure 7.5 illustrates, there were mixed levels of agreement between pupils and teachers when responding to how effective they perceived a strategy to be. The largest percentage difference in reported perception between teachers and pupils concerns the use of radicals for learning to read Chinese characters, with 36.6 per cent more teachers than pupils perceiving the strategy to be, often or all of the time, the most effective. The second largest difference in the perception of the most effective strategy between the pupils' group and the teachers' group related to the use of rote learning for reading, where 31.9 per cent more pupils than teachers found the strategy to be the most effective often or all the time. Aside from the two strategies discussed, there were no other large differences in the pupils' and the teachers' perception of the most effective learning strategies. The remaining differences in perception were less than 20 per cent, which can be considered relatively small, given that each teacher represented 10 per cent of the sample. Teachers may interpret these findings as good news and representative of the fact that both the pupils' and the teachers' perception of the most effective learning strategies are relatively well matched.

5) Is there a difference between the perception of pupils in a selective school compared with a non-selective school?

Table 7.1: Percentage of pupils from two sample schools that rated a strategy either 'often' or 'all the time' the most effective in the post-intervention questionnaire

	Non-selective mixed school (%)	Selective boys' school (%)
Rote learning (reading)	35.7	75.0
Rote learning (writing)	50.0	67.9
Stories (reading)	21.4	28.6
Stories (writing)	21.4	17.9
Radicals (reading)	21.4	39.3
Radicals (writing)	21.4	32.1

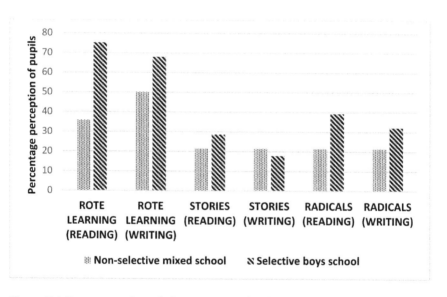

Figure 7.6: Percentage of pupils from two sample schools that rated a strategy either 'often' or 'all the time' the most effective in the post-intervention questionnaire

As Figure 7.6 illustrates, with the exception of the use of stories for both skills and the use of radicals for writing, there was little agreement between pupils from the selective boys' school and pupils from the non-selective mixed school as to their perception of the effectiveness of the three strategies. However, Table 7.1 shows that, with the exception of rote learning for reading, the percentage difference in perception between pupils from the different schools of the most effective strategies never exceeds 17.9 per cent. In light of the small sample size, meaning that 15 per cent equates to just over two pupils for the non-selective mixed school, the majority of these results do not appear particularly significant. The large difference between pupils from the selective boys' school and the non-selective mixed school in pupil perception of the effectiveness of rote learning for reading (39.3 per cent) is very interesting. One possible reason for this could be gender differences. That is, the mixed school has female pupils in the sample, and female pupils may believe rote learning not to be an effective strategy for learning to read Chinese characters. An additional explanation could be the teaching style, methods or preferences of the different teachers of the two respective groups. This could result from one teacher regularly exposing their pupils to the strategy and thereby proving or implying its effectiveness, with the other teacher rarely doing so because of their lack of faith in the strategy.

Discussion
Implications for practice
As is the purpose of any action research project, it is now essential to reflect on how the findings can be used by my colleagues and me and any future readers of this research to improve our own practice and facilitate an improved learning experience for our pupils. From my own experiences of both teaching the language and observing others teach it over the past six years, one of the largest barriers to pupils succeeding at learning Mandarin is the preconceived notion of how difficult a task it is (Scrimgeour, 2011). It is nevertheless the teacher's role to support pupils through the learning process, irrespective of how difficult it may be, so it is important to consider how the key findings of the present investigation may help teachers to do so. The key findings have been divided into three categories relating to their importance for teaching practice:

1. ROTE LEARNING FOR WRITING
Teachers and pupils from both schools were unanimous in their perception that rote learning was the most effective strategy for learning how to write Chinese characters. The first key implication of this unanimous result is that teachers should ensure that sufficient lesson time is dedicated to discussing it and supporting pupils in the effective adoption of this strategy. Teachers should not only spend time convincing pupils of the benefits of this strategy, but also prove to them that, if they are willing to adopt it, they could reap the rewards of their efforts in terms of developing their writing skills. Regarding the reasons stated by pupils as to why they find writing characters

difficult, two key themes emerged. Difficulty memorizing the characters was stated as the most frequent reason and lack of understanding of the stroke order of a character was a second significant reason for pupils finding writing difficult in Chinese. It could be argued that teaching pupils how to effectively utilize rote learning as a strategy and enabling them to experience its benefits would resolve both of these key concerns. It must be noted that the perception as reported in the present investigation relates to beginner learners of the language and that this strategy may not be perceived as most effective by either intermediate or advanced learners.

2. Differences between pupil and teacher perceptions of the most effective strategies

The differences observed in the present investigation between the pupils' and the teachers' perceptions of the most effective strategies for certain skills relating to learning Chinese have important implications for teaching practice. The most noteworthy discrepancy between pupil and teacher perception related to the use of radicals for reading. Both my colleagues and I, as well as other teachers who read the results of the present investigation, should be mindful of pupils' relative lack of confidence in the effectiveness of radicals for supporting reading compared with rote learning. Teachers should, of course, consider why this might be. It is possible that this discrepancy exists because radicals become more useful for learners who have reached an intermediate or advanced level of Mandarin: teachers are advanced learners of the language, whereas the pupils were beginners at the time this research was conducted. Nonetheless, it is the teachers' role to teach learning strategies that are most suited to their pupils' level of expertise, hence teachers should adapt their teaching to compensate for their pupils' level. Furthermore, regardless of teacher opinion, if considerably fewer pupils perceive a strategy to be effective, they are unlikely to adopt it and may even be deterred and demotivated as a result of their teacher's insistence on that strategy.

3. Pupils from different types of schools may prefer different strategies

The third and final implication for practice of the present investigation relates to the differing perception of pupils from a non-selective mixed school compared with pupils from a selective grammar school regarding certain skills. Like the observed differences between pupils' and teachers' perceptions, the main point of contention for pupils from the two different schools was the effectiveness of rote learning and radicals for reading. In both cases, there were considerable differences in perceived effectiveness. The implication of this finding on teaching practice is that teachers of

Mandarin should be aware that different pupils perceive different strategies to be most effective. Classroom activities, homework activities, and assessments should therefore be designed to cater for these differences in perception. Furthermore, a range of strategies should be presented early on in the course of learning the language, so that pupils can select the one that they find most effective for them.

Conclusion

Any research investigation can be seen to have flaws and the present investigation is no exception. Potential weaknesses were carefully considered in the design of the research, specifically in relation to validity, reliability and robustness, so that any potential limitations were minimized. However, after the data had been collected and analysed and the findings discussed, some further limitations of the present investigation's research design became apparent. It is important to acknowledge these limitations, so that both I and those who read the investigation are aware of factors that may affect how generalizable or useful the findings are.

Limitations

The first limitation that I have become aware of since analysing the results is that of sample size. The differences observed between the teachers' and the pupils' perceptions were one of the key findings of the investigation and could therefore be perceived to have important implications for teaching practice. However, as the large percentage differences in perception observed only equated to the opinions of three or four teachers, the conclusions based on these differences may be less generalizable. If the sample of teachers had been larger, the findings may have offered more robust conclusions relating to differences in pupil and teacher perception and their implications for my colleagues' and my own teaching.

The second limitation relates to the categorization of the data. Although it made sense to distinguish the most effective strategies according to whether they were selected by pupils and teachers as either 'often' or 'all the time' the most effective, this means that the data can be a little confusing. This is because a teacher could choose one strategy to be most effective 'all the time', but they could also choose another strategy to be the most effective 'often', meaning that the data could suggest that more than ten teachers perceived a strategy to be 'the most effective'. It would therefore be interesting to investigate further, maybe through a predominantly qualitative design, why one strategy is perceived by the same learner as the most effective 'all the time', yet another strategy is perceived by that same learner as the most effective 'often'.

Whilst reflecting on how generalizable the findings of the present investigation are, I became aware of a third limitation that related to the teacher group. Some teachers involved in the investigation could have had very similar training experiences and could also have had very similar learning experiences. Therefore, owing to the small sample size, the sample may not represent a wide enough proportion of the UK Mandarin teaching population. In a larger sample group, these potentially similar perceptions may have had a minimal impact on the overall result, but in the present investigation they could have had a large impact. There could therefore be an argument for further research to allow only one teacher per school to participate, which could offer a broader range of perceptions.

Where next?

In spite of the limitations of the present investigation, I hope that the findings provide answers to some of the difficult questions facing a teacher or learner of Mandarin in the UK today. The findings have certainly provided me with many new ideas about how to present learning strategies to my pupils and how a scheme of work should incorporate understanding of their importance. It is essential, finally, to return to the context of the investigation in assessing how effectively the investigation has addressed the stated problems and what more should be done to address these problems better. As discussed, the difference in pupil and teacher perception of the effectiveness of certain strategies invites further research as to why these differences exist and what can be done to address them. Teacher perception has a tendency to be overlooked, but this is done at our peril, as it is teachers who steer the learning process for their pupils. If teacher and pupil perception are not synchronized, the teacher must be aware of this to ensure that they have all of the information required to steer each pupil's learning in the right direction. Regarding teacher practice, this implies careful consideration of the learning activities and programmes planned by teachers to ensure that pupils are being presented with the most effective strategies available.

As noted in the introduction to the context of the present investigation, despite being seemingly the most effective strategy according to previous research and the findings of the present one, rote learning for writing is often one of the least popular with pupils. Further research may wish to consider how best to convince pupils of the benefits of rote learning, even if they do not perceive it to be most effective for them. An example from my own practice is that I mention that the process of rote learning is not so different from the process of preparing for spelling tests when pupils first learnt to read and write English in primary school. It is possible that if explained in positive, advantageous terms, and if pupils feel that they have already achieved something similar in their own language, they may see rote learning as a means to achievement in Chinese.

The third and final area that I feel requires further research attention, which has not been directly addressed in the present investigation, is whether a pupil's level of achievement in the subject (sometimes mistakenly referred to as a pupil's ability) may affect their strategy selection. It is not clear whether pupils from the selective grammar school are either lower or higher achievers than the pupils from the non-selective mixed school and therefore conclusions could not be drawn on this topic. However, if further research could plot pupils' level of achievement against their strategy selection, we may be able to observe patterns that enable teachers to support their pupils better, by catering more personally to their learning strategy needs. If this were achieved, pupils in my school who are in the higher GCSE set could spend more time using a strategy that is more appropriate for their advanced level, and pupils in the lower GCSE set could be supported with a strategy that suits their personal level.

On returning from a state visit to China in December 2013, the British Prime Minister commented that:

> By the time the children born today leave school, China is set to be the world's largest economy. So it's time to look beyond the traditional focus on French and German and get many more children learning Mandarin. (Watt and Adams, 2013: 4)

Although as a passionate linguist I wholly disagree with the Prime Minister's suggestion of looking 'beyond' or 'ditching' French and German, and one assumes that a statement of a similar nature would have followed a state visit to any country, there is some truth in what was said. More and more British pupils will learn Mandarin in British schools in future alongside the traditional European languages, and I hope that the present investigation may contribute in a small way to addressing some of the problems that pupils might encounter. As suggested above, there is a lot more work to be done. The responsibility for such work falls not to politicians, who may choose a language as flavour of the month and just as quickly forget about it the following month, but to the community of Mandarin teachers teaching in British schools. On a personal level, the investigation has instilled in me the importance of always being aware that different pupils may find different strategies more effective, even if some strategies appear more popular.

Furthermore, strategy selection should be presented as a key and early part of any Mandarin curriculum and should be reviewed at regular intervals throughout the course of a pupil's learning. A short list of useful reading material is provided below under 'Further reading' to support teachers who want to engage with existing research or design their own research projects.

Further reading

Chang, C. (2010) 'See how they read: An investigation into the cognitive and metacognitive strategies of nonnative readers of Chinese'. In Everson, M.E. and Shen, H.H. (eds) *Research Among Learners of Chinese as a Foreign Language* (Chinese Language Teachers Association Monograph 4). Honolulu: National Foreign Language Resource Center, 93–116.

Chen, Q. (1997) 'Toward a sequential approach for tonal error analysis'. *Journal of the Chinese Language Teachers Association*, 32 (1), 21–39.

Chikamatsu, N. (1996) 'The effects of L1 orthography on L2 word recognition: A study of American and Chinese learners of Japanese'. *Studies in Second Language Acquisition*, 18 (4), 403–32.

Chomsky, N. (1986) *Knowledge of Language: Its nature, origin, and use.* New York: Praeger.

Cohen, A.D. (2011) *Strategies in Learning and Using a Second Language.* 2nd ed. Harlow: Longman.

Corson, D. (1995) *Using English Words.* Dordrecht: Kluwer.

Crow, J.T. (1986) 'Receptive vocabulary acquisition for reading comprehension'. *Modern Language Journal,* 70 (3), 242–50.

Denscombe, M. (2007) *The Good Research Guide for Small-Scale Social Research Projects.* 2nd ed. Maidenhead: Open University Press.

Denscombe, M. (2010a) *Ground Rules for Social Research: Guidelines for good practice.* 2nd ed. Maidenhead: Open University Press.

Denscombe, M. (2010b) *The Good Research Guide for Small-Scale Social Research Projects.* 4th ed. Maidenhead: Open University Press.

Dörnyei, Z. (2007) *Research Methods in Applied Linguistics: Quantitative, qualitative, and mixed methodologies.* Oxford: Oxford University Press.

Erickson, F. (1986) 'Qualitative methods in research on teaching'. In Wittrock, M.C. (ed.) *Handbook of Research on Teaching.* 3rd ed. New York: Macmillan, 119–61.

Everson, M.E. and Ke, C. (1997) 'An inquiry into the reading strategies of intermediate and advanced learners of Chinese as a foreign language'. *Journal of the Chinese Language Teachers Association*, 32 (1), 1–22.

Everson, M.E. (1998) 'Word recognition among learners of Chinese as a foreign language: Investigating the relationship between naming and knowing'. *Modern Language Journal*, 82 (2), 194–204.

Furman, N., Goldberg, D. and Lusin, N. (2007) *Enrollments in Languages Other than English in United States Institutions of Higher Education, Fall 2006.* New York: Modern Language Association.

Guba, E.G. and Lincoln, Y.S. (1989) *Fourth Generation Evaluation.* Newbury Park, CA: SAGE Publications.

Hau-Yoon, L. (2002) 'The evaluation of a Mandarin Chinese course taught as a foreign language for distance learners'. Unpublished MEd dissertation, University of South Africa, Pretoria.

Hayes, E.B. (1988) 'Encoding strategies used by native and non-native readers of Chinese Mandarin'. *Modern Language Journal*, 72 (2), 188–95.

HEFCE (Higher Education Funding Council for England) (1999) *Review of Chinese Studies* (HEFCE Report 99/09). Bristol: HEFCE. Online. www.hefce.ac.uk/pubs/hefce/1999/99_09.htm (accessed 4 October 2017).

Jiang, X. and Cohen A.D. (2012) 'A critical review of research on strategies in learning Chinese as both a second and foreign language'. *Studies in Second Language Learning and Teaching*, 2 (1), 9–43.

Ke, C. (1998) 'Effects of strategies on the learning of Chinese characters among foreign language students'. *Journal of the Chinese Language Teachers Association*, 33 (2), 93–112.

Koda, K. (1996) 'L2 word recognition research: A critical review'. *Modern Language Journal*, 80 (4), 450–60.

Krashen, S.D. (1981) *Second Language Acquisition and Second Language Learning*. Oxford: Pergamon Press.

Kroll, J.F. (1993) 'Accessing conceptual representations for words in a second language'. In Schreuder, R. and Weltens, B. (eds) *The Bilingual Lexicon* (Studies in Bilingualism 6). Amsterdam: John Benjamins, 53–81.

Laufer, B. (1986) 'Possible changes in attitude towards vocabulary acquisition research'. *IRAL: International Review of Applied Linguistics in Language Teaching*, 24 (1), 69–75.

Li, Y. (1998) *Teaching and Learning L2 Reading: The Chinese case*. PhD thesis, Purdue University.

Meara, P. (1996) 'The dimensions of lexical competence'. In Brown, G., Malmkjær, K. and Williams, J. (eds) *Performance and Competence in Second Language Acquisition*. Cambridge: Cambridge University Press, 35–53.

Nation, I.S.P. (1990) *Teaching and Learning Vocabulary*. Boston: Heinle and Heinle.

Nation, I.S.P. (2001) *Learning Vocabulary in Another Language*. Cambridge: Cambridge University Press.

Nuthall, G. (2004) 'Relating classroom teaching to student learning: A critical analysis of why research has failed to bridge the theory–practice gap'. *Harvard Educational Review*, 74 (3), 273–306.

Oxford, R.L. (1990) *Language Learning Strategies: What every teacher should know*. New York: Newbury House.

Paton, G. (2013) 'Thousands more British students to study in China'. *The Telegraph*, 11 June. Online. www.telegraph.co.uk/education/educationnews/10114059/Thousands-more-British-students-to-study-in-China.html (accessed 8 August 2013).

Peacock, M. and Ho, B. (2003) 'Student language learning strategies across eight disciplines'. *International Journal of Applied Linguistics*, 13 (2), 179–200.

Peng, D., Li, Y. and Yang, H. (1997) 'Orthographic processing in the identification of Chinese characters'. In Chen, H.-C. (ed.) *Cognitive Processing of Chinese and Related Asian Languages*. Hong Kong: Chinese University Press, 85–108.

Rodgers, T.S. (1969) 'On measuring vocabulary difficulty: An analysis of item variables in learning Russian–English vocabulary pairs'. *IRAL: International Review of Applied Linguistics in Language Teaching*, 7 (4), 327–43.

Rubin, J. (1987) 'Learner strategies: Theoretical assumptions, research history and typology'. In Wenden, A. and Rubin, J. (eds) *Learner Strategies in Language Learning*. Englewood Cliffs, NJ: Prentice Hall, 15–31.

Schmitt, N. (2000) *Vocabulary in Language Teaching*. Cambridge: Cambridge University Press.

Sergent, W.K. (1990) *A Study of the Oral Reading Strategies of Advanced and Highly Advanced Second Language Readers of Chinese*. PhD thesis, Ohio State University.

Shen, H.H. and Ke, C. (2007) 'Radical awareness and word acquisition among nonnative learners of Chinese'. *Modern Language Journal*, 91 (1), 97–111.

Singleton, D. (1999) *Exploring the Second Language Mental Lexicon*. Cambridge: Cambridge University Press.

Sung, K.-Y. and Wu, H.-P. (2011) 'Factors influencing the learning of Chinese characters'. *International Journal of Bilingual Education and Bilingualism*, 14 (6), 683–700.

References

Alderson, P. (2004) 'Ethics'. In Fraser, S., Lewis, V., Ding, S., Kellett, M. and Robinson, C. (eds) *Doing Research with Children and Young People*. London: SAGE Publications, 97–112.

Anderson, G. L. and Herr, K. (2009) In Noffke, S. and Somekh, B. (eds) *The SAGE Handbook of Educational Action Research*. London: Sage Publications.

Bell, J. (2005) *Doing Your Research Project: A guide for first-time researchers in education, health and social science*. 4th ed. Maidenhead: Open University Press.

BERA (British Educational Research Association) (2011) *Ethical Guidelines for Educational Research*. London: British Educational Research Association.

Denscombe, M. (2007) *The Good Research Guide for Small-Scale Social Research Projects*. 3rd ed. Maidenhead: Open University Press.

Dewey, J. (1991) 'Propositions, warranted assertibility, and truth'. In Boydston, J.A. (ed.) *John Dewey: The later works, 1925–1953: Volume 14 (1939–1941): Essays, Reviews, and Miscellany*. Carbondale: Southern Illinois University Press, 168–88.

Hargreaves, D.H. (1996) *Teaching as a Research-Based Profession: Possibilities and prospects* (Teacher Training Agency Annual Lecture). London: Teacher Training Agency.

Heilbronn, R. (2008) *Teacher Education and the Development of Practical Judgement*. London: Continuum.

Klein, S.R. (ed.) (2012) *Action Research Methods: Plain and simple*. New York: Palgrave Macmillan.

McGinnis, S. (1999) 'Student goals and approaches'. In Chu, M. (ed.) *Mapping the Course of the Chinese Language Field* (Chinese Language Teachers Association Monograph 3). Kalamazoo, MI: Chinese Language Teachers Association, 151–88.

Scrimgeour, A. (2011) 'Issues and approaches to literacy development in Chinese second language classrooms'. In Tsung, L. and Cruickshank, K. (eds) *Teaching and Learning Chinese in Global Contexts: Multimodality and literacy in the new media age*. London: Continuum, 197–212.

Shen, H.H. (2005) 'An investigation of Chinese-character learning strategies among non-native learners of Chinese'. *System*, 33 (1), 49–68.

Watt, N. and Adams, R. (2013) 'David Cameron urges British students to ditch French and learn Mandarin'. *The Guardian*, 5 December. Online. www.theguardian.com/politics/2013/dec/05/david-cameron-ditch-french-learn-mandarin-china (accessed 4 October 2017).

Appendix 1: Pupils' questionnaire on learning characters

Thank you very much for your participation in this investigation. We very much appreciate the time that you will take to complete this questionnaire and hope that completing the questionnaire helps you in your learning of Chinese and helps your teacher to understand the best way to help you learn Chinese. Your participation in completing this questionnaire is strictly anonymous so you can be as honest as you want and nobody will know that it was you who completed the questionnaire. You can withdraw from completing the questionnaire at any time. Thank you.

1. **Reading characters**

   a) **How easy do you find reading characters? Please circle one word from the list below:**

   Very Easy   Easy   Moderate   Difficult   Very difficult

   b) **If you answered 'Difficult' or 'Very difficult' to question 1(a) above, why might this be? (you can circle more than one reason)**

   i) There is no similarity between Chinese characters and English words.

   ii) It's hard to link a character to its sound.

   iii) Chinese characters all look very similar and I'm confused.

   iv) I don't see/use characters very often so I easily forget their meaning.

   v) I am not interested in learning Chinese characters.

   vi) I think Pinyin is easier and I don't think I need to learn characters

   vii) Other (please specify) ....

   ....

2. Writing characters

   a) How easy do you find writing characters? Please circle one word from the list below:

      Very Easy   Easy   Moderate   Difficult   Very difficult

   b) If you answered 'Difficult' or 'Very difficult' to question 2(a) above, why might this be? (you can circle more than one reason)

      i) I am not familiar with the stroke order of the character.
      ii) I find it very difficult to memorize how to write the character.
      iii) I find it boring practising writing characters.
      iv) I don't have enough time or opportunity to practise writing characters.
      v) I am not interested in writing characters.
      vi) Other (please specify) ....

      ....

3. Speaking

   a) How easy do you find speaking Chinese? Please circle one word from the list below:

      Very Easy   Easy   Moderate   Difficult   Very difficult

   b) Do you have any additional comments to make based on your answer to question 3(a)?

      ....

4. Listening and understanding

   a) How easy do you find listening to and understanding Chinese? Please circle one word from the list below:

      Very Easy   Easy   Moderate   Difficult   Very difficult

   b) Do you have any additional comments to make based on your answer to question 4(a)?

      ....

5. Please rate on a scale of 1–5 to what extent you think the following methods are most effective in helping you to learn how to read and write Chinese characters:

a) **Rote learning** – this is memorizing characters by writing them out over and over again.

Reading: 1   2   3   4   5
         (never)   *(rarely)*   *(sometimes)*   *(often)*   *(all the time)*

Writing: 1   2   3   4   5
         (never)   *(rarely)*   *(sometimes)*   *(often)*   *(all the time)*

b) **Stories** – this is when a short story or explanation about how the character looks helps you to remember that character.

Reading: 1   2   3   4   5
         (never)   *(rarely)*   *(sometimes)*   *(often)*   *(all the time)*

Writing: 1   2   3   4   5
         (never)   *(rarely)*   *(sometimes)*   *(often)*   *(all the time)*

c) **Learning and recognizing radicals** – this is when you use the radical part of the character to support you in memorizing and understanding the character's meaning.

Reading: 1   2   3   4   5
         (never)   *(rarely)*   *(sometimes)*   *(often)*   *(all the time)*

Writing: 1   2   3   4   5
         (never)   *(rarely)*   *(sometimes)*   *(often)*   *(all the time)*

Appendix 2: Teacher character strategy questionnaire

Thank you very much for your participation in this investigation. We very much appreciate the time that you take to complete this questionnaire and hope that the results of the questionnaire will help you in your teaching of Chinese. Your participation in this questionnaire is strictly anonymous. You may withdraw from completing the questionnaire at any time. If you wish, we will share the results of this investigation through a short report. Thank you.

1. Reading characters

   a) How easy do you think your pupils find reading characters? Please circle one word from the list below:

   Very Easy   Easy   Moderate   Difficult   Very difficult

   b) If you answered 'Difficult' or 'Very difficult' to question 1(a) above, why might this be? (you can circle more than one reason)

   > *i) There is no similarity between Chinese characters and English words.*
   > *ii) It's hard to link a character to its sound.*
   > *iii) Chinese characters all look very similar and pupils become confused.*
   > *iv) Pupils don't see/use characters very often, so they easily forget their meaning.*
   > *v) Pupils aren't interested in learning Chinese characters.*
   > *vi) Pupils think Pinyin is easier and they don't think they need to learn characters.*
   > *vii) Other (please specify)* ....
   >
   > ....

2. Writing characters

   a) How easy do you think your pupils find writing characters? Please circle one word from the list below:

   Very Easy   Easy   Moderate   Difficult   Very difficult

   b) If you answered 'Difficult' or 'Very difficult' to question 2(a) above, why might this be? (you can circle more than one reason)

   > *i) Pupils are not familiar with the stroke order.*
   > *ii) Pupils find it very difficult to memorize how to write the character.*
   > *iii) Pupils find it boring practising writing characters.*
   > *iv) Pupils don't have enough time or opportunity to practise writing characters.*
   > *v) Pupils are not interested in writing characters.*
   > *vi) Other (please specify)* ....
   >
   > ....

3. Speaking

   a) How easy do you think your pupils find speaking Chinese? Please circle one word from the list below:

   Very Easy   Easy   Moderate   Difficult   Very difficult

   b) Do you have any additional comments to make based on your answer to question 3(a)?

   ....

4. Listening and understanding

   a) How easy do you think your pupils find listening to and understanding Chinese? Please circle one word from the list below:

   Very Easy   Easy   Moderate   Difficult   Very difficult

   b) Do you have any additional comments to make based on your answer to question 4(a)?

   ....

5. Please rate on a scale of 1–5, to what extent you think the following methods are most effective in helping your pupils to learn how to read and write Chinese characters:

   a) **Rote learning** – this is memorizing characters by writing them out over and over again.

   Reading: 1   2   3   4   5
            (never) *(rarely)* *(sometimes)* *(often)* *(all the time)*

   Writing: 1   2   3   4   5
            (never) *(rarely)* *(sometimes)* *(often)* *(all the time)*

   b) **Stories** – this is when a short story or explanation about how the character looks helps your pupils to remember that character.

   Reading: 1   2   3   4   5
            (never) *(rarely)* *(sometimes)* *(often)* *(all the time)*

   Writing: 1   2   3   4   5
            (never) *(rarely)* *(sometimes)* *(often)* *(all the time)*

c) **Learning and recognizing radicals** – this is when you use the radical part of the character to support your pupils in memorizing and understanding the character's meaning.

Reading: 1   2   3   4   5
          (never)   *(rarely)*   *(sometimes)*   *(often)*   *(all the time)*

Writing: 1   2   3   4   5
          (never)   *(rarely)*   *(sometimes)*   *(often)*   *(all the time)*

Chapter 8

'Checks and balances'

Using proofreading skills as an effective method to improve written Mandarin Chinese

Victoria Allen

Introduction

With the introduction of written controlled assessments in the GCSE[1] languages, I and many other colleagues face difficulties in preparing students for the task ahead, such as, for example, the level of language and grammar required, quality versus quantity, or accuracy of characters. These difficulties were what prompted me to think about action research in my classroom, and the last item became the focus of my research.

I wanted to design an action research project to measure and improve proofreading skills in my GCSE class as they prepared for a written controlled assessment. I also wanted to highlight proofreading as a skill that could and should be used by them as part of their everyday studies.

Year 11 learners (aged 16) are required to submit two pieces of controlled assessment for their AQA (Assessment and Qualifications Alliance) GCSE Mandarin examination at the end of their course. These pieces of work are over 150 characters long and must be written completely in Chinese characters, based on a task of the teacher's choosing. Such topics may be titles such as 'School', 'My Holidays', 'My Hometown', and 'An interesting weekend'.

Students are required to express themselves on one of these topics in each piece. They must show coherent expression, a full and varied range of language including timeframes, and a high level of accuracy. It is how to achieve this last point which puzzled me and has led me to undertake action research in my classroom in order to address and solve the problem.

My goal was to raise awareness with the students that accuracy on this task was an area where points would not be awarded if the characters were not accurate, if the sentences were incorrect, or if the text was haphazard or illogical. Following on from that, we explored as a class various methods for checking the accuracy of the students' work, thus motivating them to improve their controlled assessment pieces. In sum, the goal was to highlight a problem and suggest possible ways of solving it.

What incentive did the students have for undertaking the action research? On the one hand, they enjoy the satisfaction of a job well done, but also, potentially, an improvement in their accuracy grade, and hence a possible improvement to their final GCSE Mandarin grade.

What about the incentives for me as a teacher? I have a great sense of achievement, too, having equipped students with tools that they can use in many other areas of their studies and seen each student gain the GCSE grade they deserve after all of their efforts.

Puzzlement

I have been a member of our school's holistic literacy focus group over the academic year 2013–14; the group raises students' spelling mistakes and grammatical issues across the curriculum. It then considers how best to address these issues and formulates possible areas of focus. The group meets once a term to highlight any problem areas in their department, then the areas of focus are collated by the lead teacher and made into a programme for the coming term. Previous topics, for example, have focused on words that are easily confused when written or on language used in curriculum areas for examinations.

The issues raised are then tackled in English lessons and awareness is raised during tutor times and in assemblies. Additionally, there are posters for the theme of the week around school and a detailed explanation flashes up on the students' computers once they log in. It was by participating in this programme established by our school's English department that I began to think about possible action research and what I might do to help my own students with their literacy in Mandarin.

Bearing this in mind, I considered various areas for possible action in the classroom: handwriting and character legibility, variation of sentence structures, use of paragraphs when writing extended texts, the correct use of timeframes, and proofreading. Notably, one item from the list came to the fore as a key problem area: proofreading and the accuracy of work submitted for written controlled assessments.

I had noticed that in previous cohorts taking this examination (2011, 2012, and notably 2013), even high-achieving candidates did not appear to proofread their work for more than several minutes, if at all. Upon examining some copies of archived written controlled assessments for our centre (my teaching group from 2011–13, numbering 13 candidates), I saw that some candidates had made serious character errors on even simple or high-frequency characters.[2] Cross-referencing this with the grade that they received from the examination board, it was clear that candidates had lost marks due to avoidable errors. My plan was to intervene and eradicate this as a source of lost marks as much as possible.

The students do not find the tasks themselves difficult, as they usually spent six to eight weeks preparing the topic area, as suggested by the examination board. They generally feel well prepared for the task ahead. The tasks themselves are set out in English, with bullet points to enable students to think about sub-topics and select relevant information from the body of work in their exercise books and textbook. The tasks are similar or are the same as those suggested by the examination board. Any new tasks are sent to the person responsible for the Mandarin written controlled assessments for checking. From speaking to colleagues in other schools, I understand that many other schools also conduct their assessments in this way, following the AQA examination guidelines carefully.

In this study, I wanted to examine how my learners proofread and which strategies I might introduce to enable them to proofread more effectively. This would contribute to their submitting work of a higher standard and minimize avoidable errors.

Intervention

In order to help students improve in this area, I decided to intervene by trialling proofreading techniques collected through wider reading and discussion with colleagues. As the Year 11 learners prepared their final piece of written controlled assessment, I used four different techniques to assist their proofreading and prepare them for the final assessment, when they may choose to use one or more techniques.

In researching proofreading techniques, I soon discovered that there is very little written specifically for use with foreign languages. Furthermore, most of what is available is specifically for those who are checking documents for the subject of English as a native-speaker. There was little for those checking work as non-native speakers, even in the area of ESOL. I worked through various internet leads in an attempt to find additional techniques. I also asked colleagues, tutors, and contacts for assistance wherever I could.

Data collection

In the first instance I read many documents, both online and in print, for general advice on proofreading at this level of learning. Specifically, I found some detailed documents for professional proofreaders and editors very useful and inspiring for my project research (Einsohn, 2000; Lanham, 1992).

Secondly, I consulted with my mentors at the IOE for further advice on MFL-specific techniques. Thereafter, I canvassed colleagues for their ideas. These ranged from 'get students to read the whole thing through; first for gist; then for spelling' (BLP – the head of Spanish; teacher of Spanish, French and German) to 'give the students a list to encourage them to check agreements for gender and number, verb endings, tenses' (MGF – the head of MFL faculty; teacher of Spanish, German and Latin). These ideas tended to be for European languages and did not necessarily work well for character-based languages such as Chinese and Japanese.

Finally, as I am part of the school's holistic literacy project, I asked staff committee members for their input. One member of the staff group used a tin of sweets to encourage students to check and correct their work. The member of staff concerned would underline the mistakes when marking. Once the work was returned, students would correct three mistakes or more, have their work checked by the teacher, and help themselves to a sweet. Another member of staff suggested students should read their work upside down and see if that made a difference! Although it was meant as a humorous suggestion at the time, it piqued my interest and encouraged me to consider other ideas that may not have been considered for languages that do not use Roman script.

My wider reading and research gave me a shortlist of four different techniques (Einsohn, 2000; Guy, 2007; Lanham, 1992):

1. Reading work aloud – this appears to be a common strategy from my reading. It encourages the proofreader to slow down their reading and say each word aloud. Students are much faster when they read in their head and can often miss words when they read quickly.
2. Peer marking – this strategy is designed to encourage a fresh pair of eyes to look over the work. Sometimes students know their work so well that they do not read it properly, as they can predict what will come next. A peer reading another student's work for the first time will not do this.

3. Whole passage reading – this strategy is to ensure that each paragraph is logical and makes sense. Students are checking for comprehension rather than individual characters, tense, or use of constructions.

4. Reading the line from right to left to focus fully on characters – I came up with this technique in a staff meeting for holistic literacy. My colleague's humorous quip triggered the idea. If students read in an unnatural way, for example, upside down or back to front, would that encourage higher levels of concentration? Upside down might completely confuse students, I felt, so I settled for working from right to left in order to focus the students' attention on the formation of the character rather than the sense of the sentence.

I trialled these with the students in the preparation time leading up to their written controlled assessment, asking for informal feedback after each session. I introduced a technique per lesson as students were preparing and checking their work in preparation for the controlled assessment. Each technique took five minutes to explain, five minutes to put into practice, and then I allowed up to five minutes for any comments. In this way it neither impinged on lesson time, nor overwhelmed the task, nor distracted from it.

I looked at their completed tasks once they had written them to assess the accuracy of the work.

Finally, I used a series of 14 questions using a Survey Monkey questionnaire to collect the learners' attitudes towards proofreading and their opinions on the techniques and their usefulness.

The student participants were a group of 14 Year 11 male students, aged 16, who were in their final term before their GCSE examinations. I had taught most of them Chinese for four years, a few of them for only two years. There was a good rapport within the class, and I felt that I had a good working relationship with them. Indeed, it was because of the nature of the class that I felt that I could trial this programme with them, with minimum disruption to their studies.

The class was mixed ability: some students were natural linguists who worked hard and succeeded through a combination of talent and effort, some were not natural linguists but very diligent and succeeded through effort, and finally some who worked hard, had good memories, but still struggled. All of them had a keen interest in China or the Chinese language. Some had been on a China trip to Xian the previous summer (2013), some were due to go on a trip to Xiamen that summer (2014). Three of them were planning to do AS[3] Chinese when they became sixth-formers.

Before I embarked on the research, I sought permission from my head teacher, head of faculty, the students, and the students' parents.

Data analysis
Techniques trialled in the classroom
As we trialled each technique, I asked the learners for their feedback. Each time we trialled a technique, the learners worked on a different section of their controlled assessment, so the passage was unchecked each time.

Each passage was between 30 and 60 simplified characters in length. The techniques were integrated into the lessons, rather than being a bolt-on task. Lessons at the school are 60 minutes long. I do not usually teach in a dedicated Chinese language classroom, and each lesson with this class was in a different room, usually in a different department such as Philosophy and Applied Ethics or in the sixth form block.

TECHNIQUE NUMBER 1[4]

This technique required learners to read their work aloud at home or mouth the words in class to ensure that they were fully focused on the task and not distracted (James and Klein, 1994: 36, 3.2).

We trialled this in class as our first technique. I deliberately chose a technique for the first task that I felt would be familiar to the students, so that they would feel at ease with the project. In class, I introduced the technique and encouraged them to slow their reading down and concentrate on the passage. Most remarked that they felt foolish reading aloud, so I suggested that they read in their heads but mouth the sounds of the characters, so that their reading was slowed down.

Some of them felt that this would not work in an examination setting, as it would be too distracting for those around them, possibly attracting undesirable attention. I agreed, but argued that this technique could be used in other circumstances. I felt that it had worked, as most of the learners found at least one mistake.

In spite of its success, this was not a popular method with the group. They voiced their thoughts accordingly.

TECHNIQUE NUMBER 2[5]

This technique involved learners marking each other's work after an initial proofread by the author.

I introduced this to the class as a 'fresh pair of eyes' approach. I compared it to the work staff do in preparing reports and how each report is then read by the tutor, head of house, and a member of the senior management team in order to eliminate mistakes. I suggested that the group should try the same technique.

First, the peer markers read the piece once for accuracy within a sentence; then they read for a second time to check for character accuracy.

The feedback from this trial was mixed. Some peer markers found mistakes in sentences and structures that the author had missed. Some did not. When the peer markers looked for character errors, all of them found at least one character mistake.

TECHNIQUE NUMBER 3[6]

This technique encouraged learners to read their essay through to ensure that the whole article made sense and was not a series of disjointed paragraphs. Occasionally, learners become so focused on the Chinese language that they forget to follow on logically from one paragraph to another (The Writing Center, 2017b).

The learners understood the merit of this technique, yet their response after the exercise was lukewarm. Their only comment was that it was perhaps 'a helpful thing to do'.

TECHNIQUE NUMBER 4[7]

This technique provoked a much greater response as it was so unusual. It was inspired by a humorous comment in a holistic literacy meeting where a colleague suggested that learners' proofreading skills could be improved by reading upside down. I felt that this would probably not work in Chinese, but it inspired me to try the 'backwards reading' technique. This involves learners of Chinese starting to read on the right-hand side of the page in order to fully focus on the accuracy of the character, not the meaning of the sentence. This, indeed, focused the learners' concentration to the point where one learner commented, 'My brain aches!' The others in the cohort felt that it was 'helpful', 'useful', and 'good', but all of them agreed in the feedback session that it ensured their full concentration (The Writing Center, 2017a).

Overall, I had hoped for a clearer picture and perhaps a 'most favoured' technique. However, it seems that just as the members of the group had different ways of learning, they favoured different ways of proofreading.

Results

Table 8.1 details the accuracy grade for the trial group. The first two assessments were completed before the action research. The third was after all four proofreading techniques had been completed.

Table 8.1: Comparing the accuracy of written controlled assessments 1–3

Candidate reference (2012–14 cohort)	Controlled assessment grade no. 1 (score out of five marks) – July 2013	Controlled assessment grade no. 2 (score out of five marks) – November 2013	Controlled assessment grade no. 3 (score out of five marks) – March 2014
1	4	4	4
2	4	3	4
3	4	3	4
4	3	3	3
5	3	3	4
6	3	3	4
7	3	2	3
8	3	3	4
9	4	3	4
10	3	3	4
11	4	3	4
12	4	3	4
13	4	3	4

Please see Appendix 1 for the AQA grid detailing each of the accuracy grades 0–5.

Survey results

To conclude the action research, I asked the group to complete an online survey that I had created to canvass them about their experiences. In the survey, I asked them about their proofreading prior to the trialling of the techniques and after the project had ended. I also enquired as to how helpful they felt each technique was.

According to the data collected through the survey, 92 per cent of students only proofread their work sometimes prior to the project (Q1), with only 50 per cent of them proofreading their Chinese (Q2). By the end of the project, the total percentage of students proofreading their work was still 92 per cent in total; however, as a result of the project, nearly 84 per cent were proofreading their Chinese work (Q11). I feel that this is a great improvement, and even though there had not been a clear overall technique that had stood out during the research, the fact that more of the group were checking their work for errors more carefully and more frequently, is in itself a huge success. The project alerted students to what they already knew they should be doing, but possibly they had not understood previously how to apply this knowledge to MFL subjects.

When reading the results of the survey about the techniques, responses are less clear. Q3 asked about the reading-aloud technique. Sixty-seven per cent of the group found this helpful. Upon reflection, this is not a surprising result at all, as many members of the group were quite reserved, and this technique may have made them feel uncomfortable in class.

Q4 asked about the technique which involved peer marking. Sixty-seven per cent cited this activity as helpful or very helpful. A fresh pair of eyes can often help when preparing work and the students' experiences during the project seems to bear this out.

Q5 asked about reading the text for overall fluency. This question elicited a high negative response (42 per cent). I feel that this was an interesting result from the students, as the AQA 2014 examiner's report for Unit 4 (written controlled assessment) suggests that there are too many pieces of controlled assessment that are collections of stand-alone paragraphs, instead of coherent essays. The students' mainly negative reaction to this technique runs counter to the AQA examiner's suggestion.

Q6 provoked the most reaction from students, with opinion cut straight down the middle. Fifty per cent of students felt that the technique of reading from right to left was helpful or very helpful. Forty-two per cent felt that it was not helpful, with a further eight per cent citing the technique as very unhelpful.

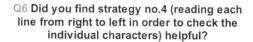

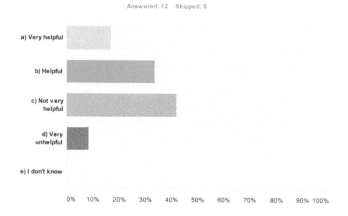

Answer Choices	Responses	
a) Very helpful	16.67%	2
b) Helpful	33.33%	4
c) Not very helpful	41.67%	5
d) Very unhelpful	8.33%	1
e) I don't know	0.00%	0
Total		12

Figure 8.1: Attitudes towards proofreading in Mandarin Chinese studies

This was certainly borne out by the ranking exercise (Q7). The students were asked to rank the techniques in order of usefulness. A clear winner was peer marking, which, although not applicable in a controlled assessment, would certainly be helpful during the preparation of it. Sixty-seven per cent of students ranked it in first or second place. Notably, the most unusual technique also turned out to be the least useful, with 67 per cent of students ranking it in third or fourth place out of four.

Conclusion

It is clear from both the assessment results and the survey results that the action research did indeed have an impact on the students. It achieved its goal of increasing awareness and providing suitable techniques for MFL students when proofreading non-Roman script assessments. As to how far this can be quantified, this remains in dispute. Most students (11/13) experienced a rise in their accuracy grade between the second and third assessments, yet as the final assessment was at the end of the course, one could argue that the students' grade could have increased in any case, as they were near the completion of their GCSE and preparing for examinations. The topics of the assessments, too, could be considered subjective: it might have been easier for students to write on a familiar topic such as 'School', which has been studied periodically since the beginning of their language learning, than on a relatively new topic such as 'Environment'. Prior learning and prior assessment would also influence the accuracy grade of a familiar topic.

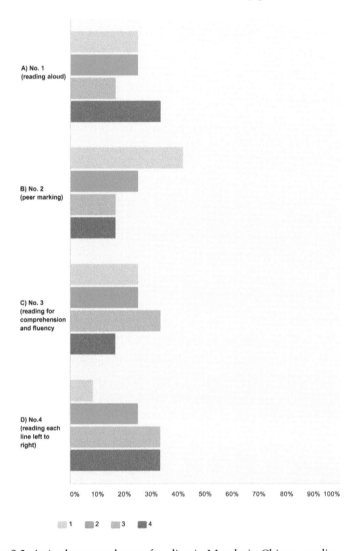

Figure 8.2: Attitudes towards proofreading in Mandarin Chinese studies

In conclusion, even though it is difficult in this limited piece of action research to see how much the research has contributed to the improvement of students' grades, I am pleased that students have adopted at least one of the proofreading skills that were trialled. As they all have varied methods of learning, so they selected varied proofreading techniques or a combination that suited them best. I feel that it is important to remember that this exercise will continue to influence not only their language learning skills in the future, but also their wider studies beyond the classroom. With this in mind, I consider this action research to have been successful.

Examination update (June 2016)

Since taking part in the action research, there have been far-reaching changes to the specifications of all UK GCSE examinations. The new GCSE Mandarin Chinese specifications delivered by both the AQA and Edexcel examination boards are for teaching from September 2017, with the first formal exams in the summer of 2019.

When testing the written section, controlled assessment will no longer be a part of the GCSE specification. In its place will be a foundation tier or higher tier paper consisting of three questions, increasing in difficulty and required length. I believe that the proofreading skills used in this action research project will continue to be as useful and valuable in preparing the students for the new GCSE specification and, furthermore, will serve them well in the exam itself.

PRACTICAL IDEAS
- Encourage students to proofread in order to spot errors: it is surprising how many students do not include this in their preparation before submitting a text.
- Ideally, students should proofread once for construction and tense, a second time for correct formation of characters, and a third time to ensure the text makes sense.
- A suggested proofreading technique could be reading aloud in order to slow down reading and focus the mind.
- Another useful technique is peer marking. Students tend to be more critical of each other's work as it is unfamiliar and thus find errors more readily.
- Reading for sense is a vital part of proofreading, especially ensuring that there are no missing characters that would affect the meaning of the sentence or passage.

- Try unusual methods of proofreading such as reading upside down or, as in this study, reading from right to left in order to focus the mind on a specific aspect of the passage such as accurate character formation.
- Make proofreading an integral part of the classroom routine in order to benefit from this fully, rather than a 'bolt-on' activity. It is not only a skill for use in Mandarin studies, but also one which can be applied across the curriculum.

Notes

[1] General Certificate of Secondary Education (GCSE) is an academic qualification taken by 16-year-old pupils in the UK in a specific subject. The results of the GCSE examinations are then used to gauge ability for employment or as entry for study in higher education. A GCSE at grades A*–C is an EU Level 2 qualification.

[2] Out of the 2013 cohort, no students scored 5/5 for accuracy, seven scored 4/5 for accuracy, six scored 3/5 for accuracy, no students scored 2, 1 or 0/5 for accuracy.

[3] AS is an abbreviation for 'Advanced Subsidiary' qualification and is a one-year post-GCSE course with a terminal examination. The AS qualification can stand alone or can be combined with a further year of study to become an A level qualification. This becomes part of the entry criteria for admission to university in the UK.

[4] 20/03/2014 – period 4.

[5] 24/03/2014 – period 5.

[6] 28/03/2014 – period 1.

[7] 28/03/2014 – period 1.

References

AQA (Assessment and Qualifications Alliance) (2014) *GSCE Chinese. Unit 4 writing*. Online. http://filestore.aqa.org.uk/subjects/AQA-46704-WRE-JUN14.pdf (accessed 3 January 2018).

Einsohn, A. (2000) *The Copyeditor's Handbook: A guide for book publishing and corporate communications*. Berkeley: University of California Press.

Guy, P. (2007) *Study Skills: A teaching programme for students in schools and colleges*. London: Paul Chapman.

James, C. and Klein, K. (1994) 'Foreign language learners' spelling and proofreading strategies'. *Papers and Studies in Contrastive Linguistics*, 29, 31–46.

Lanham, R.A. (1992) *Revising Prose*. 3rd ed. New York: Macmillan.

The Writing Center (2017a) 'Editing and proofreading'. Online. www.writingcenter.unc.edu/handouts/editing-and-proofreading (accessed 4 October 2017).

The Writing Center (2017b) 'Proofreading'. Online. www.writingcenter.unc.edu/handouts/proofreading (accessed 4 October 2017).

Appendix 1: AQA accuracy grid for GCSE Chinese written controlled assessments

AQA GCSE Chinese criteria for the accuracy part of the written assessments:

Content – out of 15 marks

Range of language – out of 10 marks

Accuracy – out of 5 marks

Total: up to 30 marks

Accuracy	
Marks	**Criteria**
5	Largely accurate, although there may still be some errors especially in attempts at more complex sentences. Time expressions are secure.
4	Generally accurate with errors occurring in attempts at more complex sentences. Time expressions are usually correct.
3	More accurate than inaccurate. Time expressions are sometimes unsuccessful. The intended meaning is clear.
2	Many errors which often impede communication. Time expressions are rarely accurate.
1	Limited understanding of the most basic linguistic structures. Frequent errors regularly impede communication.
0	No language produced which is worthy of credit.

Figure 8.3: AQA accuracy grid for GCSE Chinese written controlled assessments; reproduced with kind permission from the AQA (2012)

An investigation of the professional identity construction of Hanban teachers in British schools

Yi Xiang

Introduction

In 2015, during the Annual Chinese Teaching Conference hosted by the UCL IOE Confucius Institute, a school delegate noticed my poster about my study on Hanban teachers and expressed a keen interest in learning more. His school was about to welcome its first Hanban teacher, and he was eager to ask a series of questions: 'Who are Hanban teachers? Are they qualified teachers in China? What kind of training have they received before their arrival? What are your suggestions if we want to work with them efficiently?'

What struck me about this encounter is how little schools seem to know about Hanban teachers before their deployment, which could have a negative impact on how effectively they settle in. In their research report, Tinsley and Board (2014: 8) voice the concern that native-speaker teachers or assistants from China are under-utilized in Mandarin classrooms, and call for the provision of further training on how to use these teachers better. A first step towards better utilization of Hanban teachers is acknowledging the importance of understanding them, their context and their education.

What, then, does the current literature suggest about Hanban teachers? Some researchers recognize them as one significant type of support staff that can be deployed in the process of introducing and developing Mandarin provision in schools (Filmer-Sankey *et al.*, 2010: 3). Some appreciate the contribution they make to Chinese language teaching and the communication of different cultures (Wang and Higgins, 2008: 94–5). However, their teaching experiences have often been reported as difficult and challenging, and their pre-departure training has been viewed as inadequate (CiLT National Centre for Languages, 2007: 12; Starr,

2009: 72; Tinsley and Board, 2014: 4). Very little comprehensive work has been done to understand what real problems and challenges these teachers face, why these issues occur, how they are dealt with and how teachers develop in a new sociocultural context.

Given the practical needs and the shortage of literature on the subject outlined above, this appendix aims to provide some insight into the complex experiences of Hanban teachers in UK schools. The theoretical lens of professional identity is selected for data analysis, since it is commonly recognized as a useful frame to analyse aspects of teaching and teachers' professional development (Olsen, 2008; Alsup, 2006; Varghese *et al.*, 2005).

Learning through practice and identity

Although identity has been widely investigated by many researchers who study the experience of teachers, no consensus on its definition has been reached. Moreover, there is a certain ambiguity about the similarities and differences between identity and other concepts like self, self-concept, self-identity, soul, subjectivity or self-narrative. It seems that researchers on teachers and teacher education frequently use these terms interchangeably (Davey, 2013: 24; Gee, 2000–1: 113). They also draw on the understanding of identity from other related disciplines, such as psychology, sociology and philosophy.

I adopt the definition of professional teacher identity proposed by Sachs (2005) as my working definition:

> It provides a framework for teachers to construct their own ideas of 'how to be', 'how to act' and 'how to understand' their work and their place in society. Importantly, teacher identity is not something that is fixed nor is it imposed; rather it is negotiated through experience and the sense that is made of that experience. (Sachs, 2005: 15)

This definition depicts the multifaceted nature of identity, which contains 'how to be', 'how to act', and 'how to understand' as aspects within one frame. This indicates the deep connection between the practice of teachers and their identity. It involves the agency of teachers who construct their ideas of teaching rather than acting according to prescribed rules and behaviours. By Giddens's definition, agency refers 'not to the intentions people have in doing things but to their capability of doing those things' (Giddens, 1984: 9). Finally, Sachs's definition points out that identities are not merely mental processes within the mind of individual teachers, but also are constructed through a continuous negotiation between them and wider society, mediated by their experiences.

Hanban teachers' transitions from their previous schools involve two stages, first in the training programme, then in their UK schools; this requires a period of significant work on identity construction. The training programme and the initial teaching practice together constitute an integrated learning process necessary to become a competent Hanban teacher. In this context, I would like to explore the following questions:

- How do teachers experience the identity shift from 'a competent teacher in China' to 'a competent Hanban teacher in the UK'?
- What are the factors reinforcing or hindering this process of identity construction?

Situated learning theory, developed by Lave and Wenger (Lave, 1996; Lave and Wenger, 1991; Wenger, 1999), provides an approach to identity construction as a process deeply connected to practice. Using situated learning theory, this appendix explores teachers' thoughts on 'how to teach' in terms of the use of target language (TL) and first language (L1) in the Mandarin classroom and how their perception indicates identities developing towards becoming competent Mandarin teachers.

The use of TL/L1 in the Mandarin classroom is a salient theme that emerged from the process of data analysis rather than being determined *a priori*. This process will be discussed in more detail in the methods section. Current literature on the use of TL/L1 in foreign language classrooms tends to treat it as a pedagogical issue that concerns classroom discourse. Here classroom discourse refers to the context of 'oral interaction between teachers and their students and between students themselves that takes place in a classroom' (Thoms, 2012: 8). The pedagogical choice of teachers on their use of TL/L1 is commonly recognized as influencing learning outcomes for language learners. There is a shift in the debate on this issue, from an emphasis on maximum usage of the TL for instruction to more in-depth consideration of the role of L1 in developing learners' foreign language skills (Pachler *et al.*, 2014: 192).

However, I have no intention of joining the debate about which teaching technique is more appropriate in foreign language classrooms. Rather, I use this traditional pedagogical theme to examine systematically the teachers' changing ideas about 'how to teach' in the new landscape as well as their identity-construction work within it.

Learning through practice

A first useful concept for this enquiry is 'learning through practice'. Wenger (1999: 4) views learning 'as social participation', which is in stark contrast to the traditional view that learning is an individual cognitive process. Compared to the traditional perspective, Wenger's view adopts a different assumption about knowledge and knowing. It conceptualizes knowledge as 'a matter of competence with respect to valued enterprises' (Wenger, 1999: 4), rather than 'static subject matter', such as singing in tune, fixing machines or discovering scientific facts. 'Knowing', in Wenger's perspective, is active participation in practice, which leads to the mastery of a certain competence. Engagement in practice is both the process and the end of learning. It is the process that always leads to further advancement and it is the end that forms the very practice any individual is supposed to participate in.

Furthermore, Wenger makes explicit the links between learning through practice and the development of an individual's identity by saying, 'learning is not just the acquisition of memories, habits, and skills, but the formation of an identity' (Wenger, 1999: 96). This view resonates with what Lave illustrates earlier about the relationship between practice and a learner's identity:

> What would happen if we took the collective social nature of our existence so seriously that we put it first; so that crafting identities in practice becomes the fundamental project subjects engage in; crafting identities is a social process, and becoming more knowledgeably skilled is an aspect of participation in social practice. (Lave, 1996: 157)

Thus, this learning process concerns not only being engaged in a certain activity, but also contains the notion of development as a person. This implies a continuous negotiation of how to be a human being in the present. From being a novice to being a competent member within the community of practice, an individual is in the process of identity construction as 'a capable person, knowledgeable about problems and their solution' (Wenger-Trayner *et al.*, 2014: 43).

Identity as a nexus of multi-membership

The second important concept is identity as a nexus of multi-membership. According to Wenger, individuals do not solely belong to one community. Rather, they belong to a variety of communities, which are not just their current ones but also those that individuals have belonged to in the past. Engagement in both past and present communities contributes to individuals' identity construction to a certain degree. Thus, rather than viewing an individual's identity as a single trajectory, Wenger argues that identity should be conceptualized as a nexus of multiple trajectories that are all inextricably connected: at times, they can build upon each other, whereas at other times they might end up in conflict.

To reconcile the various trajectories within one identity requires great effort on the part of the individual. For Wenger, how much effort an individual puts into the process defines what it means to be a person. Thus, the notion of identity intrinsically contains 'multimembership and the work of reconciliation' (Wenger, 1999: 160).

As regards individuals who are leaving one landscape and joining another, they engage in a significant transition process that involves the crossing of boundaries (Wenger-Trayner *et al.*, 2014: 19). During the process, they not only acquire information about the new community, but might also have to handle 'conflicting forms of individuality and competence as defined in different communities' (Wenger, 1999: 160). Thus, the biggest challenge they encounter might be the act of reconciliation within their identities.

Similarly, Hanban teachers transition from their previous communities to their current ones and engage in activities that allow them to acquire new information about the UK school landscape. In addition, they also face situations where they have to deal with disparateness, which often conflicts with prescriptions on how to teach and behave.

In light of the concepts discussed above, my research questions can be rephrased as follows:

- How do Chinese teachers learn to become competent Hanban teachers?
- What are the interactions between different identities within multi-membership and how do such interactions influence the construction of the overarching identity?

Methods
Sampling
According to the official definition given by the UCL IOE Confucius Institute for Schools, Hanban teachers are a group of highly skilled native-speaker Chinese teachers who work across the UK, on secondment from their teaching positions in China (UCL IOE Confucius Institute for Schools, 2016). Usually, the group under the management of the Confucius Institute (CI) are collectively named Hanban teachers, while the group under the management of the British Council (BC) are called Chinese language

assistants (CLAs). However, in this study, I refer to both groups as 'Hanban teachers', since they both share many features:

- all are recruited, trained, and deployed by Hanban
- all are qualified teachers in China
- most are on secondment from their teaching positions in schools across China
- most are recruited directly from China without any formal training (leading to a qualification), working or living experiences in the UK.

My choice to include both groups in the discussion is also supported by Tinsley and Board's (2014: 131) argument that overlapping programmes, such as the Hanban teacher and the CLA programmes, should be integrated.

At a theoretical level, I use the combination of snowball sampling and opportunity sampling, suggested as an appropriate approach when it is difficult to get access to a specific group of participants (Suter, 2006: 211–5). Developing personal and official institutional trust and rapport are important to facilitate the recruitment of participants (Nordtveit, 2011: 367). However, I am aware that institutional power might bring pressure on participants and affect their willingness to get involved. With this in mind, participants were informed of their right to withdraw from the study at any point and reassured during the whole research process.

For participant recruitment, I contacted two organizations (a CI and a school) and recruited seven participants for the study. I asked the CI to send out invitation letters before the participants' arrival in the UK; six participants responded and were subsequently recruited. As to the participant from the BC programme, I was introduced to her personally by a previous participant in the pilot study and then reintroduced to her officially by her host school.

Participants

At the time of the study, the participants, who included six female teachers and one male teacher, were all aged between 20 and 50 years and spoke Mandarin as their first language. They worked as full-time Chinese language teaching assistants in a variety of UK schools. Their roles and responsibilities ranged from teaching assistants who supported small groups of students with learning difficulties or disciplinary issues, to teachers who delivered lessons to an entire class. All participants were born in China and received their bachelor's degrees there. Teacher Zheng was the only participant with a UK master's degree. Table A.1 provides some additional biographical information on the participants. The names used are pseudonyms.

Table A.1: Biographical information of participants

Name	Education background	Teaching experience prior to arrival in the UK	Year of teaching in the UK
Teacher Zhao	BA in a language discipline	5–10 years working experience as an English teacher	1st
Teacher Qian	BA in a language discipline	1–5 years working experience as an MFL teacher	1st
Teacher Sun	BA in a language discipline	1–5 years working experience as an English teacher	1st
Teacher Li	BA and MA in education disciplines	20+ years working experience as an English teacher and a teacher trainer	1st
Teacher Zhou	BA in a language discipline; MA in an education discipline	1–5 years working experience as a Mandarin as a second language teacher	4th
Teacher Wu	BA in an education discipline	20+ years working experience as an English teacher	1st
Teacher Zheng	BA and MA in other disciplines	1–5 years working experience as an English teacher	1st

Data collection

The study was conducted following a qualitative paradigm and, specifically, a narrative approach (Clandinin and Connelly, 2000). Compared with other types of qualitative research, narrative inquiry is distinguished by viewing experience over time, throughout the whole research process. It adopts 'a recursive and reflexive process of moving from field to data to interim and finally to research texts' (Clandinin and Huber, 2010: 436). Three research instruments were adopted, namely semi-structured interviews, observation and teachers' personal records.

I conducted 26 interviews with Hanban teachers, CI staff and local teachers. Three or four interviews were conducted with each Hanban teacher over one academic year, with the interviews lasting from 20 to 90 minutes. In addition, I conducted six full-day school visits to three of the target group teachers, with two days spent with each of them to acquire detailed field notes. I also participated in four events held by the CI and received 31 documents (such as teaching journals and policy documents) from both the teachers and the institutions.

Due to the limited scope and the focus of this chapter, I have analysed the interview transcripts and documents from seven Hanban teachers. Data from other sources were also used; these were not analysed systematically, but helped me gain an understanding of the field nonetheless. The data collection methods that are of special relevance to this chapter are the semi-structured interviews and documents from the teachers. I will proceed to elaborate more on what was done, and how and why it was done, in terms of those two methods.

Before the teachers started their teaching practice, I asked them about:

- their understanding of Mandarin teaching in a UK Mandarin classroom
- their understanding of living and working in the UK as a Hanban teacher
- their feelings and thoughts before starting their teaching practice.

My aim was to gain insight through these questions into their identity at the boundary between training programme and actual practice. I gave them a choice of answering the questions either by email or via internet webcam. All the participants chose to answer by email. It was through analysis of their responses that a common theme concerning the use of the TL and L1 in the classroom started to emerge.

The first set of interviews was conducted during the first month of their placement in UK schools as Hanban teachers. The following set of interviews was conducted at the end of the first term. The third and final set was conducted at the end of the second and final term respectively. The decision to carry out multiple interviews was made after considering the theoretical view that identity is something changeable rather than static. The choice of time was guided by studies (Trent, 2013) and arranged for the convenience of the participants.

Interviews were approached from a constructionist perspective, in which 'interviewers and interviewees are actively engaged in constructing meaning' (Silverman, 2006: 118), rather than with interviewees describing their experience while the researcher takes in all the information. In addition, an interview is viewed as 'a social encounter' (Cohen *et al.*, 2011: 410) and as 'part of life itself' (ibid.: 409). Thus, I have interviewed participants in casual settings such as a café or a teahouse. A short general update on our progress was always conducted before the actual interview. Field notes and reflective journals on such social encounters were kept for later analysis.

Data analysis

Based on an initial analysis of the pre-departure thoughts mentioned in the data collection procedure, I identified the use of L1 and the TL in Mandarin classrooms as a recurring theme in participants' responses. Referring to the existing literature on foreign language pedagogy, I realized this is frequently a topic of debate. Thus, I followed the development of the teachers' beliefs and practices on this matter in subsequent interviews. Data analysis proceeded through the following five steps:

1) All interview transcripts were read and the parts that concern this theme were marked.
2) The relevant parts from one participant were combined to create a sample data set. The sample data was coded into codes and pattern codes (Miles *et al.*, 2014: 73–96) using the principle of constant comparative analysis (Charmaz, 1995: 42; Holton, 2007: 277), where the aim is to 'capture, synthesize and understand the main themes in the statement' (Charmaz, 1995: 40).
3) To increase inter-rater reliability, a second reader was invited to analyse the sample data with me.
4) The rest of the data was analysed using the categories constructed from the sample data.
5) The analytical frame was drawn up. I grouped the codes into two categories i) growing knowledge shaped through practice; ii) multiple-identity tensions in the transition between communities. Within the second category, three sub-categories were developed: a) first encounter: when past experience meets the pre-departure training programme; b) second encounter: entering the actual teaching practice; c) the tension between personal and professional dimensions.

This was not a linear process. As the process went by, the properties and dimensions of each category or subcategory were constantly increasing or changing. Some new categories and subcategories were added and some of the names were also adjusted.

Findings and discussion

Growing knowledge shaped through practice

As discussed earlier, by engaging in the actual practice of a new community, a newcomer is involved in the acquisition of knowledge that can be viewed as 'a matter of competence' (Wenger, 1999: 4). This knowledge might be local to each specific community.

During the discussion of their experience on the use of the TL and L1 in Mandarin classrooms, participants tried to explain their choice, how they implemented it, and the rationale behind their pedagogical choice on this issue. The use of the TL and L1 relates to 'how to teach'. However, this is not just a matter of the technique that is being used: it has something to do with 'how to be' a teacher. It reveals the construction of identity that is in progress for teachers as they become more competent practitioners in a new environment.

It is evident that, through their participation in the teaching practice, their personal familiarity with the landscape grows. Their pedagogical decision on the use of the TL and L1 is heavily influenced by the information they have acquired in this complex environment, such as knowledge of the student-centred conception of teaching, Mandarin provision in UK schools, students and current practice in the classroom. When attempting to build a basis for how to act, different aspects of new knowledge must be considered and integrated into the teachers' personal frames of reference (Eraut, 1994: 16–25):

> Teaching Chinese has become quite challenging after coming to the UK, especially with young pupils. After saying a couple of lines in Chinese, if they don't understand you, they stop listening and even stop co-operating, which is why in the UK you must teach Chinese in English, especially when the students are young. (Teacher Zhou, interview 1)

> If the students are having conversations during class and are quite noisy, they would often say '3, 2, 1' using a different language, or some teachers would do a countdown from 5 and usually when it gets to 3 or 2 the students have gone quiet already. Then this past Wednesday in the Mandarin club I gave it a try. I have already taught them how to count from 1 to 10, so hoping that it was going to work I gave it a go and without them noticing, I said '3, 2, 1'. When I said '3', they realized that I was hinting to them to be quiet, some even gestured to others to shush and when I got to '2', everyone had stopped talking. I think this is a very effective way of classroom management. (Teacher Zheng, interview 1)

Both teachers Zhou and Zheng touched on the issue of the use of TL and L1 and its relationship with students' behaviour management. In the quote above, teacher Zhou discusses the behaviour and cognitive characteristics of his students in a UK school. He reached the pedagogical decision of using

L1 as a medium for instruction after considering their characteristics. His understanding of his students grew out of his participation in the practice. It might have been influenced by reflection and adjustment to some previously unsuccessful experiences. The modal verb 'must' shows his confidence on this matter and reveals his identity as a competent practitioner after having worked in the UK for three years.

Teacher Zheng discusses her experience in experimenting with the TL as a tool for students' behaviour management. Through participation in the new school community, she grasped a common technique shared by experienced teachers as an established behaviour management practice between teachers and students. Having correctly assessed the Mandarin level of her pupils, she experimented with this technique by adopting it in Mandarin. It turned out to be a successful experience. This anecdote reveals her identity as a novice teacher, who was still in the process of actively learning from more experienced teachers and experimenting with teaching techniques.

The two quotations reflect the work done by Shulman (1987: 8) on the seven categories of the knowledge base that are essential for teachers to enhance the learning experience of students. By entering a new school environment, participants are acquiring a body of knowledge through their participation in teaching. However, in this transition process from one landscape to another, the acquisition of new knowledge is just one task: teachers might also have to deal with tensions between 'conflicting forms of individuality and competence in different communities' (Wenger, 1999: 160).

Multiple-identity tensions in the transition between communities
The analytical lens used in this study views identity as a nexus of multi-membership. Simultaneously, teacher identity encompasses both personal and professional dimensions, which are in a dynamic interaction. There might exist tensions between the different identities that are formed in or expected to be formed by their past or present communities. When an identity that has been constructed from past experience encounters present demands on 'who to be' and 'how to act' as a teacher within a current practice, there is a tension between past and present – between 'two forms of competence whose claim to knowledge may or may not be compatible.' (Wenger-Trayner *et al.*, 2014: 18). These tensions require individuals to reconcile the different trajectories they have experienced or are currently experiencing: this provides them with the opportunity to learn and develop themselves further in a new community.

Three forms of identity tensions are discussed below. They were experienced by the target group of teachers in relation to the use of TL/L1, their identity construction work when facing those tensions and the role of agency.

The target group of teachers did not enter the pre-departure training programme as empty vessels to be filled with knowledge and skills on how to act like a good teacher (Freeman and Johnson, 1998: 401). Rather, they came with their own past professional experience as well as personal biographies. If their established understanding is in congruence with the beliefs and practices promoted by the training programme, no tensions are evoked by the encounter of the two. However, if not, tensions occur, as expressed in the following excerpts from teacher Li and teacher Wu:

> I was on a training programme at the time at X University and there was this very controversial debate going on among us. One of the teacher educators advised us to speak Chinese solely during the class, and during our first trial lecture. Because no one had any experience at the time, we spoke a lot of English. Then we were told off by our teacher that we couldn't do it this way and should have used Chinese instead, so during our second trial lecture, we spoke Mandarin only. In fact, to us it was a very big challenge ... I already thought at the time and I believed teaching foreign students Chinese in China is fundamentally different to teaching English students Chinese in the UK. Since those in China would have an advantage because of the language environment, as they would be hearing Mandarin all the time and would have the opportunity to practise. But here they simply don't have that sort of context. Coming to the UK has proven that I was right about my thought at that time. (Teacher Wu, interview 3)

> I have doubts and concerns about Mandarin pedagogy in the UK's primary and secondary schools after I got to understand it a bit more, and I feel that it is considerably different from my own beliefs on teaching that have been developed over my 20 plus years of English-teaching experience. One of the most important aspects is that here Chinese lessons are taught entirely in English. Teachers' use of Chinese is low: consequently, students' output will not be high. How efficient such a teaching

style really is interests me, and I would love to find out more. During the training programme in Shanghai, I was told by one of the Chinese teachers from France that they were often required to use as much Chinese as possible when teaching and some of her concepts and practices resonated with mine. I hope during my time here in the UK I can find an answer to this through my studies and work. (Teacher Li, pre-departure email)

Teacher Li and Teacher Wu are two of the most experienced participants. Both were expert teachers in China, with many years of teaching experience. They had already established stable professional identities not only as teachers, but also as expert teachers who have confidence in their beliefs and practices. Expert teachers differ from novice teachers, as they can more easily draw on their past experience and use it to handle issues in a new context (Sternberg and Horvath, 1995: 14). These two expert teachers are the only participants who can reflect on the principles of TL and L1 use taught in the training programme. Teacher Zhou had graduated from a prestigious programme in teaching Chinese as a second language and already had teaching experience as a Mandarin teacher. His ideas and practice are in agreement with the perspective of the training programme, so there is no tension between his identities. As for the other participants, they have comparatively less experience, as their working experience ranged from just two to seven years. However, all of them are enthusiastic about becoming better teachers. As a result, they experienced no tensions because they understood the training programme to be a crucial source for their professional development as competent Hanban teachers.

The quotations from teacher Li and teacher Wu above show that there were primarily two voices on the matter of TL and L1 use within the pre-departure training programme. I triangulated the data on this matter among participants. Other data sources (interview transcripts from other participants) also support the existence of different views within the training programme. The first perspective promotes maximum and even full use of the TL as the medium of instruction. This view is in agreement with the mainstream principle used in teaching Chinese as a second language within China. It was also adopted in some adult education programmes in France and the United States of America. The second perspective promotes the use of L1 as a medium of instruction. This was primarily described within the training programme as specific to the UK school context. It also had the support of teachers who had actual teaching experience in this context.

In response to these two views, Teacher Wu questioned the feasibility of the maximum use perspective. Based on her understanding of the differences in the language learning environments in China and the UK, she doubted that the technique of teaching Mandarin with maximum use of TL could be utilized in actual teaching. She also said she felt challenged when faced with the demands of the first perspective.

However, Teacher Li questioned the effectiveness of the second perspective. She perceived the two perspectives as dichotomous. Based on her long-held foreign language teaching beliefs stemming from her English teaching experience, she was convinced that the best learning outcome of language learners can only be achieved through maximum input of TL. Thus, she found her view was in congruence with the first perspective. However, she expressed strong feelings of confusion when considering the disparity between her own ideas, beliefs and practices and the context in which she was going to work.

Nevertheless, both Teacher Li and Teacher Wu, as experienced teachers, revealed a strong sense of agency in response to the training programme's prescriptions on how they should act. Current literature acknowledges the crucial role of agency in the construction of identity. Agency functions throughout the entire process from past creation and current maintenance, to the future development of identity (Day *et al.*, 2006: 613). Although they felt challenged or frustrated, Teacher Li and Teacher Wu did not accept the programme's prescriptions completely. Rather, they set out to exercise their agency. Faced with tensions from the outset, both planned to experiment with different ideas and identify what was best practice through actual teaching.

SECOND ENCOUNTER: ENTERING ACTUAL TEACHING PRACTICE

As participants started their actual teaching practice in UK school communities, they tended to express their professional identities under the influence of their previous teaching practices and pre-departure training programme. However, new working landscapes, as mentioned earlier, might require new forms of individuality and competence. This was likely to cause a second wave of tensions in the teachers' identities, as illustrated by Teachers Zhou and Li in the following excerpts:

> When I first came I just completely took what I did in Beijing Green Park University, which is basically using Mandarin to teach Mandarin, and used it here. But then I realized in the UK this simply doesn't work at all. (Teacher Zhou, interview 1)

I have had this thought all along, since before, when I was in China teaching English, and it has always been English only and I have never used Mandarin during class. Of course, there were teachers using Mandarin as well, but we have always thought that as a student from the start, the use of body language, the environment, and various other things can help him understand our English. So that got me thinking why couldn't Chinese be taught that way? Then during our training programme in Shanghai, we found out that in France at a University in Paris, this is exactly what they have been doing, teaching Chinese using Mandarin only, so we thought maybe the method varies between countries. So, indeed, this thought has intrigued me all along, and having taught Chinese for so many years, it was this year after coming to the UK that I realized perhaps using a target language to teach a target language is not viable, and this has got me quite confused, but because here the general teaching environment is just the way it is, I would not dare try it differently. It's true. (Teacher Li, final interview)

The word choice of 'completely' and 'at all' revealed teacher Zhou's understanding of the stark contrast between the requirements of the previous and current school communities. His professional identity constructed within the previous community did not work well in the new community. The intense tension between the two led him to shift his professional identity towards one that is more compatible with the new context.

Not so Teacher Li, whose statement reveals the ongoing conflict within her identity construction. The quote above is from the final interview conducted after Teacher Li had been teaching in the UK for one academic year. Up until then, she had expressed her confusion about the reasons why a TL could not be taught using the TL. Her persistent confusion could have two interpretations. One is that, as an expert teacher in China, her previous professional identity was so strong that it was always searching for articulation. However, as a newcomer to the current community, she lacked the agency to teach in a way that went against the good practice endorsed by the current school culture. Thus, for Teacher Li, this tension concerned not only the disparity between the previous and current practice and the shift between them, but also involved her identity, touching upon the issue of 'who to be' in a community. At the same time, she was experiencing the transition from being an expert teacher and a full member in her previous community to being a newcomer with 'peripheral participation' in her current community (Wenger, 1999: 100).

THE TENSION BETWEEN THE PERSONAL AND PROFESSIONAL DIMENSION

After working within UK school communities for a period of time, the teachers' professional identity had started shifting, which was revealed by their acceptance of current practices using L1 as the medium of instruction. However, another layer of issues relating to their personal identity emerged following this shift. As non-native English speakers, insufficient English proficiency made them feel incompetent as Hanban teachers. This tension between the personal and professional dimension of identity was expressed in the following statements:

> Sometimes I think the problem lies in our communication, because our understanding of the English language is largely insufficient. Often when teaching Chinese, my insufficient English became a constraint. For example, they would often say something like, 'the word "明天" in Chinese means "tomorrow" in Chinese, right?' to which you agreed, then they would ask, 'why is tomorrow one word but in Chinese it's two words combined?' Then you have to explain to them separately the meaning of '明' and the meaning of '天'. Perhaps this one is relatively easy to explain, but for some other words ... (Teacher Sun, interview 1)

> Another issue would be the inadequacy of my own English language, and I realized in the classes they have here, students often use English that is so different to what we normally use, especially the younger children who used the language very differently to how we normally perceive it, and compared to the English we had in China, it's even less alike. Hence, I believe, in order to communicate with our students smoothly, we really should be focusing on improving our English. So maybe after this I will find myself working hard to improve my English language and I don't mean the English language we learned from back when we were in China, but the sort of language our students are using. So sometimes I find myself purposefully asking my students how they would express a certain something in their way. What they taught me was often completely different to what I had learned in school. But I guess if you can communicate with them using their language, then we can reduce the distance between us. (Teacher Li, interview 2)

Teacher Sun reported feelings of inadequacy about the L1 vocabulary used for the traditional translation method in explaining the meaning of the TL. Similarly, Teacher Li reported on her feelings about her lack of English proficiency, especially when conducting conversations with students. However, her major concern was not about the teaching technique. Rather, it relates to the teacher–student relationship. She was concerned that her insufficient command of L1 would hinder the establishment of a better relationship with students. Facing this issue, Teacher Li exercised her agency by consciously learning L1 from her students. This might shift the teacher–student power dynamic, as she was simultaneously her students' teacher and their student.

Implications for teacher education

This appendix has examined the identity construction experience of Hanban teachers during the first year of their transition into the UK school environment. It focuses on the teachers' identity construction work around the use of TL and L1 in Mandarin classroom. Having engaged with identity construction at a more conceptual level and with the choice of instruction language at a more practical level, the discussion now turns to the implications for teacher education of these two separate but interrelated dimensions.

Identity, practice and Hanban teacher education

At an abstract level, the concepts of identity construction and learning through practice should be included in the conceptualization of Hanban teachers' education. First, Hanban teachers' learning should no longer be regarded merely as a purely cognitive undertaking for the individual: it should also concern learning how to become a certain kind of person in the school community, which entails the negotiation of social relations with other members of the community as well as the negotiation of social practices during teaching.

Hanban teachers' learning should no longer be viewed as limited to official programmes (such as pre-departure training and CPD events) and specific periods of time. Indeed, the acquisition of knowledge within the pre-departure programmes, such as subject matter, pedagogy and educational discourse in a new sociocultural environment, is crucial for preparing teachers from China to become Hanban teachers. However, the experience of participants shows that these programmes are merely the initial stage in the process of their becoming competent Hanban teachers. The first steps in their school practice requires an intensive process of learning and becoming, which involves the dynamic interaction of Hanban teachers' personal biography, teacher education and school reality. Almost every participant has experienced uncertainty and confusion around issues on 'how to act' and 'who to be' when faced with this new landscape. Learning through actual practice concerns not only the growing knowledge and competence of 'how to teach', but also their sense of confidence in their identity as competent Hanban teachers.

By considering the initial on-site practice as an integral part of learning to become a competent Hanban teacher, I have questioned what kind of induction, guidance and support at school level can be provided for this learning process, which involves significant identity construction work. This is worthy of further exploration for policymakers, teacher educators, host schools and researchers in this field.

Pre-departure training curriculum

Pre-departure training of Hanban teachers usually consists of two consecutive programmes. According to the number of trainees, these two programmes are often referred to as 'small' and 'large' training. The small training is delivered by the UK-based Confucius Institute with the support of its partner university or school in China. Teacher training is offered by staff from these partner organizations. It lasts approximately one week, with some twenty Hanban teachers who are going to work in UK schools. The large training is delivered solely by a China-based university. It lasts about one month, with roughly two hundred Hanban teachers trained within one programme. This group of teachers is typically deployed in various countries other than the UK.

Pre-departure training facilitates Hanban teachers' transition from the Chinese educational landscape to the educational environment of the UK. It provides important knowledge on how to teach in a Mandarin classroom, which is a crucial first step in providing teachers with adequate preparation, especially for those without any experience of teaching Chinese as a second or foreign language.

However, it is still insufficient in terms of the knowledge provided and demonstrates little understanding of the nature of teachers' learning in a new sociocultural environment. In particular, the pedagogical knowledge provided by these programmes is mainly theoretical, and development is based on the experience of teaching Chinese as a second language to adult learners in China. This is very different from the UK school context in terms of the language learning environment as well as the academic and linguistic needs of learners.

What works in the Chinese adult context may or may not work in the UK school context. The two perspectives voiced during the pre-departure training programme discussed above indicate the kind of different ideas engendered by different contexts. This can lead to feelings of confusion about teaching practices and a subsequent impact on teachers' confidence. Thus, echoing Tinsley and Board's (2014: 126) recommendation, I would argue for the need to develop a training programme curriculum that is better targeted and includes a greater appreciation of the UK school environment.

References

Alsup, J. (2006) *Teacher Identity Discourses: Negotiating personal and professional spaces*. Mahwah, NJ: Lawrence Erlbaum Associates.

Charmaz, K. (1995) 'Grounded theory'. In Smith, J.A., Harré, R. and Van Langenhove, L. (eds) *Rethinking Methods in Psychology*. London: SAGE Publications, 27–49.

CiLT National Centre for Languages (2007) *Mandarin Language Learning: Research study* (Research Report DCSF-RW019). London: Department for Children, Schools and Families.

Clandinin, D.J. and Connelly, F.M. (2000) *Narrative Inquiry: Experience and story in qualitative research*. San Francisco: Jossey-Bass.

Clandinin, D.J. and Huber, J. (2010) 'Narrative inquiry'. In Peterson, P., Baker, E. and McGaw, B. (eds) *International Encyclopedia of Education*. 3rd ed. Oxford: Elsevier, 436–41.

Cohen, L., Manion, L. and Morrison, K. (2011) *Research Methods in Education*. 7th ed. London: Routledge.

Davey, R. (2013) *The Professional Identity of Teacher Educators: Career on the cusp?* London: Routledge.

Day, C., Kington, A., Stobart, G. and Sammons, P. (2006) 'The personal and professional selves of teachers: Stable and unstable identities'. *British Educational Research Journal*, 32 (4), 601–16.

Eraut, M. (1994) *Developing Professional Knowledge and Competence*. London: Falmer Press.

Filmer-Sankey, C., Marshall, H. and Sharp, C. (2010) *Languages at Key Stage 4, 2009–2011: Evaluation of the impact of Languages Review recommendations: Baseline findings from the first year of the evaluation* (Research Brief). London: Department for Education.

Freeman, D. and Johnson, K.E. (1998) 'Reconceptualizing the knowledge-base of language teacher education'. *TESOL Quarterly*, 32 (3), 397–417.

Gee, J.P. (2000–1) 'Identity as an analytic lens for research in education'. *Review of Research in Education*, 25, 99–125.

Giddens, A. (1984) *The Constitution of Society: Outline of the theory of structuration*. Berkeley: University of California Press.

Holton, J.A. (2007) 'The coding process and its challenges'. In Bryant, A. and Charmaz, K. (eds) *The SAGE Handbook of Grounded Theory*. London: SAGE Publications, 265–89

Lave, J. (1996) 'Teaching, as learning, in practice'. *Mind, Culture, and Activity*, 3 (3), 149–64.

Lave, J. and Wenger, E. (1991) *Situated Learning: Legitimate peripheral participation*. Cambridge: Cambridge Unversity Press.

Miles, M.B., Huberman, A.M. and Saldaña, J. (2014) *Qualitative Data Analysis: A methods sourcebook*. 3rd ed. Thousand Oaks, CA: SAGE Publications.

Nordtveit, B.H. (2011) 'Politics, guanxi and the search for objectivity: The intricacies of conducting educational research in Chinese contexts'. *Comparative Education*, 47 (3), 367–80.

Olsen, B. (2008) *Teaching What They Learn, Learning What They Live: How teachers' personal histories shape their professional development*. Boulder, CO: Paradigm Publishers.

Pachler, N., Evans, M., Redondo, A. and Fisher, L. (2014) *Learning to Teach Foreign Languages in the Secondary School: A companion to school experience*. 4th ed. London: Routledge.

Sachs, J. (2005) 'Teacher education and the development of professional identity: Learning to be a teacher'. In Denicolo, P.M. and Kompf, M. (eds) *Connecting Policy and Practice: Challenges for teaching and learning in schools and universities*. London: Routledge, 5–21.

Shulman, L.S. (1987) 'Knowledge and teaching: Foundations of the new reform'. *Harvard Educational Review*, 57 (1), 1–23.

Silverman, D. (2006) *Interpreting Qualitative Data: Methods for analyzing talk, text and interaction*. 3rd ed. London: SAGE Publications.

Starr, D. (2009) 'Chinese language education in Europe: The Confucius Institutes'. *European Journal of Education*, 44 (1), 65–82.

Sternberg, R.J. and Horvath, J.A. (1995) 'A prototype view of expert teaching'. *Educational Researcher*, 24 (6), 9–17.

Suter, W.N. (2006) *Introduction to Educational Research: A critical thinking approach*. London: SAGE Publications.

Thoms, J.J. (2012) 'Classroom discourse in foreign language classrooms: A review of the literature'. *Foreign Language Annals*, 45 (S1), S8–S27.

Tinsley, T. and Board, K. (2014) *The Teaching of Chinese in the UK* (Research Report). London: Alcantara Communications. Online. www.britishcouncil.org/sites/default/files/alcantara_full_report_jun15.pdf (accessed 4 October 2017).

Trent, J. (2013) 'Becoming a teacher educator: The multiple boundary-crossing experiences of beginning teacher educators'. *Journal of Teacher Education*, 64 (3), 262–75.

UCL IOE Confucius Institute for Schools (2016) 'Hanban teachers'. Online. https://ciforschools.wordpress.com/about-us/confucius-classroom/hanban-teachers/ (accessed 6 July 2016).

Varghese, M., Morgan, B., Johnston, B. and Johnson, K.A. (2005) 'Theorizing language teacher identity: Three perspectives and beyond'. *Journal of Language, Identity, and Education*, 4 (1), 21–44.

Wang, L. and Higgins, L.T. (2008) 'Mandarin teaching in the UK in 2007: A brief report of teachers' and learners' views'. *Language Learning Journal*, 36 (1), 91–6.

Wenger, E. (1999) *Communities of Practice: Learning, meaning, and identity.* Cambridge: Cambridge University Press.

Wenger-Trayner, E., Fenton-O'Creevy, M., Hutchinson, S., Kubiak, C. and Wenger-Trayner, B. (eds) (2014) *Learning in Landscapes of Practice: Boundaries, identity, and knowledgeability in practice-based learning.* New York: Routledge.

Index

Index